Rain King:
The Life and Music of Adam Duritz and Counting Crows

by Geoff Harkness

Copyright © 2023 Geoff Harkness

All rights reserved

No part of this book may be reproduced, or stored in a retrieval system, or transmitted in any form or by any means, electronic, mechanical, photocopying, recording, or otherwise, without express written permission of the publisher.

ISBN: 9798218208516

First paperback edition May 2023

Cover photo by Paul Bergen, courtesy Getty Images

Cover design by GVH & KJP

Interior design by Penny Brucker

Passim Press

To my family and my friends who feel like family

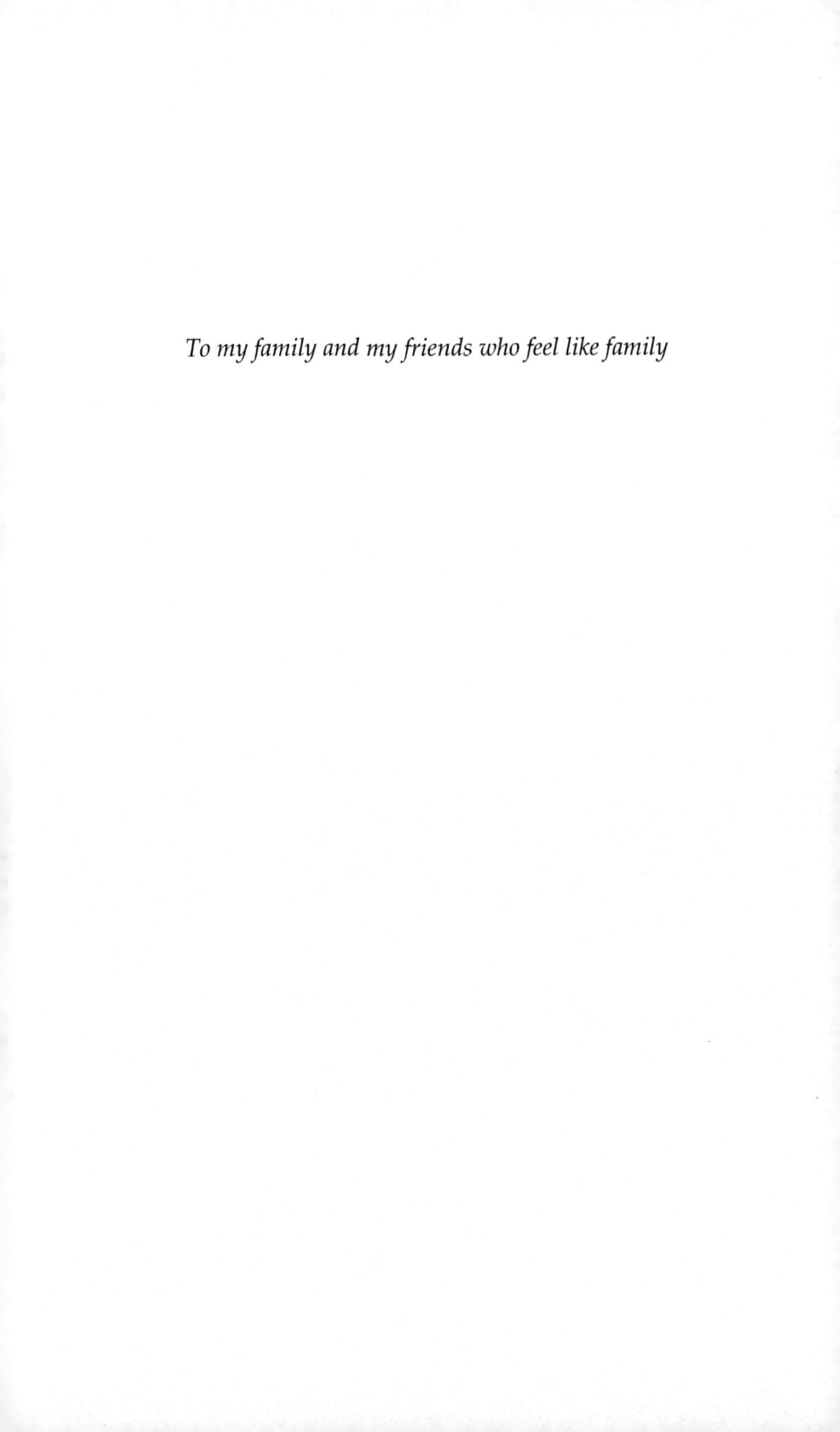

Contents

Contents v
Preface vii
Hatchlings in the Crow's Nest 1
August and Everything After 29
Recovering the Satellites 63
This Desert Life 97
Hard Candy 125
Saturday Nights & Sunday Mornings 157
Somewhere Under Wonderland 189
Discography 221
Videography 223
Acknowledgements 225
Notes 227

Preface

When Sara Gilbert introduced Counting Crows to the world, the actress did so while hosting the eleventh episode of the nineteenth season of *Saturday Night Live*. It was January 15th, 1994, and Counting Crows nearly did not perform, threatening to walk out if the show's producers made them open with their first single, a peppy pop number called "Mr. Jones." Instead, the band's singer and songwriter, Adam Duritz, insisted that the Crows play "Round Here," an emotional ballad about the pains of growing up. The singer got his way.

On the air that night, Adam sang the first few lines with his eyes closed, hands upside down at his waist, questioning. Singing louder, he slowly opened his eyes, looked to the heavens, then down at his feet. He appeared simultaneously hopeful and forlorn. The California beach bro look he had sported for years was gone, replaced by a grunge-era moppet in combat boots, tattered thrift-store shorts, and an olive-green sweater. Adam had recently sprouted dreadlocks, which he topped with a hip, wool hat. The camera zoomed in close, accentuating the singer's expressive eyebrows as he continued to wind his way through the song.

The five musicians behind Adam dragged out the opening, wringing every ounce of drama from the tune. The second verse kicked in, and the Crows took flight, launching their vocalist into the stratosphere. Adam spread his arms wide into a Jesus Christ pose before emulating a nervous tightrope walker teetering across a wire. He gripped the microphone stand with both hands, as if to keep himself from stumbling over.

The musicians slowed the song to a whisper-quiet middle section. In the pin-drop silence of 30 Rockefeller Plaza's television studio, without nightclub noise drowning them out, Adam delivered "Round Here" with previously unforeseen levels of emotional impact. Behind him, the band brought the song to a thunderous climax, with the singer wailing and crying out with everything he had.

It was a career-making performance, the instant everything changed. The group's second song of the night was the single, "Mr. Jones," a first-person account of an unknown singer who dreams of becoming a big star. But the genie had already left the bottle. By the time the Crows got to "Jones," their vocalist was no longer an aspirant pining for fame, he was a bonafide celebrity. Within weeks, the band's debut album would skyrocket to the top ten and their twenty-nine-year-old anonymous singer would become one of the most famous rock stars on the planet.

"It was weird. We weren't ready for it," Charlie Gillingham, founding keyboardist for Counting Crows, told me when I interviewed him in July 2000. "We went from selling a few thousand a week to selling 40,000 a week. It just took about five or six weeks to climb up the charts, so it was a very strange period. All the sudden, you're on the cover of all these magazines and people are yelling at you in bars."[1]

For the past three decades, Counting Crows have benefitted from the universal acclaim and massive sales of their debut album, 1993's *August and Everything After*. The record has also

Preface

been a burden of sorts—it both gave the San Francisco band a career but also meant that every subsequent effort was compared to their auspicious debut. That did not stop the hard-touring ensemble from racking up a lengthy list of Platinum albums and hit singles such as "A Long December," "Hanginaround," and "Accidentally in Love." Adam Duritz's pop sensibilities and attention to harmony echoed the Eagles and Fleetwood Mac, while his inherent sense of melancholy aligned with Brian Wilson's bittersweet vision of sun-kissed California. This book examines Adam Duritz's musical trajectory, from his earliest childhood inklings to the road-worn rock star still writing, recording, and touring today.

"Omaha" in Omaha

Like many Counting Crows fans, my initial exposure to the group was through "Mr. Jones." It was the winter of 1993, and I was working at a bookstore in Kansas City, Missouri. The store carried a magazine called *College Music Journal*, or *CMJ* for short. *CMJ* discussed everything related to alternative rock and college radio, but its true appeal was the free CD included in every issue. There were always leftover copies at the end of the month, and I would grab one and listen to the CD.

The second song of the December 1993 issue of *CMJ* featured an unknown band performing a song called "Mr. Jones." The instant "Jones" came on, I was hooked. I must have played it twenty times in a row that night, and the song remained in regular rotation for months. This exposure led me to *August and Everything After*, which I fell for along with the rest of America. The Crows' second album, 1996's *Recovering the Satellites*, took longer to grow on me, but I came to appreciate it as much, if not more, than the debut.

From 1999 to 2023, I attended ten Crows concerts. Not every show was amazing, but several were incredible, and a few were transformative. Small clubs, street festivals, outdoor amphitheaters, you name it. I've seen them headline and also share stages with acts such as John Mayer and Live. I've watched them perform at what is reportedly Adam's favorite venue, the Greek Theatre in San Francisco. I've seen Adam sing about New Orleans in New Orleans and watched them play "Omaha" in Omaha. I worked as a music journalist during part of this time, reviewing three of their albums and several live shows. In the summer of 2000, I interviewed Charlie Gillingham for a feature story about the band. I am a fan, albeit a discerning one.

For years, I have wished there was a biography of Adam Duritz and Counting Crows. It is hard to think of an artist more deserving—and Adam's story is a compelling one. They say that authors should write books they want to read, so here it is—a book I've been wanting to read for twenty-five years. I know how passionate Crows fans are, and I took the job seriously.

This book is my fourth, the third about music. I have a background in music journalism, but I also have a PhD and an MBA. When writing *Rain King*, I approached it like any other serious research topic. I scoured the internet for every magazine article, interview, CD review, concert write-up, and anything else I could find about the band. I also did a close analysis of the Crows' music, including multiple listens to every studio album, outtake, B-side, song that was released on a soundtrack, demo,

Preface

and rare recording. I also did a deep dive into the live history of the band, including scrutinizing each of their official in-concert releases as well as the hundreds if not thousands of videos that are available online. Anyone who has been to a Counting Crows concert knows that Adam likes to spin a yarn. Often, these tales contain the origin stories of his songs—how he wrote them, who they are about, where and why he wrote them. Adam's on-stage anecdotes also became source material for the book.

Beginning with chapter 2, *Rain King* is written from a chronological, real-time perspective. It means, for example, that the chapter about *August and Everything After* relies almost entirely upon news sources, reviews, and interviews published during that era. Time alters one's perspective. Looking back with hindsight, the story changes—something Adam is almost famous for.

Going through all this material, I was struck by how often the story either changed or was unclear. I have tried to accurately represent events as they took place, with the caveat that there's no possible way I got it all right. For example, at least four individuals are credited with the idea of having the Crows record their debut album in a house—and more than one of those names comes from Adam himself!

The book's focus is on Adam Duritz, not the other members of Counting Crows. Dave Bryson, Charlie Gillingham, and David Immerglück are original members of the band, with guitarist Dan Vickrey coming on board not long after. The rhythm section of Jim Bogios and Millard Powers has been in place for nearly twenty years. That longevity has a lot to do with the septet's success, as well their ability to continue drawing audiences. Adam, who writes 100% of the lyrics and most of the music, is the Crows' center of gravity, but he could not achieve his artistic vision without the band.

In the book, I focus on the Crows' musical history, including the songs, albums, and live performances that defined each of the group's many eras. I do not, however, analyze any of their lyrics. Adam's songs brim with vivid images and artful turns of phrase, but he will be the first to acknowledge that his words should not be confused with poetry. They are intended to be understood within the context of their musical backing, rather than as naked prose. In this book, the lyrics are part of the story, but not the story itself.

At the heart of this book is the music. I intentionally structured it around each of the band's six full-length studio albums, looking deeply at their writing and recording, as well as how these works were adjusted in concert. After all, it is Counting Crows' music that brought us here. I hope this book serves as both a celebration of and conversation about the musical works of art created by Adam Duritz and Counting Crows.

Chapter 1

Hatchlings in the Crow's Nest

Adam Fredric Duritz was born August 1st, 1964 in Baltimore, Maryland. He is the son of Gilbert Duritz, who at the time of Adam's birth was a twenty-five-year-old medical student, specializing in neonatal treatment of high-risk deliveries. Adam's mother is Linda Duritz (née Feldman), who eventually became a physician as well. Adam's great grandparents were Jewish immigrants from Russia. Adam's sister, Nicole, was born less than two years after him on May 14th, 1966, also in Baltimore.

Gilbert was still attending medical school in Baltimore when the children were born, but the family soon moved to Boston, so that he could take an internship at Massachusetts General Hospital. It was a pattern that became the theme of Adam's childhood: continual relocation.

The young family moved constantly. In 1969, Gilbert was drafted by the Army to assist with the Vietnam war effort. The Duritzes were stationed at Fort Bliss in El Paso, Texas from 1970 to 1972. As a boy, Adam enjoyed unsupervised forays into his El Paso neighborhood with other kids, exploring in the woods and fields nearby. The Duritzes then spent a year in Houston, a large city that the young Adam did not enjoy as much. Adam has said that the twang that sometimes appears in his singing voice stems from these formative years in Texas.

Throughout his early childhood, Adam returned to Baltimore each summer to spend time with his grandmother, Selma Feldman. Adam's grandmother was an avid duckpin bowler and would take her young grandson to league games and tournaments. "I remember doing it all the time," Adam said. "I loved it." The two would end the night by watching television together. Among their favorite shows were *Bowling for Dollars* and the youth-themed *Pinbusters*, popular duckpin-bowling programs hosted by Adam's second cousin, Baltimore broadcasting legend Royal Parker.

Adam developed an early interest in music, spending hours listening to his parents' record collection, absorbing everything from Barry Manilow to the Ohio Players. Adam's folks were not huge music lovers, but the seven-year-old boy enjoyed strumming a tennis racket and singing along to the Beatles' "Can't Buy Me Love." He recalled that, "My parents had all the Beatles albums and I can definitely remember those songs."[2]

As a child, Adam's favorite musical act was the Jackson 5. The first two records he purchased were the Jackson 5's greatest hits and Michael Jackson's 1972 solo debut, *Got to Be There*. When the Jackson 5 came to town on tour, Adam's parents took him and Nicole to the concert, held inside a vast rodeo arena. "That really knocked me out. Those songs were so good and they were so vibrant and he was such a killer singer. He was my age, a few years older than me, but it seemed like I was looking at a kid who was my age," Adam recalled. "I don't know if that made me want to write songs but it certainly made me like, 'Whoa, music is incredible.' I couldn't get enough after that."[3]

Following Gilbert's honorable discharge from the military, the Duritzes moved from Texas to Denver, so that Gilbert could complete another round of medical training. Ready to settle down, he took a job practicing medicine in Berkeley, California. Adam was ten when he moved to California in 1974, and it remained his semi-permanent home for the next two decades. Soon after, his mother, Linda, decided that she, too, would become a physician and spent several years traveling back and forth from California to Mexico to attend medical school. "All the moving around, I think, got hard on Adam," Linda told a reporter in 1994. "But to me he seemed to always make friends pretty easily. He just seemed to have that knack."[4]

In middle school, Adam was outgoing, attractive, and popular. He excelled at soccer and several other sports, which made it easier to fit in and make friends. The Duritzes' comfortable house in Berkeley was near the Claremont Club and Spa, a luxury hotel. In 1977, when Adam was thirteen, Gilbert took him to his first Cal football game, walking a mile from their house to Memorial Stadium. Adam became a lifelong sports fanatic that day and a diehard Cal supporter. Gilbert bought season tickets, which Adam has held on to ever since. They attended numerous games at Memorial, always walking. "It was just something we did together, a father-son thing. It's such a great thing to walk across Berkeley to a game." [5]

That same year, Gilbert took Adam to see Electric Light Orchestra at the Oakland Coliseum. Not long after, an inspired teenage Adam began to teach himself the rudiments of piano.

Adam was exposed to San Francisco's pre-AIDS gay nightlife scene around this time, too. "I was fourteen in '78, sneaking over there because they're not checking IDs, so we can get drunk. And the sexuality part doesn't register with me. But the freedom and the insane liberation of it does. People wearing drag, topless women. When I saw *La Cage Aux Folles* or *Moulin Rouge* later, that looks a lot like those bars when I was a kid. Everyone was really nice to us, they didn't give a shit."[6]

Adam spent the 1978-79 academic year at the Taft School, a prestigious private boarding high school in Watertown, Connecticut, whose alumni include Mary Chapin Carpenter and Phish singer and guitarist, Trey Anastasio. Toward the end of a 2003 Counting Crows concert in Hartford, Adam told a funny tale about flunking a music course when he was a student at Taft. But in 2007, he attended the twenty-five-year reunion of the class of 1982 and remembered his time at the school fondly. "It wasn't until recently that I realized that being there for a year was some of my best memories. I have a couple of really good friends I made while I was there. I went back for a reunion recently and I realized that I had had a better time there than I remembered."[7]

Back home in Berkeley in the summer of 1979, Adam and his buddies played sports, camped out to get Santana tickets, and caught the J. Geils Band at the Oakland Auditorium. "I went with my friends—we were like fifteen, and we got there really early. So, the audience was four of us stoner kids and, like, 10,000 Hell's Angels. That was a pretty great show."[8]

Adam spent his last three years of high school at the Head-Royce School, an elite private facility in Oakland. His senior yearbook photo shows a smiling young man wearing an Ocean Pacific polo and a preppy haircut. Accompanying the picture is a descriptor, written by Adam, who labels himself a "Berkeley boy" and "soccer stud" who scored a forty-yard goal at the last second to tie a match. Still, Adam insists that he was not "'one of the guys' too much growing up," adding, "The truth is you probably don't get to be an artist when you're quarterback of the football team or a cheerleader."[9]

When he was in his early teens, Adam played bass and sang in a cover band with some friends from Hebrew school. They learned the Beatles, the Rolling Stones, and Led Zeppelin from song books, playing Zeppelin's "Black Dog" at friends' bar mitzvahs.

Adam's parents practiced what he has described as "fairly intense reform to conservative Judaism," and religion played a significant role in his childhood.[10] At times, Adam has downplayed his religious upbringing, describing it as "like a lot of American Jews. I had a bar mitzvah, we ate some bagels, and I went to High Holiday services."[11]

But Adam's commitment to Judaism ran deeper than that. When he was fifteen years old, he traveled to Israel on a synagogue trip with a group of students. Adam spent time wandering Jerusalem, and the group hiked through Sinai. Adam also worked at Kibbutz Nir Oz in southern Israel. Volunteers at a kibbutz are expected to perform hard, dirty manual labor in an agricultural setting. "It taught me what work is," he recalled. "To wake up at the break of dawn every day to work with your hands."[12]

The summer after he graduated from high school in 1982,

the seventeen-year-old Adam returned to Israel, where some friends were renting an apartment in Jerusalem. Adam stayed with them and studied at a local yeshiva, a religious educational facility that shares some features with a seminary. On this trip, Adam concluded that religion was not for him. "I kind of got apostate," he recalls. "I mostly just got high and drank a lot."[13]

After weeks of intense soul-searching, Adam concluded that he did not want to make religion a central part of his life. "I realized I was more about making my own thing, rather than following someone else's ideas. But it was pretty profound and it had a big effect on the rest of my life."[14] He added that, "The next day I got on a plane out of the country, and I never had anything to do with Judaism again."[15]

Adam returned from Israel in the fall of 1982 and enrolled at the University of California Davis. He spent a year and a half there, majoring in women's studies and joining the Zeta Xi chapter of the Sigma Nu fraternity.[16] At UC Davis, Adam was assigned to read poet Carolyn Forche's book, *A Country Between Us*. "It had a really big effect on me," he said.[17] "She writes about political subjects but in a very human way. I think she's the greatest writer. The way she writes, the way she says things in understatement, the things that go between the lines, the punchline at the end of the verse. She's an enormous influence."[18]

That fall, Adam wrote his first song, a humorous ode to Nicole Duritz titled "Good Morning Little Sister." The instant the song was completed, Adam knew that he had found his calling. He began working on an old piano located in the freshman dorm lounge, skipping class and obsessively crafting original songs every day. The words and music poured out of him.

Adam's songs always began with music rather than lyrics. In Adam's mind, it separated what he did from poets like Forche. "It's music and melodies and rhythms that make me want to write lyrics," he said. "It's not poetry. These are songs. Those words are meant to bounce in between those grooves and that music. And without the music I don't know if I'd be able to think of words to write."[19]

After a few months, Adam realized that his career as a songwriter had little room to blossom at UC Davis. Most of the bands in town played covers at fraternities and had no use for Adam's growing body of original tunes. UC Berkeley's writing program was among the best in the nation, and the San Francisco music scene—cradle to legends such as the Grateful Dead, Sly and the Family Stone, Jefferson Airplane, and Journey—was world famous. Besides, Berkeley was home. Adam transferred in 1984, relocating to the Bay Area, and enrolling in courses at UC Berkeley. He had stacks of newly written songs and was eager to play them. Through some old high school friends, he connected with a group of local musicians who were putting together a band.

Mod-l Society

Adam's first band, Mod-l Society, consisted of guitarist Vincent Spalding, bassist Larry Borowsky, keyboardist Dan Eisenberg, and drummer Rob Goldsby. The musicians loved Adam's original songs and his singing voice, and over the course of several months of playing together, they bonded, becoming close friends. It was Adam's first time playing in a group, an experience he found both exhilarating and exhausting. "I was really learning to work with other musicians and learning to work with other people and writing most of the material. It was really hard and really frustrating. A lot of it has to do with being willing to get into arguments with people who are your friends and you kind of lose the friendship part of it, being the guy in charge."[20]

In 1986, Mod-l Society entered Likewise Productions, an Oakland studio, to record their first single, two songs whose words and music were written by Adam. Adam co-produced the session, alongside Likewise owner Jeffry O. Holt, who would later work with guitarist Joe Satriani.

At first glance, the two songs, "Janie" and "Back to Baltimore," are featherweight pop-rock confections that lean too heavily on Dan Eisenberg's of-the-era Roland DX-7 keyboard. Scratch the surface, however, and you'll find Adam's artful lyrics, distinct phrasing, and plaintive vocal style. Adam would later become a more emotive and technically adept singer, but his voice stood out from the beginning and, even then, made him the center of musical gravity.

"Janie" was the first in a series of songs about mysterious and frustrating women—Maria, Margery, Anna, Elisabeth—who served as muse for Adam's imaginative and verbose prose. In Adam's lyrical description, Janie is forever coming and going, dreaming, playing games, and taking spontaneous holidays to Spain. As a performance, "Janie" feels rigid and hemmed in, as if Adam and company are holding back. Near the song's conclusion, the singer offers a few minor vocal flourishes, mere hints of the mesmerizing star turns that would later conclude the Crows' classic material. "Janie's" sense of constraint could have something to do with tensions bubbling between Adam and guitarist Vincent Spalding, who quit the band in the middle of the session, recording only "Janie" before departing acrimoniously.[21]

Undeterred, Adam recruited one of his musical pals, guitarist David Immerglück, whose spidery six-string provided an immediate boost to the proceedings. The second track Mod-l Society recorded, "Back to Baltimore," hit closer to home. The musicians put in an energetic take, buoyed by Immerglück, who impressed Adam enough that the singer later invited him to join Counting Crows. Adam would name drop Baltimore on "Raining in Baltimore" from the Crows' debut album, and, like that song, "Back to Baltimore" begins slowly and takes place in a train station during a downpour. But Mod-l Society quickly kicks into a rollicking country-tinged rocker that serves as a precursor to Crows' songs such as "Daylight Fading."

Adam thought enough of the two Likewise tracks to label "Janie" side one and "Baltimore" side A—there were no B-sides here. Adam also printed the lyrics to each song on the single's foldout sleeve. A limited run of one hundred copies of the vinyl 7" discs were pressed and issued on a label hastily named after the studio, Likewise Records. (Copies of the single are exceedingly rare and trade for hundreds of dollars today.) Although ostensibly a band project, the cover of Mod-l Society's debut single featured only Adam, done up in a trench coat and sunglasses a la Prince circa *Dirty Mind*. (The photo was taken by his sister, Nicole.) Adam's placement at the front and center of Mod-l Society's first single made it clear that he was a musical artist with a singular vision, realized with a little help from his friends. A strong business acumen was also in place, with A.D. Enterprise, headed by Gilbert Duritz, listed as Executive Director for the project.

The Mod-l Society single was mastered by renowned audio wizard George Horn, whose credits include everyone from Miles Davis to Blue Cheer. Horn's involvement—and hefty fee—were indicators that Mod-l Society was a serious project that was not operating on a shoestring budget. From the early days, Adam was clearly aiming for the stars.

Mod-l Society stayed together for three years, with members coming and going. This rotation included bassist Marty Jones, famed for being the "Mr. Jones" of that song's title. Keyboardist Dan Eisenberg, who went on to play with Ryan Adams and Shelby Lynn, was asked about Mod-l Society during a 2019 interview. Eisenberg remembered the group fondly, recalling, "It was a really fun band to be a part of. The music we played was Americana based—a lot of great songs."[22]

But Mod-l Society's contentious atmosphere never sat well with Adam. In later years, Adam has said that he was not yet prepared to deal with the politics of being in a band. "The first time you really join a band, you have to work, you have to argue. There's things that are very important to you. So my first band, which I loved, was a really difficult experience for me—learning to be a bandleader."[23]

Some of these issues had to do with Adam's lifestyle, built around late nights and plenty of sex, drugs, and rock 'n' roll. "I was an athlete as a kid, and I got really far away from that," he recalled. "When I got to college, after all those years of athletics,

I felt, 'I am so tired of running around. I want to get high, get drunk,' so I stopped all that shit. So then there were years of just drinking and smoking."[24]

According to Adam, his alcohol and drug issues at this time became serious. "When I was twenty-three, I just didn't have sober days. I was falling apart. I was in a really big hole. There was a time I couldn't tie my own shoelaces–when I had to sleep in the same bed as my dad because I couldn't get to sleep otherwise...I was dangerously screwed up for a long time, and drugs exacerbated it. Lots of drinking and drugs—pot, hallucinogens."[25]

With the help of his parents and some doctors, Adam improved. "I was able to wean myself of all medication. I started to climb out of the hole a little bit."[26] But Adam never graduated from UC Berkeley. He completed all of his coursework but did not finish his senior thesis about a female American expatriate poet living in London during the Blitz. "It was the last thing and I just didn't turn it in. I was doing other things the whole time anyway. I planned to get back and turn it in. I got an extension on it, an incomplete. I just never did it. You don't go to college to get a degree. You go to college to learn something. So I learned it. I don't regret college at all. I learned a lot. And I am a writer."[27]

Shallow Days at Dancing Dog

Frustrated with Mod-l Society, in the spring of 1989, the twenty-four-year-old Adam recorded a set of newly composed songs at a local facility called Dancing Dog Studios. Dancing Dog, which operated from the mid-1980s until 1997, was owned by a pair of musicians, Dave Bryson and Lydia Holly. The sixteen-track operation was located at 1500 Park Avenue in Emeryville, near Oakland. It was the heart of the warehouse district, home to bohemian musicians and artists of every variety. Dancing Dog was frequented by local alternative rock and punk outfits such as Mr. Bungle, Operation Ivy, 4 Non Blondes, and Jawbreaker. In 1993, Green Day booked Dancing Dog to work on demos for their breakthrough album, *Dookie*.

The songs Adam recorded in 1989 explored the contours of relationships. Each one featured a different female protagonist—Eliza, Mary Jane—with Adam flitting in and about. "Love and Addiction" is not particularly observant about either topic, but love as a form of addiction would serve as the primary theme of Counting Crows' debut album. In the early demos, as well as in later works, Adam's cadre of female muses elicit different emotional reactions. In "Shallow Days," the singer plays cat and mouse with a boy toy atop shimmering singsong synthesizers.

Adam wrote all the lyrics for the earliest Crows songs, but the music is credited to Adam and the musicians who played on the sessions. The singer recruited several Dancing Dog regulars for the demos, including Bryson on guitar and Holly on keyboards and backing vocals. Adam called upon Mod-l Society's Marty Jones to handle bass, and Jones tapped his cousin, Toby Hawkins, to sit in on drums. Hawkins was a Dancing Dog regular and friends with Bryson and Holly. "I was doing a good bit of session work as a drummer at [Dancing Dog]," Hawkins recalls. "The two of us were wanting to do something together, so with my cousin, [Marty Jones], we pieced together the first incarnation of the Crows. Those first demos were downright amazing."[28]

Adam would make many changes to these initial demos in developing the Counting Crows project. The early tracks were keyboard heavy and clean, with processed electric guitars and nary an acoustic instrument in sight, save for drums and a hint of piano beneath the gloss.

But the new songs confirmed what Adam already knew in his heart—he was finished with Mod-l Society. "I hated it after a while," he said of his first band. "I was like, 'Wow this is this thing I love to do, and I'm tired of arguing with my best friends over it.' So I quit."[29]

Adam dropped out of the music scene for a time to work in landscaping and construction, saving his money to take a backpacking trip to Europe. "I was kind of drifting back then," he recalled. "To say I was in bad shape would be putting it very, *very* nicely."[30] Adam saved his paychecks and took a soul-searching journey around Europe in the summer of 1989, spending weeks riding the trains with an open-ended ticket and living out of a backpack.

Adam traveled to an island in Greece, where he met an Australian woman named Anna. Over a period of weeks, the two fell in love, knowing that the relationship had no chance. He would eventually write "Anna Begins" about this experience of being paralyzed by the weight of his feelings for the woman he met in Greece that summer.

When Adam left Berkeley for Europe, he was certain that he was done playing music forever. During the voyage, however, he came to appreciate music's significance in his life. He was also deeply envious to learn that his buddy David Immerglück had been asked to join Camper Van Beethoven and tour as opener for 10,000 Maniacs.

Adam returned to the U.S. determined to re-engage with music. He immediately got in touch with Dave Bryson, wanting to continue recording demos at Dancing Dog. They taped "Anna Begins," which chronicled Adam's short-but-intense romance in Greece. The 1989 demo of "Anna" is not markedly different from the version that was later released on the Crows' debut album. The production leans more heavily on Lydia Holly's keyboards, but the arrangement is essentially the same. Adam's lyrics are identical to the released version, an indicator that he considered each word of his songs to be essential. Nearly every vocal tic that would make "Anna" such an iconic song is already in place. All of this demonstrated how much Adam brought to the table, how his lyrics and voice are the essence of Counting Crows. When recording the Crows' debut album, Adam replaced every musician on "Anna Begins," save for Bryson, and the song did not lose a thing. If Adam is singing, you are listening to Counting Crows.

Adam and Bryson's vision for a group was a rock band founded on keyboards and effects-laden guitars. They imagined something akin to artful and intelligent outfits like the Cure or the Talking Heads and began developing songs in that vein: "40 Years" with its Love and Rockets bar-chord thrust, "Bulldog," which featured a Police-like chorus, and "Lightning" with its dramatic political overtones a la Peter Gabriel. "We sounded a lot like late Roxy Music," Adam said of the Crows' early sound. "That's kind of where Dave's guitar leanings were from, a lot of Stone Roses kind of stuff."[31] To record the new songs at Dancing Dog, Adam and Bryson enlisted fellow musicians and former bandmates to help out. Although lots of recording took place, the early version of the Crows never played a live show or moved beyond the demo-recording stage.

In late 1990, twenty-six-year-old Adam was rooming with David Immerglück in a Berkeley warehouse. One afternoon, Immerglück returned home clutching the latest issue of *SF Weekly*, an alternative newspaper. He had circled an ad in the classified section. There was a newly forming group that was in search of a singer. "Get off your ass and call these guys," Immerglück told Adam. "The ad's silly. These guys sound fucking ridiculous. They're probably the perfect band for you. Anyway, you gotta get off of your ass and play some music."[32]

With some reluctance, Adam picked up the phone. As it turned out, it was a call that changed the course of his life.

The Himalayans

The Himalayans were formed in San Francisco in late 1990 by guitarist Dan Jewett and drummer Chris Roldan, who had played together previously in a number of bands. The duo recruited bassist Dave Jankuso and began writing and rehearsing in a damp Mission District basement, crafting psychedelic soundscapes that blended R.E.M.-esque jangle pop with harder rock sounds. The trio sought a singer and lyricist, and their ad in *SF Weekly* yielded several contenders. The Himalayans had already decided on a singer when Adam rang, but they told him to come by the following night and try out.

Adam drove to the Himalayans' basement rehearsal space with few expectations. Following a brief round of introductions, the group asked the singer if he wanted to try some cover tunes. Adam demurred. "Play one of your songs and let's see how it goes." The musicians launched into their first number and Adam stepped up to the mic. "It was magic," he would later recall. Adam fit perfectly into the Himalayans' psychedelic swirl, pulling phrases and melodies, seemingly from nowhere, that soared above the cacophony. "Words just came out of me. Thankfully they were taping the audition because I think we wrote most of three or four of our first songs right there during the audition. It was like I've been playing these songs forever."[33]

Forty minutes later, they came up for air. Adam and the Himalayans stood, staring at each other in disbelief, trying to wrap their minds around what had just occurred. "Uh, you're in the band," someone said to the singer.

Mod-l Society had been rife with contention and infighting, and Adam enjoyed the Himalayans' easy-going, democratic nature. The guys would rehearse at night and then drink and dine around the corner at a small Salvadorian restaurant called Mi Mazatlan. Adam loved the prospect of not having to come up with the music, not having to be the driving force of the group. He was content to write lyrics and sing.

The Himalayans were a guitar-driven rock band, somewhere along the lines of contemporaries such as the Gin Blossoms and Pearl Jam. In fact, they were currently looking to add a second guitar to their lineup to beef up their sonic attack.

There was little overlap between the songs the Himalayans were writing and Adam's new wave project with Dave Bryson.

Adam and Bryson continued to write and record material, and beginning in March 1991, they began performing from time to time at cafes and open-mic nights around Berkeley. The pair dubbed themselves Counting Crows, taking the name from "One for Sorrow," a traditional English nursery rhyme. At these gigs, the duo would play one or two songs, appearing in a lineup of fellow amateurs and hopefuls. Adam was quickly developing into an electric live performer. He did not merely sing songs, he inhabited them, waving his arms dramatically as he wailed. Between numbers, he was extroverted, chatty, and funny. Adam and Bryson would launch into a theatrical rendition of the Himalayans' "Round Here" and bring the house down.

"I remember standing in the back of the club being stunned by this story, by these characters, and by this guy singing it," Bay Area keyboardist Charlie Gillingham recalled of his first time seeing Adam and Bryson play "Round Here" in a small cafe. "I remember feeling like nobody was noticing but this is it. This is the real thing. This is what we're all trying to do. This is genius, this is great."[34]

The acoustic structure brought out new qualities in Adam's singing, heretofore unseen nuances whose potential slowly began to reveal itself. With Bryson's acoustic guitar serving as foundation for Adam's soaring vocals, the pair would play newly written tunes alongside marvelously deconstructed versions of songs by the Cure, the Talking Heads, and the Psychedelic Furs. The pair fully commandeered the new wave covers, transforming them into what could have been original material.

As if fronting two musical projects wasn't enough, Adam

also carved out a space for himself as a backup singer in another group, Sordid Humor. Sordid Humor was a popular local rock outfit whose members overlapped with the Himalayans' network, including Adam's longtime friend and occasional roommate, David Immerglück, former Mod-l Society bassist Marty Jones, and Jones' cousin, drummer Toby Hawkins, who had played on Adam's demos in 1989. Adam regularly performed live with Sordid Humor, contributing harmony vocals and grooving along to their music. The singer also added backup vocals to several Sordid Humor studio recordings, including "Doris Day" and "Private Archipelago," which were taped at Dave Bryson's Dancing Dog. As he would later do famously with acts such as the Wallflowers, Adam's backing vocals did not blend into the surroundings. Rather, on songs such as "Barbarossa," his voice took on a prominence, offering counter lines with different lyrics that were more akin to a co-lead vocal than a backing track. One of Adam's favorite Sordid Humor songs was "Jumping Jesus," which Counting Crows would later record and perform frequently in concert.

Between Sordid Humor, the Himalayans, and Counting Crows, Adam was immersed in music around the clock. "We'd opened for each other, we'd closed for each other, we'd all played in a million bands around each other. It was a really tight scene, San Francisco. There was so much music every night. And I was in three bands, so I knew everybody."[35] Adam would later reflect that this era "was probably the greatest period of musical productivity of my entire life."

Adam's work with all three of these groups influenced what would eventually become Counting Crows. This fact was most evident in the Himalayans' penning of one of the Crows' signature songs, "Round Here." Adam's performance in the earliest known version, recorded in March 1991, is fully realized. Everything that makes his execution so remarkable in the final Crows version is already in place. Maria puts in her first of several appearances in Adam's lyrical oeuvre. The song's structure is nearly identical, save for a few lyrical differences and a guitar-heavy middle section that threatens to veer off course. The three Himalayans prove a capable backing group, with Jankuso's bass assuming a prominence that gets dialed down in later renditions. It is, however, Adam's ability to convey a sense of melancholy and despair that gives the song its emotional punch.

"Round Here," along with two other songs, were captured on a sixteen-track recorder at Dancing Dog and produced by Dave Bryson. Adam continued to perform acoustically with Bryson under the name Counting Crows.

The Himalayans took "Round Here" and other songs to the stage at 924 Gilman Street, a tiny Berkeley nightclub where the group performed some of its earliest gigs. At that point, Adam still looked the part of the California college student, with baggy shorts, tennis shoes, and a white t-shirt. His signature dreadlocks were a ways off—Adam wore his hair short, in an almost preppy cut. But his energetic and engaging performance style was well in place. Soon after, the quartet committed a longer set of nine songs to a four-track cassette recorder, including a second go at "Round Here."

Looking to expand their sound, the Himalayans moved Jankuso to second guitar and recruited bassist Marty Jones, who had played in both Mod-l Society and Sordid Humor. A May 1991 gig at the I-Beam showcased the new five-piece unit. Rather than hardening a twin-guitar attack, the group went the other direction, using an acoustic guitar to compliment new tunes such as the swelling "River Shannon." The Himalayans began performing regularly in concert, scraping together enough funds to hire a professional sound engineer to make the quintet's music and lyrics cut through as clearly as possible.

Within months, the Himalayans amassed a following, rising to become one of the top-drawing acts in the Bay Area scene. A concert on July 16th, 1991 at the Kennel Club showcased the band's growing confidence, with a powerful take on "Round Here" that was even closer to what Adam would later achieve with the Crows. With its slap-funk bass and processed guitar tones, "Someone Else's Chapstick" was a bit of a mishmash, but echoes of "Have You Seen Me Lately?" are found in Adam's lyrics and phrasing. Throughout the set, the singer sported cargo pants rolled up to the knee, tennis shoes, and a t-shirt with the slogan "Fear No Art" in bold black lettering beneath an American flag design.

Adam turned twenty-seven the following month and began to feel the clock ticking. His friends from college had graduated, taken good jobs, and gotten married. Adam was having a ball hanging around the Berkeley nightclubs and drinking with his musician buddies, but success started to seem like a long shot. "He wanted to make something of his life by the time he turned thirty," his father, Gilbert Duritz said. "That was the time limit. That was the deadline he gave himself."[36]

The hard-drinking Adam had no plan B. It was music or

nothing. "I had nothing to fall back on. All I knew how to do was write songs and play them in clubs. But I never had any interest in anything I did. And I could see that what I was doing wasn't very good in a lot of ways. I've always been self-destructive, and I thought this was the ultimate in self-destruction—building an impossible life for myself."[37]

Down at the New Amsterdam

Adam wrote all the lyrics for the Himalayans but continued to put together complete songs for his Counting Crows side project. One night, he was hanging out in a dive bar called the New Amsterdam with Mod-l Society/Himalayans bassist Marty Jones. They were there with a group of flamenco musicians who had just performed at a Mission nightclub with Jones' father, the renowned guitarist David Silva. Standing off to one side was Kenny Dale Johnson, drummer in Chris Isaak's band. Isaak was a San Francisco musician whose latest album, *Heart Shaped World*, had sold two million copies on the strength of the top-ten hit "Wicked Game." Johnson was surrounded by a bevy of three beautiful women. Adam and Jones rhapsodized that life and love would be a whole lot easier if they were big, big stars. Adam went home that night and penned the lyrics to what would become the Crows' most iconic number, "Mr. Jones."

In the song, Adam describes the scene at the New Amsterdam with specificity—he and Jones hang out with the flamenco musicians and dancers, glancing over at the beautiful women they are too intimidated to approach. Adam sings that everyone he knows wants to be famous, but for different reasons.

Eventually, he reveals his own motivation: if he can just achieve fame, he will never be lonely again. He knows it is not true, of course. Listeners put off by the narrator's overt thirst for celebrity status found it easy to empathize with his very human reason for that desire.

As Adam continued to write new songs, he would record them at Dancing Dog with Bryson under the Counting Crows moniker. The pair called upon their local musician friends to help out, slowly amassing a catalog of songs and a steady lineup to play them. Adam and Bryson's preferred roster consisted of David Immerglück on guitar, drummer Steve Bowman, keyboardist Charlie Gillingham, and bassist Matt Malley, who had played in a popular band with Dave Bryson called Mr. Dog.

Gillingham recalled that when he began playing on Adam's demos, Bryson was clearly the most established musician among them. "When the band began, here's what I actually saw: one of our guitar-players, David Bryson, was a successful engineer who owned a studio. And he was helping this guy who didn't look like he would ever be a bandleader. What he looked like was a genius who had these amazing songs, but it was unclear whether he would ever get his head together enough to start a band."[38]

Adam and Bryson recorded fifteen songs they thought were strong. Demo tapes usually consist of two to three songs. A fifteen-song demo is considered absurd by industry standards, but the tape sounded amazing, with tracks pristinely captured and mixed to perfection in Bryson's studio. Moreover, the Crows' demo contained several key tracks that would wind up on their debut album: "Mr. Jones," "Round Here," "Rain King," "Omaha," "Anna Begins," and "A Murder of One," then known as "Counting Crows."

Adam and Bryson's acoustic shows as Counting Crows began to attract more attention, sometimes drawing crowds that rivaled those of the Himalayans. By the fall of 1991, Adam was fronting two of the most popular acts in the Bay Area. Word of Counting Crows began to spread, and one night, a rep from EMI stopped in to check out the acoustic duo. Impressed, the man from EMI invited Adam and Bryson to Los Angeles to discuss working together. Adam was twenty-seven years old, and it was the first time anyone from any record company had ever expressed interest in his music.

Although the man from EMI worked in the soundtrack department, he had a vision for Counting Crows, which he laid out for Adam and Bryson at the meeting. He envisioned the pair as a sort of grunge-era Simon and Garfunkel. He offered to sign them to a development deal that included funds to create a music video for the Himalayans' song "Round Here." In the video, Adam and Bryson would dress in black turtlenecks and sport coats, and they would perform the song in a small club surrounded by a curtain of cascading laser beams.

The pitch sounded absurd to Adam, but he was forced to seriously consider it. An avowed band guy, Adam had no interest in being part of an acoustic duo. The concept video sounded laughable. Yet, Adam was in his late twenties and had spent almost a decade languishing in obscurity in the Bay Area dive-bar scene. Here at last was a real offer—his only offer—from the same record label that once signed the Beatles.

Adam reached out to his family and school networks. He got in touch with a lawyer friend of his father's, who referred him to Allen Lenard, a music-industry attorney based in Los Angeles. Adam sent his demo tape to Lenard, who ignored it for weeks before he finally felt guilt-ridden enough to give it a listen. He was floored. "It was the single best demo tape I've ever heard in my life," said Lenard, who immediately offered to represent Adam and the Crows.[39]

Lenard passed their tape to several management firms he knew, including Direct Management Group (DMG), a Los Angeles-based company founded by former A&M Records vice president Martin Kirkup and Hollywood booking agent Steven Jensen. DMG's roster at the time included Echo and the Bunnymen and Orchestral Maneuvers in the Dark, two semi-successful British new-wave acts. Both clients would have undoubtedly been admired by Adam and Bryson, who sprinkled their acoustic sets with new-wave covers and aspired to be a blend of Roxy Music and Peter Gabriel. DMG had also steered veteran Georgia new-wave outfit, the B-52s, into the biggest hit of their career with 1989's four-million-selling album *Cosmic Thing*. Kirkup and Jensen adored the Crows' demo tape and vowed to get the band in front of every major label in town.

It was clear that Counting Crows, and not the Himalayans, was going to be the project to go all the way. Wanting to capture their most recent songs, in December 1991, the Himalayans recorded eleven originals in a single-day, live-to-tape session in a Russian Hill studio. It would be the group's final outing. Bryson was also busy during this time working as engineer and co-mixer for Faith No More's *Angel Dust* album, which was recorded at a San Francisco studio named Coast Recorders from late 1991 to March 1992.

The Star Maker

Direct Management circulated the Crows demo tape, and it immediately attracted attention from prominent music-industry players. Gary Gersh, a founding partner at Geffen Records, heard about the Crows from a friend of his wife. Geffen was arguably the biggest record label in the world at that time, with a roster that included Guns 'N' Roses, Don Henley, Peter Gabriel, and many more. Gersh got a copy of the Crows demo and took it with him on a ski vacation in Utah for the winter holidays. He spent the trip listening to it incessantly. Gersh became almost obsessed with the demo and was determined to sign the band.

Gersh flew to San Francisco to check out the Crows' next gig, held January 26th, 1992, at the Paradise Lounge. He was unimpressed but met with the group the next day anyway, wanting to get a better sense of what they were all about. Gersh did not appreciate the Crows' new-wave leanings. Adam was a charismatic vocalist who wrote great songs, but the whole endeavor was missing a degree of grit.

A couple weeks later, Gersh and several Geffen executives returned to San Francisco to attend the Gavin Seminar for Media Professionals, an annual gathering put together by the Gavin Report, a powerful industry publication. The Crows were performing at a Gavin showcase on February 12th, at a nightclub called the I-Beam. Every major record company in the business had someone there to see the band. The Crows killed it, and a bidding war broke out with nine major labels offering contracts, some of which included multimillion dollar guarantees. Geffen, Elektra, and A&M were all serious contenders.

Gersh had personally signed Nirvana to Geffen and appealed to Adam's desire for artistic freedom. Gersh offered Adam a modest up-front advance in exchange for a higher royalty rate if the Crows' debut album sold well. The Geffen contract had options that enabled the company to release as many as six Counting Crows albums, with a firm commitment to issue at least three. More importantly, Gersh promised that Adam would have creative control over the music and input into the marketing and promotion of the band. Adam took the deal, signing a contract with Geffen Records in May of 1992.

Crucially, it was Adam's contract and his alone. The terms stipulated that Adam was the sole owner of the Counting Crows name and controlled 100% of the group's creative and business decisions. "It was all Adam," bassist Matt Malley said in a 2009 interview. "He could basically fire anybody without a reason. That was part of the contract. We all made equal royalties, but Adam made a lot more in songwriting."[40]

Sixteen months would pass between the time Adam signed with Geffen and the release of the Crows' debut album. But even during this time, Adam was enriched by his songwriting talent. Powerful industry figures such as radio host Bonnie Simmons took an early interest in the Crows. Simmons, who had helped establish Dire Straits in the U.S., was so taken with the Crows' demo that she featured tracks from it on the air at KPFA 94.1 FM, the local public station.

Simmons knew countless people in the business and

introduced Adam to musicians such as Bonnie Raitt, who did not write songs and was always looking for new material. Simmons co-owned a music publishing company and pushed to acquire Adam's songwriting rights. As other companies joined the fray, a second bidding war broke out, this time over Adam's publishing rights. He eventually inked a lucrative contract with EMI Publishing. Some joked that Adam should have called his band Accounting Crows instead.

In seeking a record deal for the Crows, Adam had weighed offers from every well-known record label and publishing company in town, pitting them against each other to improve the terms of the contracts he eventually signed. Thus, the already well-off Adam went into the Crows' first album a much wealthier and more powerful figure than anyone else in the group. That dynamic would influence everything to come, as Adam and a behind-the-scenes cadre of industry figures toiled to transform the Crows from promising newcomers into a well-oiled hitmaking and touring machine. What Adam and the others did not foresee was that the biggest challenges laid directly ahead.

Chapter 2

August and Everything After

Gary Gersh was convinced that Adam Duritz was a star in the making. Now that Adam was signed to Geffen Records and EMI Publishing, the record executive angled to connect the singer-songwriter with powerful musicians, producers, and industry figures who could take an unknown and set him up for stardom.

To begin, Gersh arranged for Adam to sing background on the new Maria McKee album. McKee had fronted the acclaimed L.A. country-punk outfit Lone Justice from 1982 until 1987. McKee signed a solo deal with Geffen, issuing a self-titled album in 1989 that was critically acclaimed but sold few copies. Geffen aimed to turn things around with McKee's follow-up, hiring famed producer George Drakoulias and bringing aboard a who's-who of L.A. rock royalty: Don Was, Benmont Tench, Jim Keltner, and co-founders of Americana band, the Jayhawks, Gary Louris and Mark Olson. In recent years, Adam has claimed that McKee was the same Maria he names in "Round Here" and "Mr. Jones," but Adam wrote those songs, using the name Maria, long before meeting McKee.

Adam's background vocals never made it to McKee's

sophomore effort, but he dueted with her on "Opelousas (Sweet Relief)," recorded for an album benefitting Victoria Williams, an L.A. based singer-songwriter who was diagnosed with multiple sclerosis. On Tuesday, June 16th, 1992, McKee headlined an exclusive benefit concert for Williams at the Whiskey a Go Go. At the show, McKee performed a cover of a folksy Mott the Hoople song, "I Wish I Was Your Mother." Adam would later adopt the concept for use in a Counting Crows song, "I Wish I Was a Girl."

Also performing that night were megaproducer T-Bone Burnett, his wife Sam Phillips, and singer-songwriter Michael Penn, brother of actor Sean Penn. Louris and Olson from the Jayhawks and members of Soul Asylum sat in, too. Celebrities in the audience included former Band guitarist and singer Robbie Robertson and folk legend Joni Mitchell. (In 2003, the Crows scored a hit with their cover of Mitchell's "Big Yellow Taxi.") Through his industry connections, Gersh managed to squeeze Adam and Bryson onto the bill. They would open the show, performing as the two-man acoustic version of the Crows that captivated audiences at Bay Area open mic nights two years earlier.

The pair of nobodies took the stage in front of a room full of Hollywood celebrities and industry insiders. It was a make-or-break moment for Adam, the first of many. Just like they had back in the Berkeley coffee shops, Adam and Bryson killed it. "All of the hipsters in Hollywood were there," Adam recalled. "But the thing about those moments is, you just play, because there's nothing else you can do. Or you can chicken out and fuck up. But we never did."[41]

The A-listers were astonished, completely floored. "Who *are* you?" some called out.

Despite the considerable star power at the Whiskey that night, a review in *The Los Angeles Times* singled out the obscure duo from the north: "The evening's most impressive and moving music came from a pair of unknowns, two members of the San Francisco band Counting Crows. Taut, nasal vocals and expressive body language brought out the pathos and passion of the duo's folkie story-songs, drawing the show's most sustained applause."[42]

Big Pink

Transforming the ragtag crew of Berkeley buskers into superstars was not an organic process. The six members of the Crows had performed in and around each other for years in the Bay Area, but they had not developed as a unit and had never played a single show together outside their hometown. Contemporaries like Nirvana and the Black Crowes spent months at a time on the road and could go into the studio to bang out an album's worth of new tunes in a matter of days. Counting Crows' debut was a more manufactured process, with Geffen using its industry clout (and dollars) to provide a large ensemble of producers, musicians, and other figures, who spent a year working behind-the-scenes to make the Crows into a mainstream success.

These machinations were headed up by the group's point of contact at Geffen, Gary Gersh, who Crows bassist Matt Malley once described as the "innovative business guy behind that band."[43] Gersh loved the Crows' fifteen-song demo but found it too clean and polished. The band's delivery was along the lines of Peter Gabriel or Roxy Music, but that did not suit their best material. The new-wave numbers needed to be retooled or excised, and standout tracks such as "Rain King" and "Omaha" cried out for grittier, more organic sonic foundations. As Gersh put it, "I wanted to take a bunch of demos that sounded like a record and turn it into a record that sounded like a bunch of demos."[44]

Gersh had access to every well-known rock producer in the business. He facilitated "tryout" sessions with R.E.M. producer Don Dixon and George Drakoulias, who was coming off a major hit with the Black Crowes' second album. But the tryouts did not take. Adam, too, had something different in mind than what the band captured on their initial demos. Partly due to the positive response to the Himalayans' "Round Here," working alone, Adam composed several new songs in that vein, some of which would appear on the debut album. Unlike guitar-driven rockers such as "Mr. Jones" and "Rain King," Adam's new songs—"Perfect Blue Buildings," "Ghost Train"—were somber, piano-based numbers steeped in stillness and melancholy.

Adam no longer liked the Counting Crows demos. He thought the effects-laden guitars sounded dated and his verbose lyrics were overly cute. "Since we recorded [those songs], I became much more honest," he explained. "They were clever more than meaningful, but not what I wanted out of our band. I wanted something more raw, emotional with edges. I was determined to make that kind of record, but we didn't know how to make a record."[45]

Gersh put Adam in touch with his close friend and client,

Robbie Robertson, who had a solo deal with Geffen at the time. Robertson was one of the A-listers who was blown away by Adam's performance at the Victoria Williams benefit. Gersh brought Adam over to Village Recorders, a fabled Santa Monica studio where Robertson was working on new material. Gersh had played select tracks from the Crows' demo to Robertson, who was taken by Adam's voice and songwriting. They sat around talking about the album, with Adam trying to explain the sound he heard in his head and the limitations of the Crows.

"You know what you ought to do? You ought to rent a house," Robertson advised. The Band had famously lived in a large, salmon-hued house while recording their 1968 masterpiece, *Music from Big Pink*, and Robertson believed this strategy would pay dividends for the Crows. "You all could live there, and you could make a record there. And you'll learn to play together because you'll be living together."[46]

Adam was sold on the idea, and Geffen began searching for a location where the Crows could live and record. "The last thing we wanted to do was to go into a studio where we would all know what we were doing and make a 'professional' record," Adam said. "I wanted to go to live it. To be stuck in there, trapped, where the whole world is making that record."[47]

Adam and the Crows needed to secure a producer who was willing to forgo the comforts of the professional studio and set up shop in a rental house. Bonnie Simmons, the Bay Area radio host and Crows superfan, had passed the group's demo tape to her friend, T-Bone Burnett, several months earlier. Gary Gersh, who knew everyone in the business, set up a meeting. Burnett was a guitarist and musician who built a reputation for the rootsy, natural-sounding productions he created for artists such as Los Lobos, Elvis Costello, and Bruce Cockburn. Burnett had been impressed by Adam and Bryson's performance at the Victoria Williams benefit and agreed to produce the Crows debut. Unlike other contenders, he loved the idea of working in a house instead of a traditional space. "Recording studios are breeding grounds for despair," the producer told *Rolling Stone* in 1994. "We all agreed that our favorite records had a sense of place."[48]

With Burnett at the helm, the six members of Counting Crows moved into a house in a canyon outside Santa Monica in the fall of 1992. Adam and Burnett insisted that the musicians pare everything down in order to make the songs as raw and emotional as possible. They excised Matt Malley's slick fretless basses and replaced them with antique models. Steve Bowman's huge, tricked-out drum kit was cut in half, and they removed most of his cymbals. They forbade Charlie Gillingham from using keyboards or synthesizers, limiting him to piano, Hammond B organ, and an accordion. Bryson was not allowed to use any effects on his guitar. Burnett instructed the musicians to keep it simple, to hold back, to play less. "I was pretty young," drummer Steve Bowman recalled. "I came in with more notes than were needed. He quickly cut that in half."

Adam's and Burnett's directives did not sit well with most of the Crows, seasoned professionals who bristled at being told how and what to play, and even which instruments to use. Adam claims that everyone in the band quit at some point during the making of the album. "It was brutal," he conceded.[49]

Once the musicians were stripped to the essentials, the

group had to learn to work together and be a real band. "You need to learn to play. You need to learn to listen," Adam explained. "We built a studio in a house, and we got in a circle, and we played and played and played and listened to each other. I didn't even sing. T-Bone Burnett played acoustic guitar and sang. I played harmonica, which I can't play but anyone can actually play as long as you're in the right key. And so I stood there and played harmonica until it felt like the way it was supposed to breathe. And then I went back to singing and we played the song." This arduous strategy required a willingness to try entirely new approaches to the same song. Immerglück's slashing fuzztone guitars were replaced with mandolins, pedal steels, and mandocello.

It went on like this for more than two months, with the musicians cramped up together, struggling to find the Counting Crows sound. "We had to rediscover ourselves and reinvent the music," said Charlie Gillingham, who purportedly slept on a mattress in the bathroom. "'Perfect Blue Buildings,' when we started with it, was like a pop-rock anthem. We realized in order to get to the lyric—about staying up late and contemplating suicide and drug addictions and pain—we had to bring it way down and make it very intimate. We turned out the lights and brought out the acoustic guitars and played it as quietly as we could."[50] The versions that appeared on *August* were often complete takes that were captured live in the room, including Adam's vocals. The album's long and mournful title track was worked again and again to no avail, with Adam eventually abandoning the song altogether. He kept the title, however, a reference to his life. The album would tell his story—his August

1st arrival and everything that came after.

Burnett's thumbprint is apparent on numbers such as "Omaha," whose original demo was based on a hard-rocking electric guitar lick that would not be out of place on a Rolling Stones record. For the *August* version, Burnett uses an acoustic foundation that blends David Immerglück's lilting mandolin with accordion courtesy of Charlie Gillingham. Burnett also gave Steve Bowman the last-minute instruction not to use any cymbals, forcing the drummer to rethink his entire approach just as the band was about the start recording. Burnett's musical directives perfectly complemented Adam's pastoral lyrical imagery, transforming a workaday rock tune into a homespun work of art.

A reporter who visited the house during the *August* recording sessions left unimpressed. The musicians weren't sitting around harmonizing and bonding in the woods a la *Big Pink*. They were trying to capture great performances in a soulless Hollywood mansion. The property "was a monument to '80s values—barren, white and austere. Like a lot of overpriced L.A. architecture, it had been built for millions to sell for millions more, but it had not been built for humans to live in. Now the cliffside pool was cracking and the water was running down the mountain and nothing seemed to work right. The owner had been unable to unload his crumbling Xanadu, and so was reduced to renting it to a rock band."[51]

Burnett did not restrict the recording sessions to the house or rely solely upon the members of the group. Working in four different L.A. recording studios, the producer supplemented the Crows with backing vocals from Geffen labelmate Maria

McKee and Gary Louris and Mark Olson of the Jayhawks. Robbie Robertson's longtime guitarist Bill Dillon, whose credits included Joni Mitchell and Peter Gabriel, sat in on guitar and a hybrid instrument known as a guitorgan. Burnett was also an accomplished musician and contributed guitar and other instruments to the recording. Perhaps it was the number of cooks in *August's* kitchen that caused Adam to later reflect that it was "the most produced, slickest of the albums."[52]

August's most difficult song to capture was its breakout first single, "Mr. Jones." Drummer Steve Bowman did not like the tune and could not find a groove that was acceptable to Adam or Burnett, causing frustration on all sides. The band returned to "Jones" over and over but could not capture a satisfactory take. After being asked to recut "Jones" yet another time, Bowman refused. "I don't know what I'd do differently," the drummer told Burnett.[53] The producer immediately replaced Bowman with session ace Denny Fongheiser, who nailed the drum track in a couple of takes.

Adam was ambivalent. His goal was to create an album whose songs matched his vision, despite any collateral damage. "All we could do was brutalize each other until we got it on record. It was not a picnic," he said shortly after the record was finished.[54] But the use of an outside drummer caused considerable hard feelings on the part of Bowman, particularly later when "Mr. Jones" became the group's signature hit.

Hall of Fame

In the middle of the tumultuous *August* sessions, the band pulled off an incredible coup. Van Morrison was supposed to appear at the Rock and Roll Hall of Fame ceremony, which was scheduled to take place in Los Angeles on January 12th, 1993. On January 10th, Morrison canceled. Adam claims that it was Robbie Robertson's idea to have the Crows fill in and play a Morrison song. The notion of an unknown band that had never released so much as a single standing in for Morrison in front of rock's elite was preposterous, but it was an offer the Crows could not refuse. Adam decided that he would perform acoustically, backed by Dave Bryson on acoustic guitar and David Immergluck on mandolin. On the flight to L.A. the next day, the singer selected "Caravan" from a stack of hastily purchased Van Morrison cassettes.

The 1993 Hall of Fame inductees included Cream, the Doors, Sly and the Family Stone, Creedence Clearwater Revival, and Etta James. When the Crows arrived at an L.A. warehouse for rehearsals, they overheard Pearl Jam leader Eddie Vedder singing "Roadhouse Blues" with the three living Doors. Bruce Springsteen, Eric Clapton, Jack Bruce, and Don Was were hanging out, watching. That afternoon, Adam and company witnessed Cream rehearse together for the first time in more than two decades and then played basketball with Eddie Vedder. According to Adam, the Pearl Jam vocalist was complimentary and said that he thought the two singers had a similar approach.

The ceremony took place at the Plaza Century Hotel, and soundcheck the morning of the show was more of the same: John Fogerty, Bonnie Raitt, k.d. lang, Sly Stone, and George Clinton were all on hand, checking out the Crows and congratulating them afterwards on a job well done. Funk legend

George Clinton asked Adam for his autograph, the first time it had ever happened to the singer. Adam shook his head in disbelief, telling Clinton, "You're gonna have to give me yours first, because this is too weird."[55]

When it came time to perform, by all accounts, Adam and his bandmates killed it, submitting a version of "Caravan" that did more than pay homage to Morrison's original, it extended his beloved work. Stretching the song past the five-minute mark, Adam had plenty of time to offer a complete demonstration of his vocal and performing prowess, bringing the number to a powerful conclusion with little other than his voice.

Adam did not have his signature dreadlocks at this point and spent most of the performance wrestling with a floppy hat that refused to stay in place. Regardless, "Caravan" went over well, and Adam was officially anointed by the rock royalty of the day. "What a chance, to get up and show off in front of Bruce Springsteen and George Clinton," Adam marveled a few months after the ceremony. "I'm not really scared of that stuff. That's one thing I can do—close my eyes and sing these songs. They mean everything to me."[56]

The Crows returned to their rented house soon after to complete the sessions for their debut. Adam composed one final song, "Raining in Baltimore," which he had written for Bonnie Raitt. When T-Bone Burnett heard Adam rehearsing the number on piano one day, he insisted that it replace the unfinished title track. *August* was mixed by Scott Litt, whose credits included R.E.M. and Nirvana—along with engineer Pat McCarthy. The long and difficult process of bringing *August* to life was complete.

Geffen opted to release *August* on DCG, a subsidiary label that was home to alternative superstars such as Nirvana, Sonic Youth, and Beck. Geffen had invested heavily in the Crows and were determined to put the group over the top. To do so, there was the matter of Adam, the band's 28-year-old singer, who looked more like an accountant than a rock star. The company gave him a makeover, complete with new wardrobe and the addition of what would become Adam's trademark, long dreadlock extensions that he had installed in a Berkeley salon. The singer never hid the fact that his dreadlocks were fake. "The first time I wore them was the first time I really looked like myself to me," he told *Rolling Stone* in 1994.[57] For better or worse, the dreadlocks would be forever synonymous with Adam and the Crows.

Another major shift following the recording of *August* was the departure of David Immerglück, Adam's longtime friend and fellow musician whose musical contributions are all over *August*. Immerglück was enjoying a successful indie-rock career at the time. He was the guitarist in a Camper Van Beethoven offshoot, the Monks of Doom, that landed a deal with I.R.S. Records, the label that launched the careers of R.E.M. and the Police. Adam claimed that Immerglück was conflicted, concerned about moving down into the ranks of an unknown band. Undeterred, the Crows hired axe man Dan Vickrey and moved forward. Vickrey, who remains in the group today, would appear in the music videos for *August* but did not play on the Crows' debut.

On June 19, 1993, the retooled Crows surfaced to play their first gig in months. They opened with "Margery Dreams of

Horses" and "Open All Night," promising new songs that were not included on the album. The Crows then showcased nine of *August's* eleven tracks. A few weeks later, *Sweet Relief: A Benefit for Victoria Williams* was released, featuring Adam singing backup on the Maria McKee song, "Opelousas (Sweet Relief)." It was his first appearance on a major-label album.

Triple A

That summer, as Geffen toiled behind the scenes to prepare the Crows' debut, the band scored another massive coup thanks to longtime supporter Bonnie Simmons, the San Francisco DJ who continued to feature songs from the Crows' demo on her radio program.

Simmons arranged for the group to perform at the AAA Records and Radio Convention, held in Boulder, Colorado. The convention was largely attended by radio station directors who were experimenting with a new programming format known as Adult Alternate Album (AAA). Simmons thought the AAA format, which emphasized rootsy, honest music, was perfect for the Crows. The development and popularity of the AAA format played a significant role in the Crows own trajectory. Burnett and the Crows recorded *August* at the exact time the powers that be at Big Radio were creating a new format that fit the album's sound. For the next two decades, the Crows' biggest radio hits would be on stations that programmed the AAA format.

On August 27th, 1993, the Crows played their first out-of-town gig at the Fox Theater in Boulder, Colorado. The group was the opening act at the Gavin AAA Radio Station Summit.

Introduced by the emcee as a band who was "so new, I haven't even heard of them yet," the Crows opened with "Round Here," a distinct song that made them stand out. "Rain King" and "Time and Time Again" followed, and the group also included "Caravan," which all the radio programmers had heard about from the Rock and Roll Hall of Fame show. Sharing the bill at the Fox that evening were three established artists, Rosanne Cash, Maria McKee, and Bruce Cockburn. But according to Geffen vice-president Bill Bennett, it was the Crows who won the night. "They just blew everybody away," he raved.[58]

The following day, Adam, backed by Bryson and Malley on acoustic instruments, performed live in the studio at KBCO 97.3 FM, a Denver-based radio station.

Adam and the higher-ups at Geffen clashed over *August's* first single. Everyone believed that "Rain King" was going to be the breakout track, the song that put the album and the band over the top, but first, the label needed to release an inaugural single that would introduce the Crows to the world.

Geffen hired Bay Area DJ and mega-fan Bonnie Simmons to help promote the Crows to the AAA radio programmers. Within weeks of *August's* September 14th, 1993 release date, FM stations around the country were playing songs from it, with "A Murder of One" getting the most positive response. Geffen also spent promotional funds to get the Crows played on alternative-rock radio stations, some of which began spinning "Mr. Jones."

Geffen insisted that "A Murder of One" was the perfect introductory single, but at nearly six minutes, it would have to be cut in half in order to generate airplay. Most radio stations did not accept six-minute songs, particularly from unknown acts. Adam balked at the prospect of carving up "Murder" for commercial purposes; he pressed the label to issue "Mr. Jones" instead. At a stalemate, Geffen did not issue a single at the time of *August's* release.

On Their Own

Counting Crows were virtually unknown beyond the Bay Area club scene, and now began the next uphill battle—to build a national following. Crows co-manager Martin Kirkup told *Rolling Stone* that there was no marketing strategy for the group other than to "let the record get out there and give people a chance to see the band and have the pleasure of discovering them on their own."[59]

Geffen arranged for the Crows to hit the road as openers on a bill that featured another up-and-coming act, the Cranberries, with U.K. rockers Suede headlining. They began in a van, pulling a trailer, and followed by Adam driving his father's old Datsun B210. The first show of the tour was September 9th, 1993, at the Town Pump in Vancouver, and featured just the Crows and the Cranberries.

Adam recalls that prior to this concert, he informed the group that he was going to improvise something in the middle of "Rain King" and that they should follow him. From then on, improvisation became a hallmark of the Crows live experience, with Adam blending lyrical bits and pieces of other songs into Crows' originals such as "Round Here."

The following night, the tour played Portland before hitting Detroit, Chicago and St. Louis. The Crows were finding their legs, gelling as a live, touring unit for the first time. They returned home to play an album release party at the Warfield Theater on September 17th, three days after *August* hit the shelves. A thousand revelers showed up to greet them, the band's largest hometown turnout to date.

The Crows opened with "Children in Bloom," a freshly penned composition that would appear on their second album. The group featured "Children" at shows for much of the *August* touring cycle. Next was another unreleased number, "Margery Dreams of Horses," whose lyrics include the name Anna, leading to speculation that the song was a sequel to "Anna Begins." Here again, the Crows demonstrated a knack for improvisation, a desire to vary their setlists from night to night, and hone new material on stage.

"We just had our first week of tour," Adam told the audience after the song ended. "We went to Seattle, Portland, and Vancouver. It was really rockin'. It's the first time we've ever done that. And so of course, I lost my voice immediately after. But it's back tonight." Adam attempted to clear his throat comically before introducing "Rain King." Adam brushed off his throat issues at the time, but his offhand remark foreshadowed years of voice-related problems to come.

Following "Ghost Train" and "Anna Begins," Adam addressed the crowd again. "So we had a record come out. It's the first one we've ever had. It came out a couple of days ago and this one isn't on it." The band played another unreleased new song, "Open All Night."

The show was packed with family, friends, and plenty of Bay Area musicians who had played alongside the Crows over the years. "Omaha" got a big reception, at the end of which Adam marveled, "There's a lot of people here. Did you notice that? This is the biggest show we've played here. There's probably about a thousand of you."

Next up was "Perfect Blue Buildings," which Adam introduced as his favorite song on the new album. The group ended their main set with a raucous take on "A Murder of One," before an encore that began with a pair of covers, "The Ghost in You" by the Psychedelic Furs and Van Morrison's "Caravan."

"This is our last song but I want to thank you guys for coming out," Adam told the audience. "There's like a million of you and that's just fucking great. And apparently, we sold a bunch of records last week, too, so whoever the fuck did that, thank you for that, too. We sold a bunch of records in *Reno* and I've never even been to Reno. So whichever one of you drove to Reno and bought all those records, we appreciate that, too." Adam thanked the opening act, before adding, "After we get off, I hope a lot of you stick around cause it's our release party and we want to hang out with all our friends." The following morning, the Crows departed for a gig in Denver. Things would rarely feel so normal again.

The Crows toured relentlessly in the fall of 1993, zigzagging the country and picking up whatever gigs came their way. As an opening act with one album to their name, the song selection did not change much from night to night, but Adam continually rearranged the running order of the tunes to keep things fresh. The band received positive notices, such as a brief paragraph in a larger review of the Cranberries and Suede in the Boston College student newspaper. The reviewer praised the Crows' thirty-minute set. "Their brand of classic American rock and roll came across honestly and impassioned and was an enticing preview of a band that should be turning a few heads before too long."[60] Featured on some of the Cranberries/Suede tour dates was a young Boston outfit called the Gigolo Aunts, whose singer, Dave Gibbs, befriended Adam.

In late September, the Crows played the first of two West Coast dates, opening for Midnight Oil. The group spent a good portion of the fall opening for Cracker, an alternative-rock act led by Dave Lowery that featured former members of Camper Van Beethoven. Cracker was riding high on the strength of what would be their biggest hit, "Low," and the shows went over well. Jon Pareles of *The New York Times* praised the Crows' November 12th performance with Cracker at Irving Plaza. Pareles singled out "Mr. Jones" and favorably compared Adam to Van Morrison, Bruce Springsteen, and R.E.M. vocalist Michael Stipe, calling him "a proud throwback to the days of earnest, poetic, enigma-slinging songwriters."[61]

On December 1st, 1993, Geffen issued "Mr. Jones" as the first single from *August,* and it became a minor hit on college radio. An accompanying music video generated modest airplay on MTV beginning in mid-December. The video is simple but effective, largely consisting of the band performing the song in the living room of a small apartment. The focus is squarely on Adam, who sports jeans and a t-shirt with a buckskin fringe jacket over the top. He flails and wails with exuberance before a vintage microphone as the players crank gamely in the background.

The Crows capped 1993 by opening for Cracker at the

Coach House in San Juan Capistrano, south of Los Angeles. Three weeks later, the group performed on *Saturday Night Live* and rocketed to fame.

Elisabeth

Over the past three decades, Adam and others have perpetuated the myth that the Crows were an obscure band that was not even on the *Billboard* charts when they played *Saturday Night Live*, but this is not true. *SNL* does not have a history of plucking musicians from obscurity and putting them on live television. Rather, the show prides itself on booking the hottest up-and-coming acts, which is what the Crows were in late 1993.

Thanks to MTV's playing of the "Mr. Jones" video, *August* entered the *Billboard* 200 album charts on January 1st, 1994 at number 188, climbed to number 159 the following week, and had reached 116 and sold about 120,000 copies the week of January 15th when the Crows performed on *SNL*.[62] The band's performance, along with heavy rotation from MTV, provided a significant boost—the album leapt forty-six spaces to number seventy the week of January 22nd and landed at number thirty-two a week later. *August* then spent two weeks in the top fifteen.

"That scared the shit out of me," Adam told a reporter with *August* sitting at number thirteen. "That's like Mariah Carey. That's for huge people."[63] Adam added that if things did not work out with music, "you have the rest of your life to regret your failure. And if everything doesn't fall apart you have the rest of your life to live with your fame. Either one requires a serious adjustment."[64]

August entered the top ten on February 19th, where it spent an astonishing thirty-two weeks, more than half the year. On two occasions in April of 1994, *August* reached its highest chart position, number four. The album lingered in the top ten until October 1st, when it finally dropped to number thirteen. As *August* began ascending the charts in early 1994, the Crows played a string of East Coast dates before pairing with Cracker in the West. Although the Crows were still the opener, they were outdrawing Cracker at this point.

In February, Adam introduced a new song, "Goodnight Elisabeth," to the band's live sets. He had written "Elisabeth" over the winter holidays when he returned from the first several months on the road. It was about his girlfriend, Elisabeth, who everyone called Betsy. When Adam left for that first tour, everything seemed great. He was in a successful band with a major label deal and a record coming out. He was going out on tour. He was in a solid relationship. When he returned home that December, the Crows had taken off, but the relationship was finished.

"Elisabeth" is a heartfelt piano-based ballad where Adam wishes Betsy goodnight from somewhere on the road. He is isolated, performing every night like some sort of clown in a circus. He misses her, but the temptations of the road prove too strong. He knows their relationship is over, that everything is different now. But he still yearns for her and everything they once were. "Elisabeth" would become a centerpiece of the Crows' sophomore album.

In an interview that spring, Adam explained that his relationship with Betsy was over, but the problems inherent to his having a serious relationship were not. He was still a rock star on the road—playing music every night, drinking, carousing, and being approached by women at every turn. The next day, he'd pack his bags and be off to the next town—and the next one-night stand. "That is what's going on right now, and it's still the same! I'm still leaving every day. Now I'm protected by the excuse that the band's leaving every day, but I'm not enough of a fool to think that I wouldn't do it anyway. I left a girlfriend at home when we started this. I was very much in love but it eventually became too hard to do it, and too easy to meet girls on the road. I'm not talking about bimbos, I mean really cool people. But I left behind something I thought was love. And I would do it again. Because this is what I do."[65]

In February, "Mr. Jones" began climbing the charts, moving up each week and bringing more and more attention to the band. The Crows capped this with a March 31st, 1994 appearance on *The Late Show with David Letterman*. By way of introduction, the famed comedic host held up a CD of *August* and told his audience of millions, "If you don't have a copy of this, there's something *wrong with you*." Acts on *Letterman* performed one song, and Adam selected the mournful "Round Here" over the peppy "Mr. Jones." The group offered a powerful version that demonstrated their growing confidence as a live unit. In foregrounding the lesser known "Round Here" over the then top-forty "Jones," the Crows demonstrated their breadth as a band. In doing so, Adam and company were able to steer somewhat clear of the pigeonholing that was detrimental to early 1990s flash-in-the-pans, such as the Spin Doctors and Blues Traveler.

The spotlight glared on Adam like never before. During

interviews he gave at the time, the singer came across as grateful but dazed. Adam was clearly unsure of how to react to his unexpected celebrity. "I'm in shock," he told a reporter from the *San Francisco Chronicle* shortly after the *Letterman* appearance, with *August* sitting at number four on the charts. "I thought we would make a nice, small record and tour. I don't understand how this happened."[66]

On May 14th, 1994, "Jones" peaked at number five on the *Billboard* charts. The song was ubiquitous and played in constant rotation on MTV. "Jones" was a worldwide hit, charting in Australia, France, Ireland, and Iceland. The single went gold in the U.K., Denmark, and Italy. Adam seemed increasingly uneasy with his rising stature. "I'm happy with the fame in a lot of ways. I won't deny that," he told a reporter the same week "Jones" peaked in the U.S. "But it's kind of scary. Something has definitely changed in my life, and I can't go back now if I wanted to."[67]

Adam's deeply personal songs were connecting with millions of people who believed that the singer understood their pain. "There's all these really crappy parts to [fame]. You bare your soul to all these people and you don't think about it when you do it, because it's what you do as a writer. But you're making millions of people your confidant. And then they expect to come talk to you and be your friend. That's hard, especially when people want you to be very open and personal in response."[68]

Literature Roadie

The critical reaction to *August* was positive, although not universally so. In late 1993, *The Los Angeles Times* declared the album to be "the most promising debut of the year." *Rolling Stone* gave it four out of five stars, comparing the Crows to U2 and Van Morrison and raving that *August* "communicates complex (and often desperate) emotions honestly and intelligently without resorting to cliches or cheap sentimentality."[69]

The praise for *August* was often paired with fawning portraits of Adam in the press. In 1994, a writer from *The San Francisco Chronicle* described the singer as "a deferential and earnest young man with a ready smile and a powerful appetite for music—he is collecting gospel tapes from truck stops around the country." In *Rolling Stone's* 1994 cover story, David Wild gushed that Adam was "intensely introspective and self-confident. He's open ... He's also extremely well read—having devoured Shelby Foote's entire Civil War series, assorted works by William Kennedy, James Thurber, John O'Hara, E.M. Forster, Banana Yoshimoto and, yes, Levon Helm recently. He may be the first rock star to need a literature roadie." Like many writers, Jon Pareles of *The New York Times* praised Adam for embedding literary references into songs such as "Rain King," whose title came from Saul Bellow's novel, *Henderson the Rain King*.

The media also took an interest in Adam's love life, with publications such as *Rolling Stone* speculating about Adam and two actresses he'd dated, Samantha Mathis and Mary Louise Parker. "Girls have always liked Adam," his sister Nicole said. "Why not? He's funny, he's charming, and he's passionate about what he does."[70]

The intense focus on Adam did not sit well with everyone

in the Crows. Several members were jealous or resentful and felt that the singer abandoned them in his quest for stardom. "We started off as the Beatles and turned into Elvis," they moaned to one another. When Adam's bandmates were quoted in the press, it was often in response to questions about the singer's stardom and their own anonymity. For example, during a group interview at a New York radio station, the DJ wondered if Adam might become separated from the rest of the musicians to the point where they were seen as his backup sidemen. Drummer Steve Bowman responded, "Up until now Adam's been really good about this. In fact, he refuses to stand in front of the picture and little things like that."[71] Bowman's quote appeared in the May 1994 issue of *Musician* magazine, which featured a shot of the Crows on the cover. In the picture, Adam stands in front, with the five members of the group positioned behind him. "To the outside world, I'm the cute one, I'm the quiet one, I'm the funny one, and I'm the sad one," Adam told *Rolling Stone* that spring, before insisting, "This is a band. Maybe not always in terms of decision making, but it is a band."[72]

Coming to terms with the focus on Adam was difficult for everyone in the group. "There was a year of adjustment when Adam was really the rock star and the rest of us were kind of replaceable," bassist Matt Malley said in a 2009 interview. "There was a year of people trying to find their boundaries and pushing for attention and then realizing, well, it's about Adam and we had to just face that ... It was obvious. Adam was a charismatic performer and not all of us were and we were lucky to have the job we have. But it wasn't easy. You grow up thinking your heroes, they're all equal, they're all best friends, but it's not the case at all."[73]

The unyielding attention was detrimental to Adam as well. In later years, the singer revealed that around this time he began to feel self-conscious about the way he looked. An early indicator was the beard he sported when the band played *Letterman*, a face-covering barrier that Adam would deploy with increasing frequency until it became ubiquitous.

Kurt Cobain

The Crows took advantage of their newfound popularity to perform as often as possible, in as many places as they could. A three-week run of spring European dates in April found the group breaking their sets into acoustic and electric halves. For the acoustic portion, Dan was on mandolin, Dave on acoustic guitar, Charlie on accordion. Matt played a hollow body bass, and Bowman's drum kit was pared down. They reconfigured several songs into acoustic renditions, and this retooling became another staple of the band's live concerts.

Adam had also taken to changing the lyrics of "Mr. Jones" each night. Instead of wanting to be Bob Dylan, he wanted to be Alex Chilton, acclaimed but relatively obscure member of Big Star, or Dave Lowery from Cracker. At an April 22nd show in London, Adam sang that being a big star was about as fucked up as it got, pointing his finger to his head like a gun. The performance took place just weeks after Kurt Cobain shot and killed himself.

At the Paris stop on the tour, Adam met up with a reporter and photographer from *Rolling Stone*. The Crows were going to be on the cover, which provoked anxiety in Adam. Cobain seemed to kill himself due to things like appearing on the cover of *Rolling Stone*.

Adam accepted and later declined an invitation to appear on *Top of the Pops*, England's beloved TV series, which began broadcasting in 1964 and has featured the Beatles, the Rolling Stones, the Who, Elton John, David Bowie, and more. Adam refused to lip-sync, telling the show's producers that he would only appear if the Crows played live. *Top of the Pops'* production studio was not set up to accommodate live performances. Geffen was reportedly furious over the perceived diva-like behavior from Adam.

On June 20th, 1994, Geffen issued "Round Here" as the second single from *August*. It was a top-ten hit and garnered significant airplay in the U.S., Canada, and the song reached number twelve in Iceland. The accompanying music video did not feature anyone from the Crows other than Adam, who mimed and emoted atop a set of railroad tracks, wearing a maroon sweater, baggy cargo shorts, and black combat boots. Director Mark Neale, who had recently worked on a pair of U2 videos, juxtaposed shots of Adam with conceptual dreamlike footage.

On July 5th, Geffen issued *DGC Rarities, Vol. 1*, a compilation featuring B-sides and unreleased tracks from its roster of artists, including Nirvana, Weezer, Beck, and Hole. In response to the Crows' newfound popularity, Geffen included "Einstein on the Beach (For an Eggman)," a catchy pop leftover from the Crows' fifteen-song demo. The title is identical to that of a 1976 opera by American composer Philip Glass; the subtitle references "I Am the Walrus" by the Beatles. Adam thought that "Einstein" was somewhat superfluous, but the song remains the Crows' highest charting single, reaching number one on *Billboard's* alternative airplay charts the week of August 13th, 1994. Despite this success, the group has avoided performing the song live.

Backlash

The Crows always had their share of detractors, with early critics focusing on the similarities between Adam and Van Morrison's vocal tone and phrasing. The Hall of Fame performance, Adam's use of the Morrison-like "sha la la" in "Mr. Jones," and his repetition of certain words, led to accusations that the singer was a Morrison clone. Every major feature story written about the Crows in 1993 and 1994 mentioned Morrison, necessitating that Adam continually defend himself in the press. Adam grabbed the attention of the entire rock music industry at the Hall of Fame with his passionate take on "Caravan," and the band delighted in recreating that moment for fans in concert. But by the early spring of 1994, the Crows stopped playing "Caravan" altogether, retiring the song from their live sets for more than fifteen years.

As the face and sole focus of the Crows, Adam reaped most of the rewards, but he also got singled out for the lion's share of criticism. In addition to his singing style and influences, the barbs frequently attacked Adam's appearance. "Adam has the dreadlocks of a hippie rapper and the baggy shirt of an ersatz grunge kid; on *SNL* he topped it off with one of those sock hats associated with the rave world," sneered a writer from *Entertainment Weekly* in a review. "Say what you will about a young-old-fart group like Spin Doctors: They at least look as if they'd risen out of years in beer-encrusted bars and dives. Counting Crows seem as if they'd risen out of a marketing meeting at Geffen Records."[74]

As the singer's stardom rose, so did the disparagement. In July 1994, famed rock critic Robert Christgau labeled the nearly year-old *August* his Dud of the Month, writing a scathing review that appeared in the *Village Voice*: "Adam Duritz sings like the dutiful son of permissive parents I hope don't sit next to me at Woodstock. He went to good summer camps; he doesn't eat junk food; he's confused about all the right things. And he's not going away anytime soon."[75]

Criticism sometimes came from strangers in public, who would accost the singer in bars, restaurants, book shops, and record stores. "Hey, are you Adam Duritz? Man, you out to be counting your *blessings*. You guys suck and you're so successful."[76]

"It freaked me out that someone cared enough about hating me to come up to me on the street and say it to my face," Adam told a reporter in 1996. "I couldn't go out. I couldn't go to bars. Everybody had to give their opinion of me."[77]

Former Cracker drummer (and future Crows stickman) Ben Mize spent time with Adam in the summer of 1994 and was shocked at how callously strangers treated the singer. The two musicians were walking around Berkeley, looking for someplace to grab a bite to eat. "I sensed the anxiety," Mize said. "A bunch of people recognized him, and a couple gave him a hard time. I could see what he has to deal with. People can be really cruel. They don't know you, but they have everything to say. They either attack you or pass judgment."[78]

The criticisms were personal, and Adam took them personally. In response, he seemed to retreat into himself. He refused to make any more videos for *August*, even as Geffen geared up to issue "Rain King" as a single. The band's concerts were impacted, too. The chatty, outgoing beach boy who led the Himalayans became increasingly dour and serious on stage. He sang beautifully but did so while looking at his shoes.

At some shows, Adam refused to play "Mr. Jones," the Crows' signature song and a massive hit, leaving attendees (and critics) frustrated. "Counting Crows Concert Short, Sweet, Bewildering" ran the headline in the *Chicago Tribune* after the group skipped "Jones" and left the stage seventy minutes into a sold-out performance.[79] The reviewer called the July 8th concert "as puzzling as it was rewarding" and noted that Adam failed to address the audience even once. The singer ended the night by repeatedly wailing "What do you want from me?" during "A Murder of One." The reviewer concluded that, "Perhaps life at the top of the charts isn't all that Mr. Duritz bargained for."[80]

Rolling Stoned

The Crows featured "Jones" in their setlists when they spent the first half of August playing massive football stadiums as the opening act for the Rolling Stones' Voodoo Lounge tour. The Stones' outing launched at R.F.K. Stadium in Washington D.C, on August 1st, Adam's thirtieth birthday. 70,000 fans were in attendance, and Adam had the flu.

Backstage, Adam stood next to his parents, sipping a cup of chicken broth. The singer was ushered through a corridor and into the Stones' tuning room, where he was introduced to Keith Richards and Ronnie Wood. The British guitar legends reprimanded Adam for the broth. Wood handed him a pint glass of Guinness. "Drink this," he said. Adam hesitated, but Richards gave him a nod of encouragement. The singer upended the ale and by all accounts had a great show.

The Crows followed the Stones tour to Legion Field in Birmingham, Alabama and the Hoosier Dome in Indianapolis, before spending four nights at the 82,000-capacity Giants Stadium in New Jersey.

Due to its proximity to New York City, a cavalcade of A-list celebrities were backstage at the New Jersey show, including actor Sean Penn, who was in post-production on a film he wrote, directed, and produced, *The Crossing Guard*. Penn was looking for songs to include in the movie and screened a draft for Adam.

On August 14th, 1994, following the second Stones show at Giants Stadium, Adam and guitarist Dan Vickrey stayed up late in their room at the Paramount Hotel, writing a new song, "Miller's Angels." Per custom, Adam composed the lyrics, a dark rumination on fame, where he (as Miller) stares off into space while bedding an endless cavalcade of "angels," who all but drop out the blue sky to sleep with him. These liaisons barely satisfy and never last. Miller is bored and depressed, crying out to be seen and heard. He increasingly chooses to stay at home in isolation, sleeping and dreaming the days away. Over and over again, Miller pleads to be left alone. The lyrics are not based on plot points from *The Crossing Guard*, but there are some connections—the film is about a father who mourns the death of his daughter and is haunted by a dream about her. Adam demoed "Miller's Angels" the following night in a New York recording studio. Bryson engineered the session, which featured Adam singing and playing piano by himself. The entire group later recorded the song with ex-Lone Justice guitarist Marvin Etzioni at Coast Recorders in San Francisco, with David Immerglück contributing pedal steel and mandolin. Adam created "Miller's Angels" for inclusion in *The Crossing Guard*, but when the film was released in 1995, the song was not used. Penn opted for "Missing," a Bruce Springsteen song, instead. Ultimately, "Miller's Angels" appeared on the Crows' second album.

Steve Bowman Departs

Steve Bowman's drumming did not appear on the recording of "Miller's." Adam fired him from the Crows shortly after the band's August 23rd show in Toronto. Bowman's departure has sometimes been attributed to his suffering a nervous breakdown due to the group's sudden fame, but the drummer admitted in a 2011 interview that his attitude was the problem: "I didn't get along with the singer and I was young and dumb. And I got fired."[81]

There were signs that Bowman did not get along with his bandmates in *Rolling Stone's* 1994 cover story. The writer described how Bowman was late to a photo session for the magazine's cover shoot, pissing off everyone in the group. Bowman nonchalantly claimed that he was busy doing laundry. "I was young and I wasn't ready. I wasn't mature enough to handle certain situations," Bowman would reflect later.[82] Adam has said little about Bowman over the years, telling a reporter in 1997 that, "You can't go out on a bus and tour two and a half years if you don't like someone."[83]

The Crows canceled a month's worth of headlining shows in August and September to rehearse with new drummer Ben Mize. Mize, an Athens, Georgia native, met the Crows while touring with Cracker in the fall of 1993. With Mize behind them, the Crows resumed the tour with a warmup show on September 21st at the DNA Lounge. The band then played two sold-out shows at the Greek Theatre in Berkeley and four nights at the Greek in Los Angeles.

Adam and the Crows were everywhere. On September 13th, 1994, country singer-songwriter Nancy Griffith released *Flyer*, which featured "Going Back to Georgia," a duet with Adam. Adam said that he was set up to do the session by Griffith's A&R rep, who knew he was a fan. One week later, Nashville folk label Blue Plate Music issued *The Best of Mountain Stage Live, Volume 7*, a compilation of live tracks originally broadcasted on a West Virginia public radio program. The disc included a stripped-down version of "Mr. Jones" that the Crows' recorded on November 21st, 1993.

August was Geffen's best-selling record of 1994 and was declared quintuple Platinum on December 6th, 1994, marking sales of five million. It was the fourth best-selling album of 1994, and the Crows were easily the year's top-selling rock act.[84] *August* went on to sell more than seven million copies in the U.S. and was certified Platinum in Canada, the U.K., New Zealand, and Australia. Adam was named *Rolling Stone's* male vocalist of the year in the magazine's annual awards issue.

Adam was famous, but the singer had no idea how famous until he got home from tour at the end of 1994. And nothing that happened in that first frenzied year of fame could have prepared him for what came next.

Chapter 3

Recovering the Satellites

Adam returned home to Berkeley at the end of 1994, and everything was different. The singer's once innocuous neighborhood had turned into a lively party zone, with Crows fanatics camped out on the front lawn of his apartment building. If Adam so much as peeked out his front window, they would begin shrieking, "There he is! He's right there!" Adam recalled, "I realized the party was me. They were going to the drive-in, and I was the movie."[85]

The singer could not leave his apartment without being accosted. When he did go out, most of the fans were pleasant enough, but some were pushy or even hysterical, convinced that Adam's songs were written about them. A few claimed to be suicidal. Others were rude or hostile and had no problem walking up to the singer and telling him how much they disliked his band. Adam was appalled, but he also began to fear for his safety. It was time for a change.

San Francisco was a city full of struggling artists, and Adam was now the big star he had hoped to be. At the beginning of 1995, the thirty-year-old moved to Los Angeles, a city full of working artists, where he immediately felt more at home. He rented a luxury villa at the Sunset Marquis hotel and started spending time with musician and actor friends at the Viper Room.

The Viper Room was a nightclub and celebrity hangout co-owned by Johnny Depp. The club was frequented by Depp, his girlfriend, supermodel Kate Moss, and a cavalcade of young and beautiful A-listers such as Keanu Reeves, Christian Slater, Jude Law, and Charlize Theron. Adam was a newly crowned rock prince, but he wasn't even close to being as famous as some of the Viper Room regulars. It was one of the few places where he could go and be treated like a normal person because it was normal to be a celebrity at the Viper Room. *Married with Children* star Christine Applegate was a regular who had a house for rent in Laurel Canyon. Adam became her tenant.

Adam says that Sean Penn offered friendship and mentorship during this time, too. Penn had grown up among the Hollywood royalty and introduced Adam around town. "When I moved to L.A., he showed me how to live as an artist, whereas before that I now realize I'd only known how to struggle as an artist."[86]

Adam avoided public appearances during this time. When the Crows won an American Music Award for best alternative artist on January 30th, 1995, Charlie Gillingham showed up to accept the statue. At the Bay Area Music Awards (Bammys) on March 11th, Matt Malley was dispatched to collect awards for best song and best male vocalist. The Crows were also nominated for two Grammys, for best new artist and best rock performance, but lost out to Sheryl Crow and Aerosmith, respectively.

Adam felt secure at the Viper Room and ended up there almost every night, eventually stepping behind the bar to pour drinks. Adam enjoyed bartending. You never knew who was going to show up at the Hollywood hangout, and the singer served everyone from Beat Generation author Alan Ginsberg to Butthole Surfers leader Gibby Haynes. Adam's fellow bartenders loved him because he commanded huge tips that he handed over to them.

The 250-capacity Viper Room featured live music most nights of the week. Everyone from Green Day to Tom Petty had played the venue, and the Crows put in a "working rehearsal" there on June 19th, 1995. Adam was excited to demonstrate his talents to his new Hollywood buddies and test drive some of the material he was prepping for the sophomore album.

The Crows opened with a rocking new number, "Have You Seen Me Lately?" In "Mr. Jones," Adam sings about yearning to be a big star and wanting to hear his voice on the radio. On "Have You Seen Me Lately?" he describes his reaction to becoming a big star and hearing his voice on the radio. Adam was hesitant to include material like this on the second album, wanting to avoid cliched songs about life amid whirlwind success. But he also felt that the writing was honest, a true assessment of his genuine emotions at the time he was experiencing them.

The Crows followed the opener with another new number, "Children in Bloom," which had been performed at several dozen shows on the *August* tour. The new songs incorporated Vickrey's hard-rocking influence, as well as the results of nearly eighteen months of relentless touring.

The fourth number of the night was another new one. Built

around Vickrey's rollicking Telecaster lick, "Daylight Fading" bore some resemblance to "Rain King." Its deliberate country inflections, however, added a new color to the Crows' palette that the group would continue to mien for the rest of their career. Adam worked on "Daylight's" music with Vickrey and Charlie Gillingham, but he penned the words himself. In "Daylight," Adam writes of the excitement of touring, how he can't wait to waste another year on the road with his band. At home, Elisabeth professes her love and begs him to stay, but Adam wants nothing to do with it. Ready the horses. At dusk we ride.

Also on the setlist that night was "Another Horsedreamer's Blues," whose title was drawn from a Sam Shepard play, *Geography of a Horse Dreamer*. Shepard's work is a darkly comedic tale about a man who can predict the outcome of horse races in his dreams. Some believe Adam's song took up this theme directly. For example, *Time* described the song as being about "a little girl with the ability to foresee horse-race winners in her dreams [who] is manipulated and used by those around her— a metaphor for the use and abuse of artistic talent."[87] "Another Horsedreamer's Blues" also shares a connection with "Margery Dreams of Horses," a more literary take on the subject. Fans have long speculated that these two songs are a part of a trilogy that also includes "Anna Begins." Anna is named in "Margery Dreams of Horses," and Margery is the primary subject of "Another Horsedreamer's Blues."

The Crows closed out the Viper Room rehearsal with an encore that included "Goodnight Elisabeth," which had appeared on a number of *August* setlists. Adam also called for a cover of "The Richest Man in the World," a zydeco-blues number featured on *Too Much Fun*, the 1995 album from Creole musician C. J. Chenier. The Chenier song hinted at the integral, but often overlooked, influence of New Orleans in the Crows' musical output.

Friends Zone

Hanging around the Viper Room indoctrinated Adam into the Hollywood celebrity lifestyle. His new friends were working artists—elite actors, directors, producers, and musicians striving for fortune and fame. Adam was single and the hot rock star du jour, and he had, even by Hollywood standards, an active dating life. Soon enough, some of Adam's new pals set him up with the actress of the moment, Jennifer Aniston, breakout star of the show *Friends*, which ended its first season in May 1995.

"We were set up by our friends," Adam explained in a 1996 interview. "Both of our friends that set us up told us how much each of us wanted to meet the other. They lied. But it got both of us thinking how great it is that this person likes me. And then we hung out, and she's really smart and funny and she's just a great person."[88]

In subsequent years, Adam would claim that he was on tour when *Friends* became popular and he had no idea who Aniston was when they were introduced. This seems unlikely because Aniston was one of the most famous female stars in the country at the time, featured in many of the same pop culture media that covered Adam and the Crows.

On September 21st, 1995, the first episode of the second season of *Friends* aired on NBC to massive ratings and critical raves. Eight days later, on September 29th, Adam and Aniston attended the Mr. Jenkins' Soiree, a party held at the Ace Gallery Los Angeles. The Hollywood paparazzi went nuts for the couple, snapping away as they walked the red-carpet, dressed in casually fashionable attire.

The photogenic couple looked great together, but their relationship was short-lived, lasting only a couple of weeks. Adam has been asked about Aniston for years and tends to talk about her in kinder prose as time passes. In a 1996 interview, however, he described their relationship in less charitable terms. "She's a really nice person, but I think our thing had more to do with infatuation. She's like night-and-day different from me. It was exciting for a few days, and then just difficult."[89]

In addition to their basic incompatibility was the intense interest from the Hollywood paparazzi, who pursued the couple everywhere they went. Adam found the attention untenable, and things soon fizzled between him and the *Friends* star. By early 1996, Aniston was dating actor Tate Donovan.

"I dated Jennifer for two weeks and they turned it into a huge story which led to people standing in your face with video cameras when you're kissing the girl goodnight," Adam told a reporter in 1996. "And they're saying really vile things like, 'What's it like fucking a TV star?' because they want you to punch them so their video jumps in worth from three bucks to 10,000 bucks, which is exactly what Sean Penn was telling me used to happen to him. These guys are scumbags and all this is the part of fame I really could do without."[90]

On July 18th, 1995, the Crows' cover of "The Ghost in You" by the Psychedelic Furs was featured on the soundtrack to the hit movie *Clueless*. The acoustic track was recorded live at KBCO 97.3 FM on August 28th, 1993. An acoustic version of "Rain King," recorded on October 16th, 1993, was included on a 1995 compilation titled *Live at the World Cafe Volume 1*. But these songs were merely stopgaps. The public—and the higher-ups at Geffen Records—were itching for a new Counting Crows album.

Grand Ambitions

Expectations for the Crows' sophomore effort were high, but no one had loftier ambitions than Adam. On *August*, Adam wrote about his dreams of fame and success; with *Recovering the Satellites*, he would write about achieving them. The singer was determined to compose the ultimate treatise on overnight celebrity. Adam knew he was treading well-worn terrain, but rather than seek alternatives, he took it as a personal challenge and dove in headfirst.

On November 16th, 1995, the Crows played an eighteen-song set at the Hollywood Grand, previewing nine of the fourteen tracks that eventually appeared on *Satellites*. The show became widely circulated as a bootleg titled *Launching the Satellites*.

The Hollywood Grand show hinted at Adam's grand ambitions for album number two. *Satellites* would be a double album with four distinct suites of three to four songs chronicling Adam's personal, emotional, and psychological journey in experiencing and coming to grips with sudden stardom. The band kicked off the Hollywood Grand show with the same four-song suite that would open *Satellites*, played in the same order:

"Catapult," "Angels of the Silences," "Daylight Fading," and "I'm Not Sleeping." These four songs chronicled Adam's experiences of instant fame.

"Catapult" begins with a slow burning organ drone, invoking "Round Here." The song details Adam's ending his relationship with Betsy as he is catapulted into the spotlight. He is lonely and misses her, but he is consumed by his desire to burn brightly and make his mark on the world.

"Angels of the Silences" is a hard rocker with a musical co-write from Charlie Gillingham. In Adam's lyrics, he is revisited at night by the temptresses of "Miller's Angels," who climb into his bed and consume him, body and soul, and exit without looking back. Everyone is using each other. The angels read Adam like an open book, know exactly what he wants, and give it to him without reservation. Yet, he still feels empty. In the quiet aftermath, Adam lies there, staring at the ceiling, dreaming of a relationship that provides something greater, wanting to believe that there is more than this. "It's about trying to have faith in things," Adam explained. "How do you keep that faith—in people, in God, whatever—things that you need to believe in and want to believe in. How to keep that faith when they really make you wait to pay off."[91]

"Daylight Fading" is about hitting the road and leaving everything else behind, while "I'm Not Sleeping" chronicles Adam's longtime lament, insomnia. As with many of Adam's lyrics, the notion of not sleeping assumes multiple meanings here. On the surface, there is insomnia, the exhaustion, and gray light of the television at three o'clock on another sleepless night. Adam describes the comfort and solace he once found in sleep, now gone. He also describes the insights he gained from his dreams, also obliterated. He glances at the TV, only to see an actress he once dated (rumored to be Jennifer Aniston). Adam could escape through sleep, but he can't sleep anymore. It is depressing, but something is also woken in him, a feeling he can no longer shut off.

At the Hollywood Grand preview, the Crows followed the opening quartet with two songs that would also make it to the second album, "Miller's Angels" and "Another Horsedreamer's Blues." In attendance that night was producer Gil Norton, known for his work with the Pixies, who Adam had tapped to produce *Satellites*. The record company wanted the Crows to reproduce the success of *August* by working with T-Bone Burnett a second time. Adam was not having it. He insisted on a new sound, something different that would help the band escape the trap of having such a successful first album.

1990s alternative-rockers such as Pearl Jam, who also had explosively popular debut albums, were able to level up their second time around. Other groups such as the Spin Doctors and Hootie & the Blowfish attempted to repeat the success of their breakout releases, only to be met with failure. Those acts were forever relegated to the oldies circuit, doomed to regurgitate their successful hits for nostalgia-seeking fans. Bands such as Pearl Jam were able to forge an artistic path forward that made up for any lost sales with increased credibility and cultural relevance. Adam intended to do the same with *Satellites*.

Adam has indicated that Burnett was hurt over not being invited to produce the second record, but he was firmly set on Norton. "Adam wanted to do more of a band album," explained Norton, who said he was surprised to get the call. "Because they'd toured the first album and were feeling like more of a band than when they did *August and Everything After*." This focus on hard-rocking material is apparent on "Have You Seen Me Lately?" which was also included in the Grand setlist.

Also featured that night were songs that the Crows recorded during the *Satellites* sessions but scrapped. "Chelsea" was an original that the group had been kicking around in concert. A live version was released in 1998, but a studio recording has never surfaced. "Suffocate" was a mid-tempo rocker that the band played at two shows before tossing. The Crows also ran through "Margery Dreams of Horses" for the last time. The Hollywood Grand show marks the only concert where the two "horsedreamer" songs were performed.

Late in the set, the Crows aired "Goodnight Elisabeth" and "Children in Bloom," the *Satellites* songs that dated back the farthest. These two numbers along with "Have You Seen Me Lately?" formed the second suite of Adam's four-part opus on fame. (The discarded "Suffocate" was likely part of this second set of songs, too.) "Elisabeth" and "Have You Seen" describe the downsides of celebrity from different perspectives. It is harder to see how "Children," which mentions his sister, Nicole, fit into Adam's grand concept, other than it hints of threat and danger and refers, at one point, to a fun house.

The seven songs that formed the first half of *Satellites* were in place at the Hollywood Grand show. Adam explained, "The first half of the record is really about dealing with the hysteria and some of the fears that were coming from me, and it [has] somewhat nihilistic views on things. I mean, I felt like I was fading and disintegrating—and I wanted to, in some ways, at that point."[92]

The second half of the album was less fleshed out at this stage, with only two of its seven songs making an appearance at the Grand stand. Adam closed the show by himself at the piano, playing "Good Luck," an epic ballad that he intended as the centerpiece of *Satellites*.

MTV gave the show a rave review, writing that the Crows "astonished the audience with the quality of the new material."[93] Adam was ready to bring his vision for the Crows' second album to life.

Recording the Satellites

In December 1995, the Crows convened once again in a rented Los Angeles house to record an album. This time, everything was bigger, better, and more expensive. The house was Artemesia, a 13,290-square foot mansion built in 1913 and located in the hills of Los Feliz Oaks, overlooking Hollywood. A visiting journalist described "a two-story foyer, a large sitting room, a huge ballroom downstairs, and space for the band, producer Gil Norton, and engineer Bradley Cook to stay." Adam and bassist Matt Malley both lived in L.A., so they did not reside on site with the others.

Before recording could begin, the entire house had to be soundproofed, lest the neighbors in nearby mansions complain. It took a construction crew five days to double pane windows, remove antique windows, and seal the front door with packing blankets and heavy rubber stoppers. None of the existing walls of the historic house could be touched, so an elaborate set of tents had to be erected. Dave Bryson, a successful recording studio owner prior to joining the Crows, noted, "If you could record out in the countryside, and you could find a funky old house that was a mile from any other house, it would be a cheap way to make a record. But to do it in an urban environment, which we've done both times, becomes a not so cheap way to do it."[94]

Engineer Bradley Cook was instructed to spare no expense in putting together a dream studio stocked with top-of-the-line equipment, and Artemesia's main floor was soon awash in mixing consoles, reel-to-reel tape decks, and $10,000 microphones. Renting all this equipment long-term was expensive, so the band opted to purchase everything outright.

Steve Brandon, an acoustical engineer, was hired to tune the different rooms used for the project. Brandon and his crew hung 5'x 5' sheets of fiberglass from the ceiling to help control the sound. They also built custom isolation boxes for the guitar and bass amplifiers and a massive drum riser built from four layers of drywall and plywood.

Adam insisted on hiring a documentary film production company to capture the music making and magic moments as they occurred. The film crew consisted of an unknown married couple, Jonathan Dayton and Valerie Fairs, who would go on to co-direct the 2006 indie hit *Little Miss Sunshine*.

Producer Gil Norton was taken back by the largesse, the amounts of money being spent without regard. He would later describe *Satellites* as "the most extravagant album I think I've still ever done really to this day, because they'd sold ten million albums then, which was a ridiculous amount. I wasn't very well off then at all, but I was sitting with them around the breakfast table, and they'd be checking out stocks and shares. It was the most bizarre thing."[95]

By all accounts, the recording of *Satellites* was easier than the arduous sessions that produced *August*. For the debut record, the Crows had to learn to be a band, to listen to each other and play together as an ensemble. Coming into *Satellites* was a group that had already accomplished that, followed by eighteen months on the road gelling as a live unit. Whereas the *August* songs often required endless takes to achieve perfection, many of *Satellites'* songs were completed after just a few attempts. Charlie Gillingham told a reporter that recording *August* "was like therapy. We broke every song down; it called for a lot of soul-searching. This one is more natural."[96]

Adam came to the *Satellites* sessions with more than half the songs written and ready to go. Early on, Adam brought in a new number, "Recovering the Satellites," which would become the record's title track. "The album's all about the things that I went through on the road and things that I went through in the year," Adam explained in a 1996 interview. "We called it *Recovering the Satellites* because it's about recovering our little satellite that, for me, came crashing to the ground during that very whirlwind year. It's about learning to live with everything that was happening to us, learning to want to be in a band again. That song is sort of the culmination of it. Although it wasn't the last song written for the album, it sort of sums it all up. I needed to get my satellite back off the ground."[97]

Dave Bryson recalled hearing Adam play "Recovering the

Satellites" for the first time. "When he brought it in, it was just him and a piano and we all flipped on the song, learned it and recorded it. As he was singing, he called out 'One more,' so we could have a big ending, as opposed to having it fall apart. We all kind of got attached to that moment, so we kept it."[98]

Along with "Miller's Angels" and "Another Horsedreamer's Blues," the title track completed the third suite of Adam's four-part opus. The first half of *Satellites* explored the crisis of newfound celebrity from multiple angles, the second half, Adam explained in 1996, was about adjusting to being famous. "I needed to learn to live with being an artist and being successful. Because so much about being an artist is about struggling. I needed to learn to create now, and know to feel guilty about it, and to deal with all the pressure. I'm not saying that I don't want this life. But I needed to learn to deal with it."[99] Adam added that the trio of songs that formed part three of *Satellites* were "about letting yourself feel things."[100] At this point, Adam had not composed any of the songs for the fourth suite of *Satellites*.

With the sessions off to a smooth start, everyone took a few weeks off for the winter holidays. Adam traveled to New York to see a play. On January 4th, 1996, MTV reported that pre-production was complete and the Crows planned to spend the next three months recording.[101] According to producer Gil Norton, this deadline had to be moved after Adam became ill with pneumonia. Adam spent four weeks recovering, while Norton and the band continued work on overdubs and instrumentation in the studio. During this time, *August* was declared six times Platinum, denoting sales of six million.

Between the winter holidays and his bout with pneumonia, nearly two months passed by the time Adam returned to Artemesia. Listening to playbacks of the tracks the Crows had worked on in his absence, the singer was displeased with what he heard. "When he came back, I think he just felt a bit disconnected from the whole process and didn't feel empowered with it, really," Norton recalled. "We had this long conversation about him not feeling like he was involved in it anymore. We wasted a couple of months before we were able to get back on track with the album."[102]

Norton said the sessions dragged on for another eight months, with Adam running the songs through multiple iterations to see which worked the best. "Margery," "Good Luck," "Chelsea," and "Suffocate" were recorded but left off the album. As with *August*, all variety of instruments found their way onto the tracks: Mellotron, dobro, pedal steel, mandolin, accordion, harmonica, and even a Zippo lighter. Norton recalled, "Some of the songs we did three or four times with different arrangements, different tempos, different keys. We ended up spending the best part of nearly ten months on it. It was just difficult. I think some of it was to do with focus – people being focused."[103]

At one point, Adam demanded that an orchestra be brought on board to complete his vision. He asked Charlie Gillingham to work up some arrangements. It was impractical to record an orchestra at Artemesia, so Norton and his engineers schlepped over to Capitol Recording Studios to tape the strings. Paul Buckmeister conducted, leading an orchestra through "I'm Not Sleeping," "Daylight Fading," and "Another Horsedreamer's

Blues." Despite the puffery about recording in a house, the Crows also overdubbed tracks at another traditional studio, Sunset Sound.

Adam's artistic ambition and exacting nature sometimes led to accusations that he was overly controlling; the singer claimed to have no problem with being described that way. "Why wouldn't I be?" Adam retorted when a reporter from *The Los Angeles Times* asked if he was a control freak. "I am fiercely, fiercely protective and controlling of everything that involves this band and our art out there in the world. Because I don't care about having huge hit singles tomorrow. I don't care about making a million dollars next year. I do care about being able to play in this band ten years from now."[104]

The singer's inspiration sometimes bordered on obsession. To record the vocals for "I'm Not Sleeping," an insomnia-stricken Adam woke engineer Bradley Cook in the middle of the night and asked him to run the recording gear.

Adam had composed the first ten songs that would appear on *Satellites*, but the fourth and final suite had yet to be written. Producer Gil Norton recalled that Adam was self-conscious and unsure how to write relatable songs from his extraordinary position. *The New York Times* claimed that the second album's "release was delayed for months because of Mr. Duritz's bout with writers' block."[105] *Time* magazine described this writer's block as lasting eighteen months. *The Seattle Times* went even further, claiming that Adam suffered from a two-year writer's block and a nervous breakdown.

Heartache and a Long December

As Adam struggled to finish *Satellites*, the singer got an unexpected gift from the Wallflowers. The Wallflowers were fronted by singer, songwriter, and guitarist Jakob Dylan, son of rock legend, Bob Dylan. Like Adam's band, the Wallflowers provided a name and musical backdrop for Jakob Dylan's one-man show. The first Wallflowers album had not sold well, and Dylan commissioned T-Bone Burnett to produce its follow-up, *Bringing Down the Horse*. Burnett brought in Adam to sing background vocals on a song called "6th Avenue Heartache," which featured slide guitar from Tom Petty axe man Mike Campbell. Adam worked quickly, knocking out his vocals in less than an hour.

"Heartache," released in April 1996, was chosen as *Bringing Down the Horse's* lead single. The song reached number eight on *Billboard's* modern rock charts and was nominated for two Grammys. In what may have been a nod to Adam, the song was featured on season four, episode sixteen of *Friends*, which aired in March 1998.

Not long after Halloween 1995, an acquaintance of Adam's named Jennifer got into a bad car accident. Adam's ex, actress Samantha Mathis, was close friends with Jennifer, so the two went to the hospital to visit. Jennifer's mother was recruiting volunteers to keep her daughter company and badly needed someone who could be there during the day. Everyone had day jobs except for Adam, who did not start recording until the afternoon. Although he barely knew Jennifer, he agreed to come in during the day. Thus began a two-month routine where Adam would spend his days at the hospital, record in afternoon and evening, and hang out at the Viper Room at night. Adam and Jennifer became close friends over many weeks. He brought in a VHS player and tapes of *Masterpiece Theater* and *Pride and Prejudice*, which they would watch together.

"A Long December" was written at the tail end of another extended day. Adam had been to the hospital in the morning, recorded in the afternoon, tended bar at the Viper Room that night, and hung out after at a friend's house, which everyone called Hillside Manor. The song, whose music was partly based on Adam's piano ballad "Good Luck," flowed out of him, as if the words and music were already completed and he was simply channeling them. Not since "Round Here" had Adam composed a song so quickly. Adam has said "December" is one of the most effortless numbers he has ever written. Adam recorded it the next night. The sixth take was the keeper, and the track was recorded entirely live, except for some harmonies Adam added right after the final take.

Gil Norton recalled that most of Adam's vocals on *Satellites* were recorded live with the group. Norton would scrutinize Adam's different vocal takes and compile, or "comp," the best pieces together into a final vocal to be used for the album. "Very few of the vocals were overdubs; most of them were just comped out of live performances," Norton said, "because Adam got into the vibe of it. Once Adam's in the song, then anything can happen, really. Some of the most interesting and extraordinary vocal performances we got were actually when the band was learning the songs and he was really going for things and pushing the songs along."[106]

Satellites was very much Adam's vision. Eight of the

album's fourteen songs were Adam solo writes, and on six, he collaborated on the music with members of the band. The final suite of four songs was written entirely by Adam, save for an instrumental credit from Vickrey on "Walkaways." Adam explained that, "The fourth side is about the possibilities."[107]

Courteney Loves

On March 9th, 1996, MTV reported that Adam was dating Jennifer Aniston's *Friends* co-star, Courteney Cox. "Last summer he was spotted around Los Angeles with Jennifer Aniston of 'Friends,' but that lasted about as long as a commercial break. Now it seems the dreadlocked babe magnet has made a new friend—Courteney Cox from the very same TV show."[108]

Little is known about the relationship between Adam and Cox, with most contemporary media outlets erroneously reporting that the two met on the set of the music video for "A Long December." But that video began airing nine months after MTV broke the news of their dating, indicating that Adam and Cox were romantically involved for much of 1996, a relationship that Adam's friends described as a "long and difficult liaison."[109]

According to one reporter, Adam and Cox were an item "long enough that half of 1996's *Recovering the Satellites* is about their tortured relationship."[110] This claim is not entirely accurate, but it is true that Adam and Cox dated at the same time Adam broke through his writer's block to pen the fourth suite of *Satellites*, and those songs are largely about Cox. Adam and Cox even composed a song together, a piano ballad called "Barely Out of Tuesday" that has never been released, reportedly due to the singer's bitterness over their breakup.

Adam's dating of the two *Friends* stars became an instant media trope, something mentioned in virtually every major story written about him from then on, a juicy factoid that will be part of his eventual obituary. Adam dated Aniston only briefly, but his relationship with Cox lasted longer and was more significant. Cox and Aniston are close friends. Aniston's relationship with Adam was short lived and insignificant, which is why she probably did not mind Cox dating him. Over the years, the media and Adam have lumped these two different relationships together, turning their history into a convenient tagline.

In 1996, Adam told a reporter from *The Irish Times* that, "The first half of this album is about hanging on a meat hook, which is what fame was for me; the second part deals with this new woman in my life, as in the song 'Recovering the Satellites' itself."[111]

Adam's nickname for Cox, Monkey, appears briefly in the title track to "Recovering the Satellites." More overtly, there is the song "Monkey," whose muse has the same blue eye color as Cox. With its barrelhouse piano, swooping background vocals, and winning melody, "Monkey" is a beautiful, bittersweet tribute to an unrequited love. In the song, Adam is ghosted by a paramour and wonders why he hasn't seen her around. There is a similar theme in "Mercury," where a woman haltingly and hesitatingly leaves Adam, despite his deep yearning for her to stay. On the album, Adam inserted "A Long December" here, a song that was sad but hoped for a better tomorrow. It did not come for Adam and Cox. On the album's final crescendo,

"Walkaways," she leaves, and the two are forever parted.

Adam has offered few details about his relationship with Cox over the years. "He refuses to dis Cox in print," an interviewer reported in 1998.[112] The *Friends* actress has similarly remained mum on the matter. What Cox has revealed is that she fell in love with her co-star (and future husband), David Arquette, on the set of the horror movie *Scream*. Principal filming for *Scream* took place from April 15th to June 8th, 1996, a time during which Cox and Adam were also involved.

It is plausible that Adam and Cox were only casually dating, and seeing other people, at the time Cox fell in love with Arquette. Regardless, Adam and Cox were still involved in December 1996 when Cox appeared in the video for "A Long December." Cox was a soap opera actress whose fame rose after she bopped around with Bruce Springsteen in the 1984 video for "Dancing in the Dark." By 1996, however, Cox was a massive television star who had only appeared in one other music video since Springsteen's. Cox agreed to the "December" video because she was in a relationship with Adam.

A couple of weeks after the "December" video began airing, Adam mentioned Cox at a December 12th, 1996 concert at the Wiltern Theatre in Los Angeles. At that show, Adam introduced "Barely Out of Tuesday," the song he co-wrote with Cox. By way of introduction, the singer said: "This is a brand-new song. I taught a friend of mine to play piano a little while ago, and I came over one day and she was playing all this music and it was pretty fucking good. So I stole it. I stole it and we wrote this song together. And it's brand-new and it's called 'Barely Out of Tuesday.'"

Despite these connections, it is likely that Cox eventually ended her relationship with Adam due to her more serious relationship with Arquette. According to Adam's account in the songs, it was Cox who chose to walk away. In 1998, when a reporter asked about his relationship with Cox, Adam fired back sarcastically. "I'm dating Lisa Kudrow now! Actually, now that I have worked my way through the *Friends* cast, I am on to the cast of *Scream*. I am dating Neve Campbell. Then I am going to do the *Party of Five* cast so I can date Jennifer Love Hewitt. She's so cute!"[113]

Adam's bitterness over Cox seems to have endured, at least in the short-term. At a November 12th, 1999, concert at Bucknell University in Lewisburg, Pennsylvania, the Crows performed "Monkey" for the first time since the final show of the *Satellites* tour on December 20th, 1997. Adam told the crowd that he had a great date the night before and wanted to play a song the group hadn't performed in two and a half years. He added that the song was written about someone he could not stand now, so he rarely performed it, but the date was so good, he was inspired to give it an airing.[114] Later that night, Adam concluded the concert with "Walkaways." Adam included "Monkey" in the setlists for the next several shows but tapered off again, reviving the song only intermittently over the years.

Knee-dropping Dramatics

When Adam and the Crows exited the studio that summer, they had in hand what many consider to be the band's finest album. The Crows' predilection for hard rockers such as "Angels of the Silences" and "Have You Seen Me Lately?" along with powerful slow burners such as "Catapult" and "Children in Bloom," made for a record that sounded great in concert. Adam devotees raved over tracks such as "Another Horsedreamer's Blues," where the singer led the band on a far-out musical excursion, replete with swelling orchestra strings and vocals that would not sound out of place on a jazz album. "Horsedreamer" contains some of Adam's finest singing and forever distinguished the Crows from then-popular peers such as the Gin Blossoms and Blues Traveler. Adam's vocal showcasing on *Satellites* put him into an elite echelon of singers that included contemporaries such as Michael Stipe, Eddie Vedder, and Chris Cornell. Adam was a singer's singer, and *Satellites* made that indelibly and forever clear. The comparisons to Van Morrison even ceased. *Satellites* has remained a fan favorite and popular with the group as well. Its tracks continue to be played with a frequency akin to *August* to this day.

At a September 4th, 1996 surprise show at the Fillmore in San Francisco, the band played every song from *Satellites*, save for "Children in Bloom." The show marked the live debut of the title track as well as the album's fourth suite. The performance was announced on local radio stations and sold-out in two hours. A review in *The San Francisco Chronicle* noted that, "Duritz, now sporting a beard in addition to his trademark dreadlocks, has somewhat tamed his extravagant emoting a la Joe Cocker, although there was still plenty of arm-waving, knee-dropping dramatics. He kept slipping his shirt off his shoulders so that it hung around his elbows, a bothersome affectation. But aside from such bits of divaship, Duritz delivered a stellar performance. His smoky voice turned around on his lyrics with a jeweler's touch."[115]

Four days later, the Crows played *Satellites* in its entirety alongside *August* stalwarts such as "Anna Begins" and "Round Here." The Crows would pointedly ignore their biggest hit, "Mr. Jones," at these sneak previews. The band's September 8th and 9th, 1996 concerts at the Ford Theater were filmed by a team lead by Josh Taft, who directed Pearl Jam's "Alive" video. Taft's footage was used to create a video for *Satellites'* first single, "Angels of the Silences."

Anticipation for *Satellites* was high when the album was released on October 4th, 1996, entering the charts at number one. Sales were brisk, but early reviews were mixed compared to the Crows' debut. *The San Francisco Examiner* called the album "shatteringly good," adding that, "It is always brave, and usually succeeds."[116] *Rolling Stone* gave it four out of five stars, opining that *Satellites* "doesn't so much depart from as further develop the sounds defined by the Crows on their debut ... This is a deeply satisfying album and that satisfaction deepens over time."[117] MTV compared the Crows to R.E.M. and Pearl Jam, extolling the record as "even deeper, more ambitious, and more challenging than the Crows' debut."[118]

Other reviewers were less generous. *The Washington Post* criticized *Satellites* for its self-focus. "The album blares me me me." *The New York Times* dismissed it as "an album that tries too hard to achieve too little."[119] *Entertainment Weekly* graded it a "C" and hammered Adam for his "trite downer lyrics" and mistreatment of women: "Females here tend to be either pathetically unhappy or condescended to."[120] College newspaper *The Daily Collegian* opined that *Satellites* was "jinxed with the sophomore curse," stating that the songs sounded too similar and that Adam's "whining" ruined the few promising numbers.[121] *The Independent* was scathing, negatively comparing the Crows to Hootie & the Blowfish: "Adam Duritz operates at a peculiarly strident pitch of self-pity; investing the most innocuous of lyrics with excessive emotional drama. A classic solipsistic soul-barer, he just won't shut up about himself."[122]

Adam's two-halved, four-suite concept was lost on virtually everyone, save for a reviewer from *Rolling Stone*, who dismissed the concept as unclear and pretentious. The twin-sided, double-LP structure did not work when *Satellites* played as a single piece on CD, the format of choice for most listeners in 1996.

At the onset of *Satellites*, swept in on the residual goodwill from *August*, Adam and the Crows were feted. In October 1996, *August* was declared seven times Platinum. In November 1996, Adam was invited to Yale University as the featured guest of a College Tea. Yale's Teas, formerly known as Master's Teas, "provide an opportunity for a relatively intimate group of students—as well as Yale community members and members of the public—to interact with distinguished visitors from the worlds of politics, the arts, academia, social movements, business, and media in an informal setting in the living room of the Head of College House. Teas are casual affairs during which the guest speaks to students, and takes questions, about lifelong passions and experiences."[123] Adam told a reporter that the Tea was one of the best times he ever had, that the small, intimate setting was easier than the mobs of fans he encountered in his day-to-day life.

Adam did not care if someone found his high-concept

albums or his pontificating to Yale students pretentious. "I always felt like I was meant to do something extraordinary," he told *The New York Times* not long after *Satellites* was released.[124] If Adam was miffed about the media's focus on his romantic life, it did not deter him from casting Courteney Cox to star in the video for "A Long December," issued as a single on December 2nd, 1996. "I'm a Hollywood kid now," Adam told a reporter from *The Times* upon the video's release.[125]

Adam was due for a drubbing and got it when *The Times* fired back in a review of the Crows' December 2nd show at the Beacon Theater, portraying Adam as a self-absorbed Eeyore, whining even after selling seven-million records. "Long-suffering guys like Mr. Duritz have always been part of pop [but his] sad-sack persona is relentless."[126] *The Times* went so far as to dig up aggrieved ex-drummer Steve Bowman to take a shot at his former boss. "It's like he's created a role for himself in a movie where he's the star. He may enjoy some of the drama, but I think there's a lot of pain that goes along with great intelligence."[127]

Variety was similarly merciless in reviewing the Crows' December 12th, 1996 concert at the Wiltern Theatre in Los Angeles. The reviewer claimed that the Crows had no sense of being a band, just a front man and his anonymous sidekicks. "Duritz exudes a degree of charm, no doubt but his stream of problems is so steady that eventually you pray for a lyrical dam. There's no danger, no edginess here … nothing but self-pitying artifice."[128]

These were the media sentiments as the Crows took the stage at *The Late Show with David Letterman* on December 11th, 1996. The comedic host introduced the group earnestly and with enthusiasm, stating that in 1994, "They played a song from their first album and they blew the roof off of this dump. It was one of the most exciting moments, musically, we've ever had on this program." Before the Crows got to the first note of "Catapult," Letterman asked them to return the following night. The host's invitation came across as semi joking, but the Crows returned the next evening and played, "A Long December." It marked the first time in history a musical act performed two nights in a row on Letterman's show. A week later, *Satellites* was certified Platinum, marking one million records sold.

In later years, Adam has been philosophical about the early criticisms of *Satellites*. "You don't get to write songs complaining about being famous without getting trashed for it," he said in a 2016 interview. "Even though [fame is] an experience that people go through. Because it is such a weird thing to suddenly become famous that inevitably, people write about it. But then everyone says, 'Oh, fuck him—he's whining about being famous.' But you know, the truth is, it's what your life is. You can only write about where your life is. Or I can only write about where my life is. So I knew it was coming. This is what all of the songs were about. I knew I was going to take a hit for that."[129]

On the Road Again

The Crows had stayed at home for all of 1995 and most of 1996. In 1997, the band returned to the road to play more gigs than any other year in their career. The *Satellites* tour launched January 23rd, 1997 in Houston with Fiona Apple opening. The Crows setlist featured eleven of the fourteen *Satellites* tracks. The group inserted a four-song acoustic showcase into the middle of their performance, highlighting "Miller's Angels" and "Mercury," but also incorporating "Mr. Jones" back into the set.

On the *August* tour, Adam and the Crows learned to improvise, with the singer inserting the lyrics of different songs into originals such as "Rain King" and "Round Here." On the *Satellites* tour, they took it a step further. The band would regularly deconstruct and reinvent their own material in significant ways. For example, the group took their hardest-rocking song, the six-string slasher, "Angels of the Silences," and reimagined it as a harmony-drenched acoustic ballad awash in mandolin and accordion. Adam and the Crows would make such deconstructions a regular part of their repertoire for the remainder of their career. Doing so kept the songs fresh for the band, but it also enabled longtime listeners to hear familiar material in a completely new light.

The Crows played throughout the southern U.S. in the early months of 1997, moving north as the weather warmed. After Fiona Apple departed the tour, Ben Folds 5 was brought on board. There was a growing sense that *Satellites* was not going to be a smash of *August* proportions. In March, *The Seattle Times* wrote, "The new album is doing well, having sold about two million copies, but is not the blockbuster it was expected to be. Perhaps Mr. Duritz's worries about stardom are eased by that; then again, maybe not."[130]

Reviews of the tour were mixed, with most of the attention focused on the singer. At a homecoming show in Berkeley, held April 4th, 1997, Adam was described as triumphant. "What Duritz gives you is his soul, and it's hard to fault a man for being willing to throw his psyche dead-on in your face—if it's done with sincerity, which is never in doubt with Duritz's delivery."[131] But a few days later, at a show in Irvine a few hundred miles south, Adam was disparaged for his theatrical performance style. "His stage presence itself was problematic. Lying on his back or flailing his arms, he seemed to mistake motion for emotion."[132]

On April 10th, 1997, the band played "Daylight Fading" on *The Tonight Show with Jay Leno*, with Adam adopting a "professional artist" look in a long-sleeved button-up shirt. Adam and the band starred in a moody psychedelic music video for "Daylight," directed by Howard Greenhalgh, whose credits included Elton John, Sting, and the Pet Shop Boys.

In May, the group departed for a six-week European tour. Geffen issued "Daylight Fading" as a single on May 19th. That same day, the Crows played the Pinkpop festival in Holland, with Adam incorporating his Courteney Cox collaboration, "Barely Out of Tuesday," into a ten-plus minute version of "Round Here."

On June 6th, *Satellites* was declared double Platinum, marking two million records sold. The Crows returned to the U.S. and went back on the road for a summer tour co-headlining with the Wallflowers, a double bill that was popular enough to play two nights in some cities. The tour began June 21st in Fort Worth, Texas with the Gigolo Aunts, the Boston alternative-rock outfit that had toured with the Crows early on, slated to open.

The Wallflowers had become one of the hottest bands in the land. In 1997, they were nominated for two Grammys, were featured on the cover of *Rolling Stone*, were tapped to open for the Rolling Stones, and sold about five million records. Similar to the Crows, Jakob Dylan was the sole focus of virtually all of the public's passion and criticism. "We see them going through the same things we did a few years ago," Adam said as the tour hit Florida. "Particularly Jakob. He's the target of the attention. All of them seem to have handled it well."[133]

As for Adam, he claimed to have adjusted to life in the spotlight. "No huge regrets or anything," he said. "I wanted to do this my whole life and now we're doing it. I wouldn't trade it in for anything. But it still took some adjusting, because you can't know what that's like until you get there."[134]

From July 20th-24th, Adam had to bow out of four gigs in Boston, Toronto, and Buffalo due to swelling vocal cords. *Rolling Stone* reported that Adam "ha[d] nodes on his vocal chords [sic] and could permanently damage his voice if he strain[ed] it too much."[135] The Wallflowers opted to play anyway, and the co-headlining shows became Wallflowers solo gigs. No one seemed to mind all that much. "We were still going to be in Boston anyway," Jakob Dylan told MTV. "We wanted to work anyhow, people would still come and the venue wanted us to play."[136] Adam and the Crows returned to the tour for a July 26th show in New Jersey. A writer from the *Courant* praised Adam's "inspired" performance at a July 29th show in Hartford. "Although he sipped water in the middle of every song, the Crows' distinctively braided frontman was in very good voice."[137]

On August 12th, 1997, the Crows performed before a small audience at Chelsea Studios in New York City. The show was recorded for *VH1 Storytellers*, where artists explain the background and writing of their songs in an intimate setting. The band concluded the set with "Chelsea," an unreleased number. "I don't usually write spare songs," Adam explained. "If I complete something that we play on tour, it usually finds a place somewhere on an album."[138] VH1 aired the Crows' performance on October 1st as the sixth episode of *Storyteller's* second season.

At a September 18th show in Las Vegas with the Wallflowers, Adam described his recent breakup with Courteney Cox, reminiscing about his split with Betsy in the winter of 1993. To introduce "Goodnight Elisabeth," Adam explained, "I've been on the road a year now, which can screw any relationship in the ground. This is a song about the first time we ever went on tour and the consequences of not coming home for a long time, and since it's happened again to me yesterday, I'm going to play it tonight."[139] During "Round Here," Adam seemed to be singing directly to Cox, "Hey Monkey, why you wanna leave me? Why?"

Adam's animated performing style during these songs became another point of critique. Reviewing the band's September 21st show at the Shoreline Amphitheatre in Mountain View, California, a writer carped, "Despite his wide range of theatrical rock-star gestures—hitting his forehead with his fist, clutching his chest, holding out a pleading hand—Duritz seemed to put his heart on his sleeve only opportunistically, seeking a response more than offering true emotion."[140] On September 27th, the Crows played the final gig of their co-headlining tour with the Wallflowers.

The Crows' November 6th show at the Hammerstein

Ballroom was recorded for *Live From the 10 Spot*, a weekly concert series that aired on MTV. The band then returned to Europe at the end of November to play a month of dates. Adam was exhausted from the touring. "A year and a half is a lot of your life," he told a reporter, adding that when the final European dates were finished next month, he was taking some time off. "I'm going to the movies. I want to catch a matinee."[141] Adam stated that his plans also included hanging out with friends, working on a failed relationship, and writing some new songs.

On November 26th, 1997, the Crows played an intimate set in front of two hundred die-hard fans in Amsterdam. The show was taped for a live-performance TV show called *2 Meter Sessies* (or *Amsterdam Sessions*). The Crows delivered four songs from *August* and four from *Satellites*, beginning with a perfunctory, low-energy take on "Daylight Fading." They then switched over to acoustic instruments for "Angels of the Silences" and another five songs, reverting back to the electric devices for "Anna Begins." Adam wore a button-up shirt and a bucket hat, and he sported the goatee and mustache that he wore through much of *Recovering's* writing, recording, and touring cycle.

At the end of the show, the Crows were supposed to play one final song, but Adam walked off stage. The camera crew followed him backstage, where the singer told them he was burnt out from the endless touring. The interviewer asked Adam what he missed the most, and he replied, "I miss my friends a lot. That's the main thing. I used to have a girlfriend. I don't have that anymore—too much time away. But I like playing. We got into this to do that. It's the only thing I really like to do." Adam was eventually persuaded to play one last song, a solo rendition of "A Long December."

The critical backlash to *Satellites*, along with the significant drop in sales, took the Crows down a notch. By choosing artistry over commerce with *Satellites*, however, the Crows put themselves on a path to longevity, enabling the group to continue well after the popularity of their first album diminished. The albums that followed *Satellites* would sell even fewer copies, but they continued to satisfy fans with material that was sometimes as strong as that found on the first two releases. But Adam's determination to succeed on his own terms put him at odds with everyone, from his record label to his bandmates, and sometimes even his fans. The singer would spend the next several years navigating the Crows' career through a period of significant turmoil and change.

Chapter 4
This Desert Life

Adam seemed almost shellshocked by the relative commercial and critical failure of *Satellites*. In reaction, he spent the next few years trying to regain lost terrain with the Crows and pursuing creative business endeavors outside the band.

For starters, Adam and his managers, Martin Kirkup and Steve Jensen, founded a boutique record label, E Pluribus Unum. The Latin phrase means "out of many, one" and was the title of a 1969 album by folk guitarist Sandy Bull. Among Adam's early signings was the Gigolo Aunts, the Boston rock outfit that had toured with the Crows several times over the years. Aunts singer Dave Gibbs was friends with Adam, carousing and crashing at the singer's L.A. pad a good deal of the time. Adam then signed Joe 90, a Los Angeles band with whom he had become friendly. E Pluribus released their debut album in 1999, featuring the lead single "Drive," with Adam on backing vocals. The label never went far, and *Billboard* reported that Adam sold E Pluribus Unum to Geffen in 2000.

Adam also became involved in non-musical pursuits around this time, partly owing to his proximity to Hollywood and his friendships and romances with TV and movie stars. In

1997, Adam served as co-executive producer on *The Locusts*, a drama starring Vince Vaughan, Paul Rudd, Ashley Judd, and Kate Capshaw. The movie tanked at the box office, but the experience piqued the singer's interest in film.

In January 1998, *Burn*, a feature film co-executive-produced by Adam and Crows' co-manager Steve Jensen, screened at the Sundance Film Festival in Park City, Utah. One scene in the film featured "Good Luck," the epic piano ballad Adam had earmarked for *Satellites*, before he replaced it with "A Long December." The studio version of "Good Luck," which has never been released, features Adam accompanied by a lone piano, augmented by horns a la "Chelsea."

Adam chalked up his creative interests outside of music as a product of moving to Los Angeles, the city for working artists. In San Francisco, Adam told a reporter around this time, "people talk about art a lot, down here it's all about doing it. That works for me."[142]

The Crows only played a handful of gigs in 1998, most notably a two-night stand at the Viper Room in April for friends and family. At the first show, billed under the name Trial By Fire, the Crows performed with electric instruments. They returned the following night and played an all-acoustic set under the name the No Brainers.

At the Viper Room shows, Adam introduced three new songs: "St. Robinson and His Cadillac Dream," "Sundays," and "She Don't Want Nobody Near." All three numbers would eventually be released, each of them on a different project. Adam explained that he was not a prolific songwriter and that when he played new material in concert, he planned to record it. "I never write and perform any songs that I won't intend to release at some point," he said.[143]

Crows co-manager Martin Kirkup told the press, "Playing live makes them feel much more like a band again. They finished touring in December, and for the past three months, they've been literally scattered all over the world, taking a break. They wanted to get together and play a couple of gigs. They already had a couple songs ready that they started writing while they were on the road last year, so they played [three] new songs. The new songs fit into the uptempo electric mode. But just based on three songs, it doesn't mean the whole album is going to be like that."

The Crows' principal songwriter offered few predictions for the group's third record, besides that fans could expect more of the same. "I have a lot of ideas for the next LP, but it's hard to say now how it's all gonna come out. It's pretty standard Counting Crows as I can tell so far."

Across a Wire

On July 14th, 1998, Geffen issued *Across a Wire: Live in New York City*, a double CD set comprised of songs from the band's acoustic *VH1 Storytellers* performance on August 12th, 1997, and their electric set recorded for MTV's *Live From the 10 Spot* at the Hammerstein Ballroom on November 6th. The two discs covered the biggest hits from *August* and *Satellites*, as well as the mournful unreleased fan favorite, "Chelsea." Crows co-manager Martin Kirkup stated that the group released *Wire* to satisfy demand and to curb the spread of overpriced, poor-sounding bootlegs.

Adam used *Wire's* acoustic/electric structure to highlight the group's differing approaches to songs such as "Round Here" and "Angels of the Silences." Those numbers and two others appear on both discs, in acoustic and electric form. "The record is like an encapsulated perfect version of a song," Adam explained not long after *Wire's* release. "With a live gig, you're really just filtering the songs through the day and however you are that day. The songs change every day, and grow. They're constantly metamorphosing, and I like that ... We were trying to discover other sides of the songs, trying to find other textures and facets to the songs"[144]

Hunger for Crows product was high, and *Wire* charted in nine countries, reaching number nineteen in the U.S. The album quickly went Gold, indicating sales of 250,000 double CDs. But it would take until 2005 before *Wire* reached Platinum status, evidence that the millions who snapped up *August* and *Satellites* passed on their live counterparts.

Overall, the reviews for *Wire* skewed lukewarm to negative. In one of the more positive assessments, a critic from *Amuzine* rated *Wire* seven out of ten stars, stating of the *Storytellers* disc, "The understated instrumental backing thrusts Adam Duritz's expressive voice and yearning lyrics into the spotlight and the poignancy of these songs is emphasized."[145] *All Music* gave *Wire* three out of five stars, praising the group's rearrangements as "fascinating and entertaining," but also "odd," adding that "skeptics can't help but wonder if a double-live set is necessary."[146]

To critics, *Wire* was a water-treading money grab that looked back, rather than forward. Joining forces with VH1 and

MTV (their logos appeared prominently in *Wire's* liner notes) gave the appearance of a band that was wholly in bed with major corporations. *Wire* was seen by some as yet another declaration of the group's self-importance. The usually laudatory *Rolling Stone* assigned the album 2.5 out of five stars, calling the release "an extraordinary act of hubris." Asserting that *Wire* lacked musical revelations, critic Greg Kot dismissed the *Storytellers* set as "jug-band reverie" and called Adam out for supposedly hating fame, yet "releasing an album in conjunction with the two music-video channels most responsible for making him a pop icon."[147] *Salon* trashed the release. "The arrangements on the first, VH1-sponsored disc are mature and eclectic—which means: add accordion parts and string bass; destroy all hooks. [The CD] demonstrates what a professionalist, music-bizzy outfit the Crows are in real life: studio-slickoids, not weirdo-beardo Frisco prodigies ... The studio albums – all two of 'em – are far more definitive."[148]

Recording Desert

In June 1998, the Crows announced that Cracker singer-guitarist David Lowery would co-produce the group' third album in partnership with Camper Van Beethoven producer Dennis Herring. Lowery was, of course, an old friend, but he had also earned accolades recently for his production work for Sparklehorse and other indie outfits.

To record their third album, *This Desert Life*, the Crows again opted to lay down tracks in a Los Angeles mansion. Crows co-manager Martin Kirkup explained, "The writing is going really well and quickly. David did about two weeks of work in May at a house the band rented, helping them with some pre-production work, giving them advice about structure and how they want to make the album."[149]

Early reports indicated that the Crows had a dozen songs ready to record for album number three, but it was far from the truth. In reality, for the first time, Adam and the Crows were entering the studio almost empty handed. Unlike *August*, where the group selected the best songs from their years-in-the-making demo, and *Satellites*, where the Crows began the sessions with half the album written and road tested, Adam had almost no material prepared for *This Desert Life*. Rather than spend a prolonged period penning new songs, the plan was for Adam and the band to write the album in the studio, as it was being recorded. It was intended to give the sessions a spontaneity that was absent from the deliberate crafting of the first two releases. The liner notes for *Desert* include credits for handclaps and "drunken backing vocals," an indication of the lighter vibe they were trying to create in the studio.

Interviewed during the *Desert* sessions, Adam explained, "David got here really early, and we sat down with no preconceptions. We had only written a few things, and I wanted to see how it would work to just start from scratch. I think this record will sound really different."[150]

Any illusions that recording in a house required roughing it were put to rest with the report from a San Francisco journalist, who dropped in on the sessions and found a family friendly setup where the musicians spent time between takes shooting hoops on a regulation-sized basketball court. High-stakes poker games took place frequently, with *Desert*'s liner notes stating that the album was recorded "on a casino on a hill in Hollywood" and thanking David Immerglück for his contributions to the pot. A personal chef was on hand, serving generous helpings of gourmet fare, including lobster ravioli, endive salad, and tiramisu. Adam explained to the reporter that, "We're here all day, and no one has time to cook. Also, if we didn't have [a chef], we would eat way too much pizza and burritos. Not healthy."[151]

Desert's comfortable writing and recording sessions continued into the fall of 1998. In September, Adam and company quickly put together a new song that played over the closing credits of the Matt Damon-Edward Norton drama *Rounders*. "Baby, I'm a Big Star Now" was a medium-tempo rocker buoyed by dashes of country and funk and lifted by the same type of strong harmonies the Crows would deploy to winning effect on "If I Could Give All My Love (Richard Manuel is Dead)." The six-minute "Big Star Now" was catchy, but it mostly forewent the anthemic pop hooks found in the Crows' more commercial material and concluded with an impassioned Adam losing himself amid his bandmates' slashing. It was a killer performance of a great tune. Adam insisted that the Crows retain "Big Star Now" for *Desert*. He would allow the song to be used in *Rounders*, but not on its accompanying soundtrack. Ultimately, Adam excised the number from *Desert*, and a *Rounders* soundtrack was never released. "Big Star Now" was issued as a bonus track on some editions of the Crows' fifth album in 2008 but remains one of the band's great lost songs.

Interscope

In January 1999, the Crows' record label, DGC, was part of a merger that resulted in the formation of a single umbrella organization, Interscope Geffen A&M, owned by Universal Music Group. Dozens of artists were dropped from their labels, and nearly 300 jobs were eliminated. Thanks to their back-to-back multi-Platinum albums, the Crows hung on, but the reorganization underscored the economic realities of the music industry at the turn of the century.

Furthermore, Adam suddenly found himself signed to Interscope, home to hardcore acts such as Eminem, Nine Inch Nails, Snoop Dogg, and Limp Bizkit. Adam's new twenty-something bosses at Interscope were not sure what to do with a folksy rock band fronted by a thirty-five-year-old white guy with fake dreadlocks.

A team of label executives stopped by the mansion and asked to hear the material the Crows were working on for the new album. Adam played them "Mrs. Potter's Lullaby," an eight-minute acoustic-driven number that the group hoped to release as a single. The session did not go well. "The new Interscope guys came in and listened to what we'd done so far, and they were not hugely impressed," Adam told a reporter not long after the meeting took place. "They liked it but didn't *love* it. They liked 'Mrs. Potter' but couldn't relate to an eight-minute single; things like that."[152]

The impasse threatened to derail the entire record, but Adam stood his ground, going to the head of Interscope and asking that the company stop interfering with the Crows' recording process. The company backed off. "The secret of dealing with these huge companies is not to be adversarial, but to know what you're up against—and communicate firmly," Adam said. "I'm not always a nice guy; I'm mean sometimes. But I make things happen."[153]

On March 5th, 1999, the movie *Cruel Intentions* was released. The teen drama starred young Hollywood A-listers Sarah Michelle Gellar, Ryan Phillippe, Reese Witherspoon, and Selma Blair. The film featured a steamy sex scene set to a new Counting Crows ballad, "Colorblind," giving the group an unexpected boost. It probably helped the Crows' standing with their skeptical new bosses at Interscope, at least temporarily.

On May 5th, 1999, Adam and David Immerglück played a surprise acoustic gig at the Shim Sham Club in New Orleans. Adam sported baggy shorts, combat boots, and a short-sleeved button-up shirt, alternating between sitting on a stool, standing to sing, and pounding out chords on a piano. On a music stand next to the singer were notebooks filled with lyrics. During the show, he called for covers by Camper Van Beethoven, Cracker, Guided by Voices, the Kinks, and more. Adam also previewed two new songs from *Desert*, telling the crowd that the band had just finished recording the album that week and that it would be released sometime between August and Thanksgiving.

For "Four Days," Adam brought a drummer and bassist from the Continental Drifters, as well as two female singers to handle backup. The song's lyrics reference Ohio because Adam was dating a woman from that state at the time. To introduce "Mrs. Potter's Lullaby," Adam said, "This may or may not be our first single. Probably not 'cause it's too damn long but it's our favorite song on the record." The loose, informal Shim

Sham shows became an annual tradition for a few years, giving Adam and friends an opportunity to try out new material, play rarely-attempted cover songs, and basically just have a good time (and lots of drinks) on stage.

Hanginaround

This Desert Life was a deliberate pivot, a move away from some of the things that the Crows got knocked for on *Satellites*. Gone were the hard-charging rockers, replaced with mid-tempo grooves and airy production that contained lots of space. *Desert* was the first Crows album to be recorded digitally, rather than on reel-to-reel tape. This change reduced the cost, but it also removed some of the organic warmth that made *August* and *Satellites* stand out.

At ten songs, Adam kept *Desert* short and to the point. When the singer decided, at the last minute, to add the campfire rocker "Kid Things" as an eleventh track, he deliberately kept the song's name hidden from the track listing. Crucially, *Desert* was not a retreat or an attempt to recreate the moods and themes of *August*. By deliberately moving away from both *Satellites* and *August* and into new terrain, the group was able to maintain a sense of artistic purpose that lent credence to Adam's claims that he was not simply looking for hits. Like the first two records, *Desert* was excellent but for entirely different reasons.

He may not have been out to top the charts, but Adam was clearly out for a reset, to alter the public's perception of the Crows as rock's dourest hitmakers. Adam enlisted comic book artist Dave McKean to design *Desert's* cover art, inspired by a children's book he illustrated called *The Day I Swapped My Dad for Two Goldfish*. *Desert* begins with a song that surprised even longtime fans. The Crows were known for their serious originals, but sometimes used cover songs to demonstrate a subtle sense of humor. By contrast, "Hanginaround" sounds like it was deliberately written for dancing and drinking at an outdoor amphitheater on a hot August night. The lyrics to the meatball stomper celebrate a life of leisure and malaise atop piano loops and a funky hip-hop beat, the penultimate anthem for suburban America at the turn of the century.

The video for "Hanginaround" furthered the newly upbeat Crows image, with Adam seated at a park bench while jugglers, construction workers, and little kids passed by. It was juxtaposed with footage of the band performing the song in a crowded apartment living room, presumably recreating the types of Berkeley house parties Adam and company attended back in the day.

"Hanginaround" was intended to set a tone, and it did. On *Desert*, Adam followed it with "Mrs. Potter's Lullaby," a winning up-tempo number with few commercial considerations. The Crows made a music video for "Potter's," too, with the group performing in an apartment the day after the type of raucous blowout that was thrown in the "Hanginaround" video. Clocking in at nearly eight minutes, the catchy tune had no prayer of being played on the radio. If Adam was trying to make the Crows more appealing to the masses, he was doing so on his own terms.

"It's a little more joyful album than the other ones have been," he said shortly after *Desert's* completion. "It's a little less heavy in its mood as well. There's a little more yearnings that are a little more upbeat, tinged with the possibility of getting what you yearn for."[154]

Much of *Desert* sounds positively featherweight, floating by on a mélange of unobtrusive acoustic and electric instrumentation. On the surface, breezy numbers such as "Four Days" and "High Life" are indistinguishable, tinted in the same buttery beige color scheme as the album's cover art. Scratch the surface, however, and you'll find hidden treasures and rich details that make each unique. The head-bobbing "Sundays," an outtake recorded for *Desert*, retains this same sense of high altitude. The song would eventually appear on the Crows' fifth album in 2008.

As Adam did previously, he enlisted a small army of additional players to flesh out *Desert*. David Immerglück returned for the third time to add bass, mandolin, guitar, and pedal steel. There were multiple violin and cello players, working from arrangements created by Charlie Gillingham. "We finally sound like we've always intended to. We finally figured out what Counting Crows sounds like," Gillingham told me the summer after *Desert* was released. "The first two records, you can hear us trying different things to see what we might sound like. It works in some ways, and in other places I don't really think it works. On the second record, there is a lot more instrumental stuff going on, but it's a little confused and a little loud. On this record, the instrumental stuff is perfect. It compliments the song, and it's connected very deeply emotionally."[155]

Adam concurred with Gillingham's assessment. "We've grown musically by leaps," he said in an interview around this time. "On *This Desert Life*, we have gone into an area sonically that has incredible complexity. We're using bigger guitars and louder drums, and place those elements in contrast to the quiet stuff—sometimes from song to song, sometimes within songs."[156]

Like *Satellites*, *Desert* is steeped in Southern California mythos, with its themes of freeways, the Pacific, sunshine, Sunset, Laurel Canyon, the Hollywood hills, and more. "I Wish I Was a Girl" pays tribute to Mott the Hoople's "I Wish I Was Your Mother" as well as Prince's gender-reverse classic, "If I Was Your Girlfriend." Like Prince, *Desert* serves up songs that are presented like jewel boxes—small and shimmering and practically magical when opened. The lolling "St. Robinson and His Cadillac Dream" contains a million-dollar, harmony-laden chorus that the group took their time getting around to playing. *Satellites* sounds like a band trying as hard as they can and winning; *Desert* is a triumph because the performances seem positively effortless.

In a July 1999 interview, with *Desert* finished, Adam explained how the new record differed from the others, "The second album was a lot more guitar-heavy than the first album, and [*Desert Life*] is sort of stranger-sounding, I think. It's not quite as heavy, and it's not quite as mopey either. We were just in a different mood when we were making this album. It's a little lighter in tone but not lighter musically. It's pretty dense musically. There's a lot more stuff going on."[157]

By the Time We Got to Woodstock '99

The Crows toured North America in summer of 1999, prior

to the release of *Desert Life*, hitting outdoor amphitheaters and festival stages. On the summer tour, they served up a crowd-pleasing mix that leaned heavily on the popular cuts from *August*. Depending on the venue, the band sometimes incorporated a brief acoustic mini set into the larger show. The group almost always opened with "Mr. Jones," a song they spent their first couple of years trying to disown.

Another change was the promotion of David Immerglück, who became an official member of the band, creating a permanent place for himself between Bryson and Vickrey. With multi-instrumentalist Immerglück on board, the Crows could retain their two-guitar wall of sound, while adding a third instrument to the mix, filling out their material in ways previously unimaginable. At other times, Immerglück simply strapped on a third guitar and let 'er rip. "Immy has come out with us," Adam enthused to a reporter that summer. "I get sooooo much out of our friendship, it's like having a party every night on the road. We rearranged all the songs for three guitars, and it completely revitalized our live show. There's so much stuff in it now."[158]

On July 6th, 1999, the Crows gave a first live airing to "Hanginaround," which Adam described as being about "my twenties in Berkeley—that blasé, going-nowhere life."[159] Adam recalled that back in Berkeley, he was stoned all the time. "I was thinking I had no future and wondering what the hell was going to happen. So I was sort of semi-celebratory about that, but also [thinking] 'Where am I going?'"[160] "Hanginaround" became a mainstay of the group's setlists that summer and onward.

The Crows' North American summer tour culminated with a July 24th appearance at Woodstock '99, held on an Air Force base in Rome, New York. The band went on during the day to the strains of the Beatles' "Magical Mystery Tour." Adam, attired in a short-sleeved navy-blue button-up shirt, his dreadlocks longer than he wore them before, and looking more filled out, greeted the crowd of 220,000 excitedly: "What's up!"

The Crows opened their Woodstock '99 set with a snippet of the Byrds' "So You Want to be a Rock 'N' Roll Star," segueing into a crowd-pleasing "Mr. Jones" as beach balls and frisbees flew. Adam did his best to project to the sun-screened throng, standing atop the floor monitors, arms spread wide, and putting everything into a setlist consisting of upbeat rockers and popular ballads such as "Round Here" and "A Long December."

The Crows shared the stage that day with everyone from Wyclef Jean to the Dave Matthews Band. Rage Against the Machine and Metallica headlined. The Crows' mellow catalog and predilection for mandolin and accordion led to incongruities, such as members of the audience crowd surfing during "Anna Begins," but the band was well received overall.

Woodstock '99 gained infamy for riots, assaults, and fires that took place on the third day, Sunday, July 25th. The Crows set on the second day occurred without incident, and their appearance was largely overlooked in the media coverage of the third-day events. Also under the media radar were a handful of lucrative South African dates, including an August 8th performance at the controversial Sun City. The shows unanimously sold-out.

On October 9th, the Crows returned to Giant's Stadium to perform as part of Net Aid, an anti-poverty mega-event modeled on Live Aid, with high-profile acts performing at benefit concerts simultaneously taking place on three continents. The U.S. lineup featured Sting, Bono, the Black Crowes, Wyclef Jean, Puff Daddy, and Sheryl Crow, among others. Despite the celeb-heavy roster, Net Aid's U.S. show was characterized by low turnout. A review in *The New York Times* noted that, "Although nearly all the performers have sold at least a million albums each, the scattered lineup didn't fill the stadium; the top tier was empty, as were expanses of the lower tiers and the field."[161]

The Net Aid acts played abbreviated sets that were simulcast on MTV, VH1, and online. The Crows performed four songs, including the still-unreleased "St. Robinson and His Cadillac Dream" and their party-hearty anthem, "Hanginaround," which had been issued as a single a few weeks earlier. Adam suffered from back pain throughout the Net Aid gig, recalling a few weeks after the concert, "I was a mess for the event—completely whacked out on Flexaril. Skull, gone. I did some interviews that I read later, and I was amazed I made any sense at all. I did this entire interview for MTV with Serena Altschul, whom I used to date, and it was so bad."[162]

On Halloween night 1999, Adam wore a full-sized bunny costume on stage at the Orpheum Theater in Boston. The fuzzy outfit was light pink with long ears and an oval-shaped stomach made of white fur. "Is it weird to hear a pink bunny rabbit sing these depressing songs?" the singer asked the crowd. The entire band was dressed up that night. Matt Malley donned a long robe and Yoda mask; Dave Bryson was done up as a soldier. David Immerglück wore a red devil outfit, and the concert became known as the Devil and Bunny Show. Adam and Immerglück sometimes performed together under this name, and the singer would later reference a bunny suit in the song "Holiday in Spain."

Light and Breezy

When *This Desert Life* was released on November 1st, 1999, "Hanginaround" was number one on *Billboard*'s AAA charts. The album debuted at number eight. The critical response was mixed, with positive reviews praising the Crows' lighter approach. *CMJ* wrote that, "Each track on *This Desert Life* is compelling, powerful and poetic."[163] *The San Francisco Examiner* called the album "seductively charming" and praised the band's "light and breezy" turn.[164] *The South Florida Sun-Sentinel* raved, "The Bay Area sextet reinvents itself with an hour of originality and deep introspection ... Piano replaces heavy guitar as the central instrument, and the result is a bunch of hummable melodies minus the noise."[165] *Rolling Stone* scored it 3.5 out of 5 stars, saving its highest praise for "All My Friends" and "High Life," where "Duritz rises to the occasion of a stellar arrangement featuring discursive strings, spacey synths, and river-deep basses."[166]

Other reviews were less charitable, with some critics openly dismissing the once-revered act. *Spin* gave the album 6 out of 10 and asked, "Is the charismatic singer/songwriter burdened by his two Platinum albums and his relationships with lovely TV stars, or is there some secret store of dread leaking from those locks?"[167] *The Los Angeles Times* scored the album 2.5 out of five stars, writing that, "As relentless bummers go, *This*

Desert Life is pleasant enough. The band has managed to write some endearing melodies to go with Duritz's whine [and] mannered jive."[168] *Entertainment Weekly* opined, "The shining moment for mournfully melodic roots rock has passed, making this unsurprising third studio effort from Adam Duritz and Co. relevant for die-hard fans only."[169]

This Touring Life

The *Desert Life* tour began on October 13th, 1999 in London, England, before stopping in Holland and Germany. At the opening show, the Crows played "I Wish I Was as Girl" for the first time in concert. "Girl" is another song Adam composed about Betsy, the subject of "Goodnight Elisabeth." "Girl" is about Betsy's fear that Adam is sleeping with other women. Adam explained to the audience in London that being unfaithful was "something that I didn't ever do, but she was kind of crushed by that thought when we were going out. This song is about how I wish I was a girl so you would believe me [that I was not cheating]. If I was your friend you'd probably actually believe me when I tell you this."[170]

In Holland, the Crows premiered another *Desert Life* song, "Colorblind," which became a staple of their sets for several years to come. From the Netherlands, the group returned to the U.S. for a round of headlining dates on the East Coast. It included a November 4th stop at *Late Night with Conan O'Brien,* where the group performed "Hangingaround." It was the Crows' first appearance on O'Brien's program, and they showed up with two extra bands—Adam's E Pluribus Unum signees, the Gigolo Aunts and Joe 90—in tow. That put fourteen musicians on the stage, making for a crowded and chaotic singalong. A few weeks later, on November 18th, the Crows performed the song by themselves on *The Late Show with David Letterman.*

On December 10th, *This Desert Life* was certified Gold, denoting sales of 500,000. Two days later, the Crows performed a sold-out show at the Warfield San Francisco. A review described the band's seeming exhaustion: "Ups and downs considered, the Counting Crows' latest homecoming show aptly reflected their music. It was engaging, intimate and ripe with tradition, but hardly inspired."[171]

Adam was unfazed by such assessments. "I feel more confident about the music and myself than I have in a really long time," he told a reporter the week of the Warfield show. "You're always having to prove things to yourself and others, but this time I'm not so worried about it."[172]

The first leg of the *Desert Life* tour culminated with a two-night stand, held December 20th and 21st, at the Wiltern in Los Angeles. After a month off for the holidays, the tour picked back up in Chicago on January 20th, 2000. Four days later, *Desert Life* was awarded Platinum status, indicating one million records sold. It would be the last time a new Crows studio album would earn a Platinum distinction.

On February 9th, 2000, the Crows appeared on *The Tonight Show with Jay Leno*, inexplicably choosing to play a four-guitar rendition of "Kid Things," *Desert's* hidden track. The performance was solid, but the odd choice of song probably didn't motivate many viewers to pick up a copy of the new record.

Seeking to salvage things, Interscope issued the unabridged

"Mrs. Potter's Lullaby" as a single on April 3rd, 2000. The lengthy track enjoyed some mild radio play, reaching number three on the alternative radio charts on May 27th, but did not revive *Desert's* commercial prospects.

Live Forever

Hoping to convert fans the old-fashioned way, the Crows hit the road like never before. Immediately after *The Tonight Show*, the band traveled to Ireland, where they launched a two-month series of European dates. The group took just a couple of weeks off before returning to the U.S to crisscross the Midwest with Cracker opening. They played the New Orleans Jazz & Heritage Festival on April 26th, followed by their traditional drunken covers gig at the Shim Sham Club.

Outdoor festivals in Birmingham, Nashville, Atlanta, Memphis, and New York followed, and on June 5th, the band returned to Europe to play summer festivals, including Holland's beloved Pinkpop on June 12th and England's famed Glastonbury on June 23rd. The Crows were barely able to catch a breath before it was back to the U.S. for a three-month run of outdoor amphitheaters with Pennsylvania rockers Live as co-headliners.

The Crows-Live tour launched from Kansas City on July 28th and wrapped up at the end of October. Some viewed the matchup as odd—one critic called it "hopelessly incongruous."[173] Live was a self-serious alternative quartet fronted by vocalist Ed Kowalczyk. Adam and Kowalczyk both lived in Los Angeles and would frequently run into each other at bars and industry gatherings. Like the Crows, Live had enjoyed a number of hits but were struggling to maintain the mass popularity those chart-toppers brought them.

Prior to the start of the tour, Kowalczyk explained, "I was on a video set in January, and Adam called and said, 'What are you doing during the summertime?' We talked about it and talked to our bands about it and decided to go ahead."[174] "We were determined to do everything evenly, down to splitting the money," Adam explained.[175] "We want to make it the same for both, exact same set length, everything even."[176]

The Crows and Live alternated as headliners, depending, Adam said, on "where we are, on who's bigger in that city. When we're opening, I'll find a bar for us to hang out in after the show. When Live's opening, Ed's married and I'm not, so I need some help, so he'll say nice things to girls about me."[177]

Adam and Kowalczyk aimed to keep things distinct, ensuring that each act had their own production and stage setup. "The emotion thing we do [onstage] is very similar, but the way we approach the look onstage is very different," Adam explained. "We want to capture that so Live doesn't look like a Counting Crows show and vice versa."[178]

Each group played an abbreviated seventy-five-minute set, meaning a dozen or so songs from the Crows. Adam adjusted the band's setlist each night but always included "Hanginaround," which he viewed as their best shot at re-engaging fans. "We're definitely going to beg them to help us with 'Hanginaround,' because we need people for that," Adam said shortly before the tour started.[179] *Rolling Stone* reported, "'Hanginaround' has become a ritual that emphasizes the tour's collaborative nature: Members of Live, along with each band's road crew and the tour's opening act ... clamber onstage for a mass singalong free-for-all."[180]

Hammered out in beer-soaked amphitheaters on hot August nights, "Hanginaround" contributed to the frat-party vibe that took over some Crows concerts that summer. Once the revelry began, it could be difficult to contain. Adam would sit at the piano to perform a delicate solo version of the Oasis ballad "Live Forever," only to be drowned out by his own audience. On the tour's opening night in Kansas City, the singer struggled to get through the middle section of "Round Here" uninterrupted. A review of the show described the scene: "Adam implored the throng to be quiet, sshhh-ing them and trying to pull them into his emotional space. The unruly crowd just screamed and poured beer over each other, prompting the exasperated singer to finally give up in disgust, saying 'Shut the fuck up.' The audience howled. 'You shut the fuck up!' one drunken concertgoer yelled back."[181]

It was clear that the Crows' third album was not going to give *August* or *Satellites* a run for their money in terms of sales or cultural impact. Critics of the band began to turn sharper around this time. Previewing the Crows-Live double bill in St. Louis, one journalist asserted that the Crows were a successful act whose commercial fortunes soured after rush-releasing *Across a Wire*, a move "frequently seen as a career summing-up or a surrender ... The Crows' commercial fortunes have foundered a bit since ... Live is stalled in similar commercial doldrums right now, but having something like that in common is hardly the stuff off which a mutually beneficial tour is made."[182]

Defensive over criticisms that the Crows were on the decline, Adam pushed back philosophically, admitting to one reporter that, "What hooks in the minds of the majority of America may not be my songs this year. One year, you're going to be the center of the universe—if you're lucky. The next year, you won't be ... Even though we're on the fringes of the universe, we're still selling over a million records."[183]

The Crows stayed on the road in the U.S. for the remainder of the summer and most of the fall, finally calling it quits after an October 28th appearance at the Voodoo Music Experience in New Orleans. This relentless gigging meant the Crows overplayed some markets, appearing two or three times in several metropolitan areas during *Desert's* touring cycle. Teaming with a peer for a run of co-headlining shows was calculated to keep things from becoming stale, but that strategy reduced the band's stature because it aligned the Crows with lesser acts or artists whose popularity was declining.

Pussycats

Adam and the Crows took a much-needed break, returning to their various homes and families for the winter 2000 holidays. Adam spent time penning tracks for the Crows as-yet-untitled fourth album. He also contributed to the film *Josie and the Pussycats*, whose musical director, Kenneth "Babyface" Edmunds, was tasked with writing material that would be performed by the fictional band in the movie. It was a songwriting-by-committee project, and Babyface enlisted a small army of musicians to assist, including Adam Schlesinger, Matthew Sweet, Jane Weidlen of the Go-Gos, and Adam's buddy and roommate, Gigolo Aunts singer-guitarist Dave Gibbs. The songwriting team's efforts were not yielding many new tunes, so Adam and Gibbs spent a weekend cooking up ten new songs. They passed these along to Babyface, who brought in even more songwriters, and assembled the demos into *Pussycats* tracks. Ultimately, five of the Duritz-Gibbs collaborations made it to the film and its soundtrack. It included "Spin Around," an energetic ditty that shared qualities with "Accidentally in Love," a song Adam would later write for the *Shrek 2* soundtrack. The *Pussycats* soundtrack was released in March 2001 and was more successful than the film, hitting number sixteen on the *Billboard* charts and earning a Gold record.

Hobnobbing with Hollywood celebrities was now commonplace for Adam, and the singer claimed to be more comfortable with his status as a celebrity these days. "I was unable to handle big success when it happened. I'm much better adjusted to it now. I'm probably more famous now than back then, but the 14-year-old-girl mania was stronger then."[184]

In early 2001, Adam and the Crows split with DMG, the management firm that had handled the band from the beginning. A blurb in the April 14th, 2001 edition of *Billboard* magazine stated, "Counting Crows are now managed by Gary Gersh and John Silva's G.A.S. Entertainment. The group, which is in the studio working on a new album, was formerly handled by Direct Management."[185] Adam did not mention the split publicly, but partnering directly with Gersh made sense, given that the powerful industry figure had signed Adam to Geffen and steered the Crows' career ever since.

Whiskeytown

Three songs into the annual drunken acoustic covers

blowout, held April 28th at the Shim Sham Club in New Orleans, Adam introduced "Winding Wheel," by a semi-obscure singer-songwriter named Ryan Adams. Adam met Ryan Adams during a boozy jam session at the Viper Room. Adams was in town recording his second solo album, *Gold*. The pair immediately bonded over their mutual love for Americana music, hard partying, and one-night stands.

"This is a song by a friend of mine," Adam told the Shim Sham audience. "He used to be in a band called Whiskeytown. He's doing solo stuff now. His name is Ryan Adams. Pretty much my schedule during the day is I work all day in our studio and then I go at night to his studio, and then we kind of go streetwalking down Hollywood Boulevard, stopping at all the bars. Ryan, while being a very good drinker, is also probably a better songwriter than I am. In any case, he's a lot of fun."

In May 2001, the Crows hit the road without a new album, just the two-year-old *Desert Life*. Having worn out their audiences via relentless touring, Adam sought new venues, including wineries, casinos, and events at colleges, in addition to the summer festivals that always seemed happy to add the Crows. Rather than presenting themselves as a contemporary band, the Crows began to be relegated to nostalgia-act status. Even the concerts for young college students were framed this way. "We wanted to bring this group in because of their popularity in the 90s," said Ed Chatal, who helped book the Crows at Sam Houston State University for a performance. "Hopefully, they will be able to hit our college age group. Most of our students were brought up on that kind of music."[186]

The Crows used the summer gigs to try out new material

written for their fourth record. On May 2nd, they played a student-only concert at the University of Arizona's 2400-capacity Centennial Hall.[187] Because the show was for students and ticket prices would be sold at cost, the band agreed to perform for a reduced rate of $50,000.[188] (Their rate for a student concert at Yale later that year was "between $55,000 and $65,000."[189])

At the Arizona concert, Adam called for several new songs, including three that would appear on the group's fourth album, 2002's *Hard Candy*: "If I Could Give All My Love (Richard Manuel is Dead)," "Goodnight L.A.," and "Black and Blue." The Crows also premiered two new songs that would not be released until their fifth album, 2008's *Saturday Nights & Sunday Mornings*: "Los Angeles," and "1492." Perhaps growing weary of their originals, Adam filled out the set with covers by the Ramones, Warren Zevon, Big Star, and Oasis. In the end, about half of the songs performed that night were unreleased.

At a July 6th, 2001 show in San Diego, the group premiered four new songs that would appear the following year on *Hard Candy*, including the show opener, "Miami," as well as "Carriage," "American Girls," and "Butterfly in Reverse." Adam also included "Richard Manuel" and "Black and Blue," which meant that about a third of the setlist consisted of new material from *Hard Candy*. The remainder of the show featured a mix of covers and songs from *August* and *Satellites*, but only one *Desert Life* number, the ubiquitous "Hanginaround."

The Crows' West Coast run included wineries, which would become a staple of the band's touring cycles. A July 18th show at the Chateau Ste. Michelle Winery in Woodinville, Washington found the group in what one critic described as an "unusually buoyant" mood. "This is a really weird tour for us," a giddy Adam told the sold-out crowd of about 4,000. "We've never toured wineries before. Wineries are great because they have wine. I'm into it."[190] A reviewer opined that, the forthcoming album appeared to be "a stronger effort than its 1999 predecessor," adding that, "The catchiest of the new songs was 'American Girls,' a quirky guy-girl love song with some strange twists. It has hit-single potential."[191] A blurb in *Billboard* noted that the Crows were weighing several potential producers for their next album, including David Lowery, Dennis Herring, and Steve Lillywhite.[192]

On September 25th, Ryan Adams released his second album, *Gold*, which featured Adam guesting on a track, "Answering Bell." The song garnered mild interest for its *Wizard-of-Oz*-themed music video, which prominently featured Adam, along with former D-Generation's Jesse Malin, Adams' girlfriend, singer-songwriter Leona Naess, and a cameo from rock legend Elton John. On February 26th, 2002, Adam joined Ryan Adams on *The Tonight Show with Jay Leno*, grooving along and singing backup in a brown jacket.

Their summer outing had wrapped up, but the Crows were not finished, adding thirty-four dates to their calendar and extending the tour into November. As the group's album sales declined, performing live became their central source of revenue, requiring that they stay on the road much of the year to keep afloat financially.

Reviews of the fall trek were generally positive but began to focus on what would become a central theme of in the second half of the band's career, Adam's changing physical appearance. It didn't just come from the tabloids. Music journalists and critics had spent years discussing Adam's hair, but now, it was the singer's body that sparked their analysis and critique. An October 2001 concert review praised Adam and company's performance but described the singer as "noticeably heftier."[193] Another review from later that month depicted the bearded 37-year-old vocalist as "a more burly, imposing figure than in previous appearances."[194]

This Desert Life did little to resurrect the Crows' fortunes, selling half as many copies as *Satellites*, which was considered a disappointment after it stalled at sales of two million. The band remained a potent live act that continued to draw fans, but it also meant endless roadwork. Adam was approaching forty, gaining weight, and competing for audience share with picturesque twenty-somethings such as John Mayer, Matchbox 20 vocalist Rob Thomas, and Dashboard Confessional's Chris Carabba. All of this put immense pressure on Adam to turn things around with the band's fourth album. Little did he know that his most significant challenges were just around the corner and had nothing to do with music.

Chapter 5

Hard Candy

Adam rarely wrote while the Crows were on tour, finding it too distracting to concentrate. With his calendar increasingly filled with concerts, it was harder to find time to write at home. Because Adam was the Crows' sole lyricist, the other musicians had to wait until the muse struck. As Charlie Gillingham told me, "Adam doesn't like to write on the road. We've tried, but it never seems to work out. Adam writes in these spurts where he'll write eight songs in a weekend and then nothing for eight months. That's kind of the way he is."[195]

Adam explained, "It's like you eat when you're hungry. I write when I'm moved to write."[196] Adam claimed that penning all the words himself gave a consistency to the Crows' catalog that would be otherwise absent, that it was difficult to sing other people's words to one of "his" songs. "I find it's hard [to share]. It's like having multiple personalities—too many points of view."[197] Adam tackled the subject of writing on the *Candy* tune "New Frontier." The songwriter explained, "I describe how much the world around us is made of plastic, how fake everything is and how many differences there are between you and me, between who writes the songs and who listens to them."[198]

Adam said that memory was the underlying theme of *Hard Candy*. "The album is thematically about memories," he explained, "the way you use them to substitute for living sometimes. Some memories are sweet, but tough and painful too. And they're not good for you."[199]

Adam clarified that his lyrical motifs arose naturally, rather than being part of some sort of creative master plan. "I don't write with [themes] in mind," he said. "You don't sit down and say, 'Today I'm going to write a song about memory.' I'm more likely to, as in the case with a song like 'Hard Candy,' pull a photo out of a drawer and look at it and think about everything in the photo—and then write about it."[200]

"If I Could Give All My Love (Richard Manuel is Dead)" approaches memory from a different vantage point, dating to March 4th, 1986. "This record is very much about memories, and several songs are about things that happened a long time ago. This song in particular was born from the memory of the day Manuel died," Adam explained.[201] He and a girlfriend had been out drinking all night, stumbling home as the sun began to rise. On the way in the door, Adam grabbed the newspaper, which reported that Manuel, singer and pianist for the Band, had hung himself in a Florida motel room at age forty-two. "It just had this striking effect on me, you know, the utter impermanence of things. I really got the sense that you can't afford to go on forever just playing footsie in your life, dipping your toes in, because your life will pass you by."[202] Adam added, "I remember thinking that you can't let things slip by you, because one day they're gone. The girls that you can't get your act together for, they go off and marry someone else."[203]

Adam explained that the writing process itself was fundamentally about creating lasting impressions in a world filled with constant change. "In a sense, writing songs, you're making meaningful, permanent memories, so that things that come and go out of your life don't just fade. The people in the songs understand that however transitory things were, they meant something to me. Anna knows. Elisabeth knows."[204]

This Desert Life was loose and expansive, with songs that breezed well past the dictates of pop radio. Adam was committed to reining himself in on *Candy*. As he told *Billboard* magazine, "For whatever reason, I was really in love with writing gems, perfect songs, and getting the things I had to say [out] in less time. Sometimes I feel like writing eight-minute songs. And on this album, I was really obsessed with great, perfect pieces."[205]

In addition to the lyrics, Adam frequently composed all the music as well. When he collaborated with the other musicians, it often began with one of his ideas. Adam writes music on the piano, bringing the basic chord changes to the band. Guitarist Dave Bryson explained, "Nine out of ten times, by the time we're done, [Adam's] piano part goes away completely. Everyone rewrites and comes up with their own signatures. And it's those signatures that make the song."[206]

Recording Candy

Like the first three records, *Hard Candy* was recorded primarily at a house in the Hollywood hills, with the Crows avoiding traditional studios unless absolutely necessary. "We've never done a record in a studio," Adam explained. "I hate studios. Studios are really claustrophobic to me. I hate the whole vibe, sitting in some bland lounge when you're not working."[207]

That doesn't mean *Candy* was a studio-free creation. The band laid down overdubs and orchestral arrangements in two traditional recording studios: Ocean Way Recording in Hollywood and Westside Studios in London. "We work in them, we have to be in them, but I just don't like being there," Adam said. "They're fine for a day, but they're not a place to build or feel."[208]

Adam originally enlisted Smash Mouth producer Eric Valentine because the singer liked the sound of his pop singles. Ultimately, Valentine proved to be too detail-oriented for the Crows. Adam also tried out Ethan Johns, producer of Ryan Adams' *Gold*, with whom he worked on "Answering Bell." That did not pan out entirely either, so Adam retained famed producer Steve Lillywhite, whose resume included the Rolling Stones, U2, and Dave Matthews Band.

"I have no idea what Steve does, but I can tell you he's really fucking great at it," Adam raved to *Rolling Stone*. The singer claimed that he had forty records in his collection that were produced by Lillywhite. "There's a reason why he's been producing records for twenty-five years now. The best producers just bring a certain atmosphere to the studio. They create a vibe where it seems magical, and it seems like you're making this very special thing that's classic and timeless."[209]

Ethan Johns continued to do production work on the project, with Steve Lillywhite at the helm. "I wanted two producers because I like to give things a bit of movement," Adam said.

"With this way of working we can make the things we do fresher. You can work more intensely and even faster."

The Crows recorded in a house, but the *Candy* sessions differed from the making of the first three records. Historically, the group compartmentalized recording and touring, and would take time off the road to record. For *Candy*, the Crows never stopped playing live. They would hole up in the studio for six weeks, then hit the road for a month, return to L.A. for another few weeks of recording, and then go back on tour.

On February 25th, 2002, the Crows played an unannounced six-song show opening for Ryan Adams at the El Ray Theatre in Los Angeles. Later, Adam joined the headliner during his set for "Answering Bell." The band also took time off from recording to perform at lucrative corporate gigs, which they played frequently, on tour and off. On March 12th, they put in a seven-song set at the National Association of Recording Merchandisers (NARM) Awards Banquet, held at the San Francisco Marriott. Vocalist Vanessa Carlton was selected to open, with standup comedian Jack Gallagher emceeing.

The Crows spent four months completing *Candy*, much faster than they typically took to make an album.[210] Adam explained, "We stopped and started again so many times: going into the studio for a week and then taking a break for a few days allows you to focus better on your work. I think this record, for the actual time we spent making it, was done in a pretty short amount of time."[211]

Recording a new song typically began with a basic track, after which Adam and the band would layer instruments, vocals, and other accouterments. "Carriage" and "Up All Night" were captured in one or two takes. Songs such as "Richard Manuel" were more labored over, with the band recording multiple versions, laid down over many weeks. "Once we're done getting a good band performance, we work on all the colors, harmonies, horns, strings, banjo—whatever the extra colors are gonna be," Adam explained.[212]

It was through collaboration that Adam resolved the difficulties he was having with an upbeat number named "American Girls." He explained, "The chorus sounded too anthemic, and it wants to be relaxed, sort of sexy and breezy."[213] One day, the singer was sitting in the office of Interscope co-founder Jimmy Iovine, who was playing him Sheryl Crow's forthcoming record, *C'mon, C'mon*. Adam told Iovine about the problems he was having with "American Girls," which everyone hoped would be a single. "That song is really derogatory," the singer said, "It's a very seductive, nasty song. I was having huge problems with the way it sounded."[214]

Iovine recommended adding Crow, who got her start as a backup vocalist for Michael Jackson. Adam recalled, "I called her up and said, 'Can you come over and try this?' She listened to it, liked it, put the headphones on, sang the harmony, note-perfect, doubled it, note-perfect and moved on to the next section. She did the entire song in an hour. That could have taken all day with somebody else. Backup singing is a totally different art. The kind of shit Sheryl did, I can't do that."[215]

Adam called upon other famous friends and acquaintances to help out as well, including backing vocals from "friend of a friend" Matthew Sweet on the album's title track and Ryan Adams' paramour Leona Naess on "Black and Blue."

Adam also collaborated directly with Ryan Adams on "Butterfly in Reverse," a tune he had been wrestling with for months. He had written music for the song and lyrics for its chorus but could not figure out where to go from there. Ryan Adams stopped by one afternoon and the two finished it on the spot. "We ended up brainstorming and doing the whole song," Adam recalled. "We just went line for line then, trading lines through the whole song. It took us fifteen minutes. And I wanted him to sing it with me because we wrote it together."[216]

Adam collaborated with Ryan Adams and Dave Gibbs on a song titled "Los Angeles" that did not make it to *Candy*. "It was written as an unapologetic fuck you to anyone who wanted to criticize our lifestyle because we loved what we were doing," the singer said. "We were working on *Gold* half the days and *Hard Candy* half the days, and then Ryan and I were wandering Hollywood Boulevard from bar to bar, all night long. So at the time, it was about our particularly debauched lifestyle."[217]

Other songs did not make the cut, either. In March 2002, *Billboard* listed "1492" and "Mr. Deeds" as forthcoming tracks on *Candy*, but both numbers were ultimately excised.[218] "1492" was an up-tempo rocker featuring David Immerglück on bass that would open the Crows' next album. "Deeds" became "Goin' Down to New York Town" and was issued on the soundtrack to the Adam Sandler comedy *Mr. Deeds* in June 2002. The two-minute rocker's working title, "Going to Town," was taken from its chorus. *Billboard* also claimed that the Crows had recorded an album's worth of cover songs, including a version of Pure Prairie League's "Amie."

The covers project was conceived as a live-in-the-studio

Shim Sham show, with fun and serious songs blasted out in a single take. One cover that made it to *Hard Candy* was the Crows' contemporary spin on Joni Mitchell's "Big Yellow Taxi." "It was meant to be a lark," Dave Bryson explained. "We were recording covers, mostly by friends of ours. But when we did 'Big Yellow Taxi' it was apparent to everyone it was kind of special."[219]

Produced correctly, a Crows cover of "Taxi" could be a legitimate hit. "If we recorded in a more polished way, radio might be willing to play us more," Dave Bryson said, adding, "We took it to Ron Fair and asked him to develop it and make it groovier, a kind of hip-hop sound."[220]

Fair was a record executive and super-producer, known for his smashes with Christina Aguilera, Black Eyed Peas, and Mary J. Blige. Fair was just coming off a monster hit with Vanessa Carlton's "A Thousand Miles," issued in February 2002. Fair souped up "Big Yellow Taxi" with a hip-hop rhythm and synthesizer blasts, giving *Candy* another track that strayed somewhat from the Crows' traditional sound. Adam seemed unsure what to do with "Taxi," so he included it at the end of *Candy* as a hidden track a la "Kid Things," the unnamed closer to *Desert Life*.

Coca-Cola

In the months before *Candy* was released, Geffen approached the band about partnering with Coca-Cola as part of a summer advertising campaign. "American Girls," *Candy's* lead single, would be used in an advertisement starring Adam and the group. Adam was horrified. "My first reaction was absolutely not. And then I started thinking about it. I really hate to make knee-jerk reactions. You really need to think about things."[221]

Geffen and the band's management pressed him to take the deal. Musical acts routinely paired with big-name brands. Besides, this was not Marlboro or Jack Daniels, it was Coke. "We felt comfortable with it," Dan Vickrey told a reporter. "Who doesn't drink Coke, you know? We've been approached to do beer commercials, and we've turned them down for obvious reasons."[222] Adam added, "We, as a successful band, have a great responsibility towards our audience. We know that we are 'specially watched' by millions of teenagers in America and around the world."[223]

But advertisements were an increasingly viable way for rock artists to deliver new material to the public. In a hyper-competitive music industry dominated by gangsta rap, boy bands, and Britney, a Coke commercial could help keep the Crows name in the spotlight. "It's a great marketing tool nowadays," Adam said. "It's so hard to get yourself out there for everybody and we're not a bunch of 16-year-old kids, which is what (record buyers) want to see right now. So a company as big as Coke wants the Counting Crows—and I love Coke—then why not? What's the harm?"[224]

Adam and the group agreed to do the advertisement, which was shot on a beach in Southern California that spring. In the commercial, "American Girls" plays in the background as a shirtless young man delivers a bottle of Coca Cola to actress Kayla Ewell, who is tanning on a crowded beach. "Who are those guys?" she asks. Adam and the Crows, dressed in stage wear, smile down at them. "Counting Crows. They came with the Coke," the young man shrugs. "Cool," she responds, smiling. The closing shot features Adam and the Crows seated around the woman. Adam is laughing and smiling. "That's the whole joke. Rock band on the beach," the singer explained to *Rolling Stone*.[225]

"American Girls" was released to radio in May 2002, airing in the Coke commercial soon after. The campaign worked, and *Candy's* debut single hit number one on *Billboard's* AAA charts on June 22nd.

Adam claimed that he and the band were paid virtually nothing for appearing in the Coke ad. Featuring the group's latest single in a national advertising campaign was considered payment enough. "The thing that's being misconstrued is that we made all this money," Adam said. "Not that there's anything wrong with that, I'm kind of (angry) they didn't pay us a ton of cash. I was like, 'I've been waiting for all these years, not doing a single commercial while other people made millions of dollars, and you tell me I'm doing it for the exposure.' Well, I guess the exposure's good, but I'd sure like the cash."[226]

In other interviews at the time, however, Adam claimed that he had no problem earning a paycheck from the Coca-Cola corporation. "Of course, we took some money. So? You also work for a company, which I assume pays you. We did the same thing: we worked for Coca Cola, which paid us. I really don't understand this hysteria around artists who give their songs to advertisers: many have done it."[227]

Whatever gains the Crows made from the commercial were not enough to make up for the backlash from fans, the press, and fellow musicians. The Crows were, after all, a group that prided themselves on integrity and once threatened to walk out of *Saturday Night Live* because the showrunners wanted them to open with their latest single. This was a band that declined to play hits like "Einstein on the Beach" at their concerts, that turned down *Top of the Pops* because their singer refused to lip-sync.

The forums on the Crows website exploded with derisive comments over the Coke ad, and the group even gained some high-profile detractors. In an interview that took place not long after the commercial began airing, Pearl Jam lead singer Eddie Vedder ranted, "I saw something with Wyclef Jean last night for some fucking product and Counting Crows for Coca-Cola or something. Fuck them. Busta Rhymes for anti-perspirant? What the fuck is that? Why? They have a set of morals they can run with and that's fine but I'm just gonna say, 'Fuck you.'"[228] Adam fired back at Vedder not long after: "I think the whole fame thing is a huge issue for Pearl Jam because they got flagged from day one as being wannabe Nirvana."[229]

Adam refused to back down or apologize, but he did post a defensive message to fans on the Crows' website. "I'm truly sorry if it upset some of you, but that's the breaks," he wrote. "As long as we make music the same way we always have and as long as business concerns never affect the way we make our art, then I think you are truly rude to accuse us of selling out just because we made a commercial for a product we actually like."[230]

Five-star Fare

Hard Candy's effervescent opening title track hit a sweet spot, joining the ranks of the band's best upbeat fare without resorting to the guitar histrionics Vickrey and Immerglück sometimes employed. "Miami" was founded on a simmering castanet-based rhythm that refused to quit, building to a violin and vocal climax that featured a standout performance from Adam. "My songs are so specific. I use place names, people's names," he said. "People are always asking me why I use the names. It's really simple, because those are the names, you know? That's what the song is about. It seems crazy not to use them."[231]

For longtime fans, however, it was Adam's wholesale return to balladry on *Candy* that made the album a classic. The ballads he wrote, all of them solo compositions, were grounded in piano and weighted with melancholy and sorrow. Musical artists typically feature one or two such tracks on an album; Adam insisted on four. "Good Time" is a yearning ode to feeling like an outsider in every setting, with Adam climbing into a beautiful lyrical crescendo. "Goodnight L.A." is a 3 a.m. ode to insomnia that captures the condition's sense of loneliness and flat despair. "Up All Night" also tackles insomnia but sounds hopeful and light. That year, Adam told a New York audience that "Holiday in Spain" began as "this really stupid song about getting drunk and staying up all night," but ended up being, "a beautiful slow song about waking up with a hangover."[232]

The wealth of five-star fare on *Candy* made it a standout release that has endured, but it has detractors among Crows adherents, and even the band itself. *Candy* was the first Crows album to include a number of tunes that missed the mark. Maudlin mid-tempo sludge such as "Butterfly in Reverse," "Carriage," and "Black and Blue" were among the least compelling songs Durtiz ever cooked up and gave his critics plenty of ammunition. "New Frontier" attempted to recreate the Crows' early new wave sound but did little other than prove that the group was wise to leave that style behind.

Hard Candy was released July 8th, 2002, with "American Girls" still riding high on the charts. The album debuted at number five. *PopMatters* hailed it "their best, most mature, and most vital effort to date."[233] Kansas City alternative newspaper *The Pitch* praised it as their "fourth consecutive home run."[234] *Drowned in Sound* ranked it seven out of ten, calling *Candy* "focused experimentation, full of catchy hooks and a complete right angle to their previous Americana-tinged efforts."[235]

Advancing the lead single of their new album with a Coke commercial, however, meant that it was often the focus of the review. For example, *The Washington Times* began with a paragraph about the ad. "It's pretty clear that the members of Counting Crows weren't happy with the sales or airplay of their third album, *This Desert Life*. So when it came to marketing their latest album, the band took the unusual step of appearing in a Coke commercial."[236]

The Coke ad signaled the end of the band's days of widespread critical acclaim. The gloves were now off for those who never liked the Crows in the first place. In his review of *Candy*, Chicago music journalist Jim Derogatis dinged the group for "compromising their earlier principled stands (no lip-syncing; no 'selling out' man) by appearing in a Coca-Cola commercial and avoiding some of the more ambitious, Van Morrison-style experiments of the last few discs."[237]

Entertainment Weekly graded *Candy* a B-minus in a review dripping with snark. "That Coke ad was no fluke: Adam Duritz and underlings really mean to go for the gold this time, leaving the mopiness of recent duds largely behind in favor of sprightly tunes that all but scream 'follow-up single.'"[238] The once laudatory *Rolling Stone* scored it three out of five stars. "This is a supremely confident, fastidiously arranged, masterfully played record with a slightly prefabricated feel."[239] *Billboard* offered a lukewarm review, dismissing "American Girls" as "radio-friendly frat fare" that attempts to "rock the suburbs."[240]

Hometown paper *SF Gate* hated the entire thing. "There's nothing hard and not much mouthwatering about Counting Crows' fourth studio album."[241] *The New York Times*, which had praised the Crows to the heavens less than a decade earlier, now dismissed them as hopelessly passe. "The group writes jangly, earnest songs that might appeal to young listeners everywhere, if only young listeners weren't more interested in hard rock, hip-hop, dance pop and other genres that aspire to novelty or innovation."[242]

Adam claimed that critiques about the Crows declining cultural relevance had no bearing on his artistic decisions. The band was a business, but he was not motivated by sales. "The real pressure is to make good albums; that's hard. The pressure is to play good shows; that's hard. Whether people are going to accept it or not, well, that doesn't have anything to do with me."[243]

Touring Candy

On April 26th, 2002, the Crows performed at the New Orleans Jazz and Heritage Festival, playing three songs from *Candy* in a thirteen-song set. The following night Adam and friends packed the Shim Sham Club for their annual cover-song extravaganza. It included "Big Yellow Taxi" from *Candy* as well as Pure Prairie League's "Amie," Teenage Fanclub's "Start Again," and The Faces' "Ooh La La." Adam was happy to be on the road, playing music with the band. "The truth of the matter is, I express myself much better in music than I do in speech or day-to-day life; I'm much better onstage than I am in the rest of my day."[244]

The Crows appeared at festivals in Nashville, Atlanta, and Memphis, and then took part in MTV's Rock and Comedy Concert at the Tribeca Film Festival on May 10th. The show featured comedians Robin Williams, Whoopi Goldberg, and Jimmy Fallon and musical acts that included David Bowie, Wyclef Jean, and Sheryl Crow, who joined the Crows onstage to sing "American Girls."

Adam was photographed sharing a laugh backstage with Fallon, whose 1998 audition for *Saturday Night Live* included an impression of Adam. "I met Jimmy years ago," the singer explained. "We were in a bar, and Jimmy came over. He let it slip out that he did this impersonation of me, and I was like, 'Shut up!' He said, 'Yeah, I play guitar, do some songs, funny stuff.' I said 'Well, we've got a gig tomorrow night at fucking Hammerstein Ballroom, Mr. Funny Guy, why don't you come down and play, see if you can do it in front of a whole house of Counting Crows fans.'" Fallon took Adam up on the offer, opening for the

Crows with his loose-limbed impression of the singer. "He came out on stage and embarrassed the fuck out of me. It's such a horrific impersonation of me. But imitation is a form of flattery."[245]

Following a month of spring shows in Europe, beginning in late June, the band opened for the Who on four West Coast dates, including a July 1st stop at the Hollywood Bowl. The Who sets were fairly short, seven or eight songs split among the four albums. Every concert featured their most enduring hits: "Mr. Jones," "Hanginaround," and "A Long December."

The Who mini-tour culminated with a July 6th stop at the Gorge Amphitheatre in George, Washington, 150 miles east of Seattle. Pearl Jam vocalist and Seattle resident Eddie Vedder is known to be a massive Who fan and was backstage that day. The singer was still upset over the Crows' appearance in the Coca-Cola commercial and left Adam a book detailing Coke's problematic relationship with elementary schools. Adam thumbed through Vedder's offering but remained unmoved. "What the book said was that Coke was willing to pay all this money to put Coke in the cafeterias. It doubled the amount of money this particular public-school system could spend per child. I appreciated what [Vedder] was trying to say, but to me, it's a no-brainer."[246]

The Crows played a few promotional dates on the East Coast, including an acoustic show at Tower Records in Philadelphia on July 9th. A couple of weeks later, the band returned to Europe for another round of festivals. Like "Omaha" before it, *Candy* songs that named New York, Los Angeles, Miami, and Spain were guaranteed crowd pleasers for the heavy-touring group. Adam explained, "You forget and then you sing the name of the city, and the people go crazy, and I'm always like, 'Whoa, what happened?'"[247]

The group traversed the States from September until the end of the year. In October, *Hard Candy* was declared Gold, denoting sales of 500,000. It was half the sales of *This Desert Life*, which had also been considered a commercial disappointment. *Candy* was the final Crows studio album to earn a Gold award. The band continued to draw fans to their concerts, including three sold-out shows in October at the Hammerstein Ballroom. *The New York Times* reported that Adam got a big response after informing the audience that he had recently bought an apartment in New York.[248]

New York, New York

Adam's relocation from Berkeley to Los Angeles was an upheaval, but one that made sense. In some ways, his move from his beloved working artists town to New York City was more surprising. After all, he was a musician who was synonymous with the West Coast. But after writing four albums that paid tribute to Southern California, Adam was ready for a change.

"I'm a single insomniac living in L.A.," he said, just after the Hammerstein Ballroom shows. "I don't sleep very well in L.A. and I'm moving to New York. I'm sure that New York will become more present in the songs because of that. You just write about who you are."[249]

Adam explained that he had grown tired of the languid, traffic-jammed Los Angeles lifestyle. He sought the anonymity and twenty-four-hour excitement of New York, where no one cared that he was the singer for Counting Crows. Adam purchased a giant apartment in Manhattan and planned to move there soon. "New York is a huge city and with that many people packed in, it's just not a big deal for me to be there," he explained. "It's just a different vibe. I'm going there for a lot of reasons. I'm feeling a little [uninspired]. You want to be invigorated by your life. Because what I found in L.A., I'm a workaholic and then I go home and watch TV. And that's not how your life should be."[250]

Adam did not just buy any old apartment. He purchased a palatial spread the size of a basketball court. It was located in Astor Place, one of the swankiest blocks in the city. "He lives more like Batman," wrote one journalist upon visiting.[251] If you pressed a button on the shelf of the library, it activated a hidden door to the singer's bedroom. There was a game room with arcade classics and a ping pong table. Gold and Platinum records hung in the bathroom.

Adam sectioned off one piece of the apartment as a garden. It was "carpeted in Astroturf, complete with wooden outdoor chairs, a swing hanging from the ceiling and a picnic table with a blue umbrella." A huge antique railroad clock stood nearby. Adam explained, "Outdoor space is so hard to find in New York, and it's really expensive. So I thought, why not just create my own backyard?"[252]

The move to New York seemed to be about a successful celebrity escaping boredom and burnout in Los Angeles. "Sometimes at the end of the day, I just can't believe that's all there is," Adam confessed. "Is that as good as it's gonna get today? So I'll stay awake and watch TV and read books and keep spooling time out as if something was gonna come along at four or five or six in the morning, and there ain't nothing coming. But you have to practice a certain discipline to make yourself go to sleep when you're that way."[253]

Adam explained that he was using exercise as a way to counter some of the mental health issues that were troubling him at the time. "I've been boxing a lot, which I've been doing for about a year," he said. "It started off that I wanted to get in shape, and there's different ways to do it, like running, biking, but that shit bores me. I'd rather shoot myself than do something tedious like that."

Adam knew that he was not the young, fit rock star he was when "Jones" ruled America's airwaves. "I'd always been in good shape, but in the last ten years I found myself in less and less good shape," he said. "I didn't want to be that way. I wanted to be like a 'rock star' rock star."[254]

Yellow Taxis and Films About Ghosts

At a December 10th concert at the Universal Amphitheatre in Los Angeles, drummer Ben Mize became ill in the middle of the show, causing Adam and Immerglück to hastily improvise an all-acoustic closer. A review in *The Los Angeles Times* asserted, "There's a staid predictability to both the [Crows'] music and lyrical imagery. Having to cover for the missing drummer took the band out of its game and put it into the moment."[255]

The Crows closed out 2002 at the Warfield in San Francisco, where they played five sold-out shows, with Toad the Wet Sprocket opening. On the first night, Adam kicked things off with a cover of "San Francisco (Be Sure to Wear Flowers in Your

Hair)," Scott McKenzie's 1967 hippy anthem. "Nothing could have better warmed the crowd or placed more grins on faces," *PopMatters* declared.[256]

The Warfield shows were the last concerts the group would play with drummer Ben Mize, who departed to spend more time with his family. He was quickly replaced by Jim Bogios. Bogios was a Bay Area native and a former bandmate of David Immerglück. He had played with Sheryl Crow for several years and had toured with Ben Folds, Eric Clapton, Prince, and others.

SF Gate offered faint praise for the Warfield opener, noting that despite the run of sold-out shows, "The group's national following has shrunk dramatically since [the 1990s], witnessed by dismal sales for its new album."[257] Adam seemed unconcerned about album sales. "We may have sold less records," he told a reporter in November. "But while other people are hemorrhaging money, we're packing 'em in."[258]

Adam wasn't kidding. Within weeks, he and the Crows set off for a tour that took them on a two-month trek that included Europe, then Australia and New Zealand. These shows featured the band's latest hit, a surprise that few saw coming.

In late 2002, about six months after *Hard Candy* was released, super-producer Ron Fair remixed the Crows' "Big Yellow Taxi" for use in a new Hugh Grant, Sandra Bullock romantic comedy *Two Weeks Notice*. The film was released just before Christmas 2002, and Fair's remix included the addition of background vocals from his client Vanessa Carlton. *Two Weeks Notice* did reasonably well at the box office, and in February 2003, the Carlton version of "Big Yellow Taxi" began to generate airplay. Geffen sprung for a music video, directed by Liz Frielander, whose credits included Alanis Morrisette, U2, and R.E.M.

On March 22nd, "Taxi" peaked at number two on *Billboard's* AAA charts. The song was a significant worldwide hit for the Crows, charting in thirteen countries outside the U.S., landing in the top ten in five of them. When Geffen realized they had a hit single that was not on *Hard Candy*, they replaced the original Crows-only version of "Taxi" with the Carlton remix and listed the formerly hidden track on the album's cover art and liner notes. The Crows had a new hit to include in their playlists, and "Taxi" joined the ranks of "Jones," "December," and "Hanginaround" as stalwarts of the group's live sets.

The group's Australian setlists were hindered by the absence of bassist Matt Malley. "Our hands are a little tied," Dave Bryson told a reporter during the Crows' Australia trek. "Our bass player's father is ill, and he's had to take a break from touring. Right now we're all playing bass, and it's really restricted our repertoire. Ordinarily we have about fifty songs to draw from. Right now we're down to around twenty or so."[259]

Two weeks after returning from Australia, the Crows were in New Orleans to launch a six-week round of theaters, halls, and college campuses, culminating in their annual stop at the Shim Sham Club on May 3rd.

In June, Geffen issued "Richard Manuel is Dead" as the fourth single from *Candy*. An accompanying music video juxtaposed live footage with B-roll of the band horsing around backstage and on the streets of Amsterdam. Adam appeared noticeably heavier in the video.

The Crows hit Europe for the summer festival circuit, including a June 18th stop in Vienna opening for the Rolling Stones. A week after that, the group was in Colorado to launch a two-month co-headlining tour with John Mayer. The jaunt with Mayer, which ran from July 7th to September 2nd, was another shotgun wedding, matching the Crows with an incongruous peer. The Crows-Live lineup paired two recently popular alternative rock acts for a night of instant nostalgia. The two bands' popularity in any given city determined that night's headliner, with the Crows generally coming out on top. John Mayer, by contrast, was a hot new singer-songwriter whose star was ascending, a twenty-five-year-old heartthrob who packed the sheds night after night with screaming teenage girls.

The Crows opened nearly every show. A review of the July 11th gig at the Gorge Amphitheater noted the preponderance of "giddy girls pining for a closer look at John Mayer. Mayer is now a bona fide pinup pop star. The immense collective shriek that greeted his arrival on stage may not have been on par with Beatlemania, but it was loud enough to drown out the opening chords."[260] By comparison, the Crows and their 39-year-old vocalist seemed old and out of touch. They got pounded by critics. In a review of the Los Angeles stop, *Variety* opined that Adam and company "appear to have lost whatever momentum (or inspiration) they achieved" with *August*. The reviewer called Adam's dreadlocks "the silliest rock star tonsure since A Flock of Seagulls. But it has more personality than the band's material, a lumpy mélange of classic-rock cliches."[261]

On November 2nd, 2003, Geffen issued *Films About Ghosts*, a compilation of hits from the group's first four albums, plus

"Einstein on the Beach" and the Vanessa Carlton version of "Big Yellow Taxi." Two new songs, "She Don't Want Nobody Near" and a cover of the Grateful Dead's "Friend of the Devil," were also included. The new tracks were produced by Brendan O'Brien, who came to fame as Pearl Jam's producer and had since worked with newcomers such as Stone Temple Pilots and veterans such as Bruce Springsteen.

The Crows promoted the new release by performing "She Don't Want Nobody Near" on *Good Morning America*, *The Tonight Show with Jay Leno*, and *The Late Show with David Letterman*. Geffen funded a music video, which featured Adam, minus the Crows, miming the song outdoors in the desert. "Nobody" was a hit, reaching number one on *Billboard's* AAA charts. *Ghosts* was certified Gold in the U.S. and the U.K.

On November 19th, 2003, Adam appeared on *The Howard Stern Show*, performing an acoustic version of "Mr. Jones." The group closed out the year by playing five sold-out shows at the Warfield in San Francisco and four sold-out concerts at the Wiltern in L.A. At the December 12th Warfield gig, Adam, performing solo at the piano, played the title track to *August and Everything After* for the first time.

Accidentally in Love

Gary Gersh knew the Crows needed a shot of adrenaline, so he got to work behind the scenes to put Adam into the movies. He tapped the songwriter to compose the theme song for the forthcoming sequel to the animated children's film, *Shrek*. Like the first movie, *Shrek 2* was being produced by DreamWorks, which was co-owned by David Geffen; the film's soundtrack would be released on Geffen Records.

Shrek 2's theme song would open the film and serve as the lead single to its soundtrack. It was a high-visibility placement, an all but guaranteed hit. The first *Shrek* movie, released in 2001, had grossed nearly $300 million in the U.S. and won the Oscar for best animated feature. Its accompanying soundtrack sold more than two million copies.

Adam visited DreamWorks, where he watched about half the movie, including the opening montage. The executives told Adam that the song had to be uplifting and gave him a key instruction: "Don't write a song about Shrek, write a song that's about you."[262] Adam would joke at a press conference for *Shrek 2* that this directive was easy because, "I was falling in love with a girl who kept turning into an ogre at night." [263]

Kidding aside, Adam found the songwriting assignment difficult. "I was really struggling with it," he recalled. "I generally don't write songs on demand, and I almost got to the point where I thought I wasn't going to do it."[264] Adam was not used to being told what to do by corporate executives. "When I work on my own records, the record company generally doesn't try to fuck with me. But when you're doing a movie, the people who do the music are considered the bottom crawlers. So much money is involved in these movies that someone somewhere is going to try to screw you."[265]

Adam returned to New York but couldn't come up with anything. Then, he wrote half the number in an afternoon, basing the lyrics on a recent romantic experience. "The song ended up reflecting a lot of what was going on in my life at the time: falling in love with someone you're not supposed to fall in love with because it's inconvenient."

Adam was due to depart for the band's latest international tour, with dates booked in Europe, South Africa, and Australia. A week and a half later, he finished the song in a hotel room in Manchester, England.[266] The ultra-catchy track was packed with sunshine and earworms a-plenty. Adam said that the line about ice cream brought everything together. "The 'strawberry ice cream' turned the song around. I wanted it to be more colorful. Animation presents a world that is far more brightly colored than the one we live in, and (that's) why they're fun to watch. I wanted the song to feel like an explosion of color and feelings."[267]

To accompany his words, Adam envisioned a soundtrack along the lines of the Cure's "Just Like Heaven." "That exuberant flow of words, an explosion of words. It's like someone who is experiencing that sort of joy and is about to lose it all."[268] To get the music right, Adam recruited David Immerglück, Matt Malley, and Dan Vickrey to help out. Production was handled by Brendan O'Brien. The finished track was the most overtly pop song the Crows had ever released, but it aligned with "Einstein on the Beach," the songs he co-wrote for *Josie and the Pussycats*, and *Hard Candy's* pop-rock forays.

Selma

On March 28th, 2004, Adam was waking up in a hotel in Perth, Australia when his mother called with the news. Selma Feldman, Adam's grandmother, had passed. She had suffered a stroke five years earlier, and her health had been on the decline ever since. Selma's funeral would be held on March 30th in

Pikesville, Maryland, outside of Baltimore. Adam had barely put the phone down when he received a text message—his current girlfriend was breaking up with him. Two crushing losses, back-to-back.

Adam was overwhelmed by a sense of loneliness, worsened by his isolation in a remote city located in one of the far corners of the world. The Crows had a string of shows lined up, and Adam intended to push through and fulfill what he viewed as obligations. He flew to Adelaide, setting up shop in the glass-walled penthouse on the thirtieth floor of a luxury hotel.

Adam couldn't sleep. He was wracked by guilt for always being on the road, always missing important life events. Birthdays, holidays, family get-togethers. Touring caused him to forgo being there for the birth of his sister Nicole's twins, who arrived a trimester early. He had barely interacted with Selma in the past five years—and when Adam saw her on holidays, Selma was taken aback. The adorable grandson who came to visit Baltimore in the summers had been replaced by a burly, bearded, dreadlocked rocker who made her nervous.

This time would be different, Adam vowed. He called the Crows' road manager and ordered him to cancel the rest of the Australian tour. He then called his travel agent with a clear directive: "I need to fly to Baltimore by this time tomorrow. Whatever you have to do, find a way."[269]

Adam flew to Tokyo, where he caught a direct flight to Baltimore. Nicole picked him up at the airport, and they drove straight to Selma's funeral, arriving fifteen minutes after the proceedings began. Adam served as a pallbearer. He felt remorse. He was close with his grandmother as a child, but being a globetrotting rock star made it hard to keep in touch. Now, it was too late.

At his darkest hour, Adam's sunniest song was soaring, taking his career to unforeseen heights. "Accidentally in Love" was released as a single on May 3rd, 2004, two weeks before *Shrek 2* premiered. It played over the opening montage of the film and appeared as the first song on its soundtrack. A review in *Billboard* hailed "Accidentally" as "the perfect kickoff to summer [that] will tickle the tots and their parents, too."[270] The song was a hit, spending five weeks at number one on *Billboard's* AAA charts. The accompanying music video features an animated rabbit who has Adam's hair and facial expressions, dancing around the apartment of a couple who are just waking up.

The Crows performed the song on May 26th on *The Late Show with David Letterman* and May 28th on *Today*. The group also appeared in *Inside Shrek 2,* a feature that aired on VH1. "My songs for Counting Crows are mature and generally don't get a chance to reach kids," Adam said in an interview around this time. "To be part of something like that is pretty cool."[271] The songwriter added, "The chance to do something timeless like that is rare. Movies for kids don't seem to get old if they're really good, and *Shrek's* really good. Look what happened with 'Someday My Prince Will Come.' It becomes a standard. Then it becomes a jazz standard. Then it's the title of a Miles Davis record, y'know what I mean? It has all kinds of life. That's pretty cool to me."[272] The song was added to later editions of the *Films About Ghosts* best-of collection. "Accidently" would go on to be performed by Kidz Bop, another indication of its reach to previously untapped youth audiences.

"Accidentally" was nominated for a Golden Globe, a Grammy, and an Oscar for Best Original Song. Adam and his bandmates attended the 77th Academy Awards ceremony, held February 27th, 2005, at the Kodak Theatre in Los Angeles. Adam appeared on the red-carpet wearing sunglasses and a shiny, blue suit over a rainbow-striped shirt and a bright green tie. His dreadlocks were swept up into what could be described as a pineapple. Later that night, he and the Crows performed "Accidentally" live, but their song lost to "Al Otro Lado Del Rio" from *The Motorcycle Diaries*.

Matt Malley Departs

Missing from the red-carpet on Oscar night was bassist Matt Malley, who departed the Crows in late 2004. Like Adam, Malley was frustrated that he spent most of his time alone in hotel rooms, while life's most important events were taking place back at home. Malley had a four-year-old son who he barely saw, and a second son had just been born.

Although Malley claims that he quit the Crows, Adam stated in a 2008 interview that, "no one has ever quit" the band other than Ben Mize.[273] Malley's exit from the Crows was undoubtedly hastened by a letter the bassist wrote to *Rolling Stone* that was published the week of the 2004 presidential election. John Kerry, the Democratic nominee, was running against George W. Bush, who was up for a second term. Kerry appeared on the cover of *Rolling Stone* that week. Malley wrote, "I am Counting Crows' bass player. I believe that you're cheating your readers by offering a one-sided argument regarding the upcoming election. George W. Bush is one of the greatest presidents in our country's history. After 9/11, he knew that America had to show the world that nobody should have tolerance for fanaticism and evil. You should present the facts with balance. Matt Malley, Sherman Oaks, CA."[274]

Malley's support for a Republican president was at odds with his Berkeley-bred bandmates during a contentious election, but it also ran counter to his own hippy roots. Malley, who was born in Oakland, discovered meditation in 1987 when he was twenty-four years old. "I was a seeker. I wanted to find an answer. Something that could allow me to shift gears, spiritually, so I don't have to get on this wheel of mediocrity that people who aren't seeking have to go through in life."[275]

Malley attended a lecture by a guru named Sri Magaji Nirmala Devi, who practiced something she called sahaja yoga meditation. Malley quickly became a student and fervent devotee of Devi. They became so close that the guru even arranged Malley's marriage to another follower. "Sri Magaji suggested that I marry a girl named Sesh who was also in sahaja yoga. So I met her and we liked each other, and soon after we were married, with a hundred other people in a traditional Indian wedding."[276]

By the time Malley joined the Crows, he was married and a devoted practitioner of meditation. From the beginning, it put him at odds with hard partying bandmates such as Adam and Immerglück. But as the group took off, Malley says his meditation practice kept him grounded. "It kept me in balance. I just had a moral compass that a normal person in a rock band doesn't have. So I got to hold on to some balance during those crazy years."[277]

Malley's commitment to sahaja yoga meditation did not wane during his time with the Crows. In the liner notes to *Hard Candy*, his final album with the group, Malley thanked "Sri Magaji Nirmala Devi for allowing to taste the ambrosia of divine love." The bassist said that his spirituality and desire for enlightenment ran counter to some of *Candy's* baser material. Malley thought "American Girls" was especially trivial, particularly in the wake of the September 11th, 2001 World Trade Center bombings, a somber time. "It felt so shallow. There was a time there spiritually speaking where it was really embarrassing to be playing a couple of songs, two or three."[278]

Malley also claims that he never fully adjusted to Adam's dominant role in the Crows. "Adam was really the guy in charge—he owned the name and everyone else was kind of equal under him. He made some smart decisions, we had a lot of success, so no one complained. But nothing was in our control, it was all in his … It never felt like I was part of it. I just had to worry about the bass parts and show up for work and get paid."[279]

Despite getting a big payday for his help writing "Accidentally in Love," Malley was discouraged by the band's declining popularity and what he perceived to be low pay. "We had our success on our first two records, especially our first one. The second album came along and it did pretty well, but it was a downhill ride after that. If we had kept our level of success, I would have thought twice about leaving. But we'd had some dry years and I got a family to support, so I gotta start thinking of a way to make a little income. That had a lot to do with it."

It is possible that things were coming to a breaking point

with Malley, that he was unhappy and wanted to be at home with his family. But the bassist's public support for George Bush, using the Crows' name, is likely to have been the last straw. Adam wanted him out. "Honestly, the band could tell before I knew, I'd just had enough," Malley confessed.[280]

Like ex-drummer Ben Mize, Malley was quickly replaced. Adam brought on former Ben Folds bassist Millard Powers, who played his first show with the Crows on April 22nd, 2005, at the Paramount Theater in Denver. It was one of just a handful of dates the group played that year.

Malley's career floundered after his exit from the Crows. He made a few minor guest appearances and released a 2008 sahaja yoga meditation-themed solo album, "The Goddess Within," that flopped. In a 2009 interview, Malley talked about needing to return to work, having exhausted his savings. In 2011, the former Crows bassist completed training at Dootson School of Trucking and became a certified class-A big-rig driver.

Disney Hall

On October 25th, 2005, Adam and the Crows were accompanied by the Hollywood Bowl Orchestra at the Walt Disney Concert Hall in Los Angeles. The symphony show was part of a corporate concert series, sponsored by Argent Mortgage. Looking to raise its visibility, Argent teamed with a company called Elevation Entertainment to stage a series of one-off concerts that paired pop musicians with symphony orchestras in elite venues. Argent had previously contracted with Lee Ann Rimes, Seal, Duran Duran, and Jewel. In a press release promoting the event, Jeff Gillis, executive vice president of operations for

Argent Mortgage Company, stated, "This musical convergence of world-class orchestras and top performing artists offers an uncommon and innovative experience to pop music and classical music enthusiasts alike."[281]

At Disney Hall, the Crows played a fourteen-song set that began with "Round Here" and ended with "Chelsea," the rarely-performed number from *Across a Wire*. The Crows featured songs that spanned their catalog, with emphasis on *August* and *Satellites*. The orchestra was led by Vince Mendoza, whose resume included Joni Mitchell, Bjork, and Robbie Williams. Some adherents consider the Disney show to be the holy grail of Crows concerts, and there have been entire fan sites petitioning for its release on DVD.

In October 2005, the band's *Across a Wire* live set was declared Platinum, denoting sales of 500,000 copies of the double album. It was the last Platinum album the Crows would ever receive. Adam did not care at this point. The singer was about to enter his darkest period yet.

Chapter 6

Saturday Nights & Sunday Mornings

On April 22nd, 2006, Counting Crows performed on a temporary stage in a Kansas City parking lot to celebrate the grand opening of a shopping mall. Between songs, Adam informed the audience that the group was contractually required to play "Big Yellow Taxi" that night. "They actually insisted that we play that song, which is strange to me because that song is all about how bad it is to make parking lots. And here we are in a parking lot."

A parking-lot concert practically screams Spinal Tap, but the Crows reportedly drew a crowd of 8,000 to 10,000 that day.[282] Regardless, the endeavor underscores how far the Crows had fallen and the band's willingness to take any gig that came their way.

It was a dark time for Adam. "The end of 2005 and beginning of 2006 were pretty bad," he recalled. "I have gaps in my memory from the meds."[283] The singer spent most of his days in bed. He found it difficult to write new songs, blocked by the self-consciousness that came alongside the spotlight's glare. He was drained by the music industry, sick of catering to radio programmers. He was debilitated by the media's degrading treatment of him.

More than anything, Adam was tired of his career getting in the way of his personal life, of his even *having* a personal life. "There's a structure to your life when you're in a rock band—you write the songs, you make the record, you go on tour. I kept screwing my life up because of the way my schedule works," he said. "I lost the girl I was in love with. And I almost skipped my grandmother's funeral. I sure didn't see her for the last four years of her life. So I decided to pull back for awhile until I could figure out what was going on. We still played and toured some, but I wasn't sure about making a record. I didn't know if I would ever do it again."[284]

Adam had lost his inspiration. "All of our records are, like, you're driven to do this because you have something to say. But I didn't want to say anything for years. I was afraid to say anything. I went crazy."[285] Four years had passed since the last Crows studio album and Geffen had run out of ways to stall. The Crows had released almost every song they had ever recorded, but there were a few leftovers in the can. "1492" was a salacious rocker from the *Hard Candy* sessions that had not made it past the demo stage. Adam did not think it fit *Candy's* theme of memory and scrapped it. The singer described "1492" as "the hardest, darkest song we've ever played. It's about my utter disintegration—alcohol and blow jobs in underground bars in Italy and a total loss of self."[286]

Adam played the demo of "1492" over and over again, coming to believe that he could build an entire record around the castaway tune. "There's this album here," he thought to himself.[287] "An album about disintegration, and about everything that had brought to my life to that point, and where I thought my life was going."[288] Adam decided that he had to make a new record. "We have to go in the studio now. Right now," he declared.

In April 2006, a couple of weeks before the parking-lot gig, Adam blogged about the possibility of a new album. "Things are brewing. We may even see the inside of a studio soon. Things are stirring. It may even be possible to get me out of my house. Kicking and screaming and being dragged… but out."[289]

Adam itched to record, but he was almost completely ensconced in his Manhattan apartment, preferring to spend most non-gig days in bed. "I still wasn't capable of leaving home," he recalled.[290] There was no way he was going to make another record in a Hollywood mansion. So, the band came to him, laying down nine tracks with Gil Norton at Avatar, a famed Hell's Kitchen studio, better known by its former (and since revived) name, the Power Station. "You have to understand," Adam said, "we have never made a record in a studio before."[291] The Power Station was chosen, in part, due to its proximity to Adam's apartment, which was only six blocks away. The Crows also worked in nearby Looking Glass Studios.

Adam pulled together every scrap of leftover song he had: "Come Around," which the group had played once back in 2003, "1492," and "Los Angeles," which were demoed for *Hard Candy*, and "Sundays," an outtake from *This Desert Life*. The Crows' former rhythm section of drummer Ben Mize and bassist Matt Malley can be heard on "Sundays," with Mize also appearing on "Los Angeles."

But Adam's fit of inspiration only yielded four new tunes: "Hanging Tree," "Insignificant," and "Cowboys," all of which would appear on the Crows' fifth album, *Saturday Nights & Sunday Mornings*. There was also a Rolling Stones-esque number, "Sessions," that was included as a bonus track on some editions of the finished release.

By all accounts, Adam was almost completely out of his mind during the *Saturday Nights* recording sessions. "I was having a lot of trouble staying conscious. The meds put me in a sort of narcoleptic, insensible state. I would just collapse and pass out, but I could still hear everything that was going on around me, and sometimes I'd even speak. I'd be asleep on the couch in the control room but I could hear Gil Norton and Jim Bogios talking. One of them would say, 'We should ask Adam,' and the other would say, 'He's out,' but then I would answer the question."[292]

Two and a half weeks later, the band had nine songs in the can, just enough to qualify for a new record, which Adam decided to call *Saturday Nights*. The singer also envisioned adding a companion piece, a set of Sunday-morning songs that would showcase the group's softer side. But it never came to fruition. "We went on tour, and afterward I just went completely down the pipe and we never went back to work on it."[293]

Goo Goo

It had been four years since the Crows' last studio album and more than three years since the group had released the *Films About Ghosts* best-of compilation. The band had spent the bulk of that time on the road, crisscrossing the U.S. and Europe, playing many cities several times annually. Guitarist Dan Vickrey insisted that the Crows were not overplaying these markets; they were building a lifelong fan base there. "If they get to see [you] three times and you give them an amazing show three times, I mean, I think that's something that sticks with people and they end up growing with you."[294]

With no new album on the horizon, on June 19th, Geffen issued the Crows' second live release, *New Amsterdam: Live at Heineken Music Hall February 4–6, 2003*. The record drew from three 2003 Holland shows. The disc opens with "Rain King," which appears twice on *Across a Wire*, but *New Amsterdam* mostly avoids songs from the first live disc, focusing on tracks from the third and fourth albums, both issued after *Wire*. It entered the *Billboard* charts at number 52, disappearing three weeks later.

A review in *PopMatters* was lukewarm at best, taking the band to task for refusing to alter the formula that made them successful: "This live set confirms that as pleasant as their jangly anthems are, it's about as adventurous as a high school reunion. You're excited to go back at first, show everyone your new self, and revel in the good old times. Then you realize it's the same old halls, the same smell of industrial-strength floor disinfectant, the same graffiti, and then it's time to go home."[295]

On May 28th, 2006, the band played a festival in Columbia, Maryland, followed by a co-headlining summer tour with fading 1990s hitmaker, the Goo Goo Dolls. The fifty-one-stop trek began June 17th in Las Vegas and wrapped on September 9th in Dallas. The Goo Goo Dolls had just issued a new album, while the Crows were four years away from their last studio effort.

Adam was noticeably heavier on the Goo Goo Dolls tour. "I

gained 70 pounds from the meds I was taking initially," he recalled in 2008. "You can see that pretty easily in photos of me from the past few years. I went from athlete to fat guy. Then I had to read in the tabloids about how fat I was."[296]

In addition to picking on his appearance, some journalists expressed concern about the singer's declining creative output. Ben Wener, a music critic for *The Orange County Register*, called Adam out in a lengthy op-ed titled "For Adam Duritz, Creative Daylight Fading." Wener wrote about his longtime fandom of the band, whom he felt had squandered their talent. Wener dismissed *Films About Ghosts* and the latest live album as "stopgaps" and wondered why the Crows' output was so paltry compared to their more productive heroes like Van Morrison and Bruce Springsteen. The Crows, Wener wrote, had almost as many live albums as studio releases. "Rather than retreat, finish up a rumored double-album, they have taken to touring. Again. And with, of all acts, the Goo Goos. Didn't Duritz insist—to me and anyone else who interviewed him last year—that they weren't coming back until a new album was done? This development is pathetic, and troubling. It suggests Duritz is creatively washed up and willing to pick up a paycheck by teaming with an inferior touring partner ... Is he done? Is he just in a lull?"[297]

Wener reviewed the Crows show a couple of weeks later and concluded that Adam was not washed up, just slow to create. Wener noted Adam's "alarmingly hefty frame" but conceded that the singer remained a compelling performer of his well-worn material. Wener had just seen Radiohead try out eight freshly composed tunes at a recent show, and he took the

Crows to task for the absence of songs from *Saturday Nights*. "Rather than use this summer outing as a chance to test out completed material, Adam and his six steady collaborators aren't touching the new stuff. It's hard not to be disheartened by that ... That the Crows weren't willing to treat longtime devotees to even one new morsel suggests they have no faith in their fans' attention spans."[298]

A review of the July 29th show outside of Boston noted that the Crows had a new album in the works, but "with no songs showing up on this tour, the jaunt seems either a labor of love or money." The reviewer, however, left convinced that Adam and company still had it, heralding their "strong, thoughtful set" that "seemed to be searching for greatness beyond hit songs."[299]

A reviewer at the August 7th show in Saratoga Springs was less enamored. "Duritz, in what seemed to be some sort of Counting Crows therapy session, totally changed the planned set list and went primarily acoustic." The singer reportedly told the crowd, "I know this is a weird set, but it's exactly what I want to sing tonight." The reviewer praised the band's artistic intensity but wrote, "It was clear that the performance was not really what everyone expected as midway through the set a steady stream of people began heading for the exits."[300]

On October 7th, the Crows performed at Andre Agassi's Grand Slam for Children 2006 in Las Vegas, followed by a December 9th appearance at Vail Snow Daze in Colorado. Adam was at an all-time low. "I felt a lot better that summer when we were on tour, but I deteriorated again in the fall and was truly disastrous by the end of '06. I was pretty much Brian Wilson, weighed in at 250 pounds, hadn't been out of bed for a long time."[301]

Adam claimed that his medications were driving most of these issues. "The meds make you gain weight," he said. "There's nothing you can do. I've tried to work out and eat right. I've boxed for seven or eight years, but there's nothing you can do. It changes your metabolism."[302]

Adam decided he needed to change his life. "I hit this place in December, and I thought 'You're in a lot of trouble now, you've gone as far as you can go without this being a really serious issue.' So I had to get my shit together."[303] Adam went cold turkey and stopped taking all medications. "It's easier to go through physical withdrawal than the mental withdrawal of going off something slowly," he said, recalling, "I spent Christmas '06 insanely sick—just horrific. I mean, I quit doing recreational drugs so long ago. I never thought I would go through a drug withdrawal again, twenty years later. I'm sitting there shaking, thinking, 'What the fuck is this?'"[304]

Sunday Mornings

Things began to improve slightly after the new year. Adam began seeing a different psychiatrist, who completely changed his medication regimen and even recommended that he look into electroshock therapy. "We tried new meds and found the right stuff. Then I started working harder, really trying to figure my life out," he recalled. "Things really weren't much better early in 2007. I had a certain determination about things, some progress, but I knew I needed to stay home and get better."[305]

In early 2007, Adam launched a boutique label,

Tyrannosaurus Records, which issued the debut CD from a Chicago rock band Blacktop Mourning, as well as *She Likes the Weather*, a collection of seventeen remastered Himalayans demos. He also took over the Counting Crows Twitter account around this time and began to use it to make announcements and interact with fans.

In mid-January, Adam called Gil Norton and the Crows back to the studio to spend a month completing *Saturday Nights*. Adam began to focus more deliberately on its companion piece, the softer songs that countered the raucous *Saturday*. "As things were turning around in my life, I had the idea for *Sunday Mornings*," Adam recalled. "While we were recording the second batch of work on *Saturday Nights*, I began to introduce to the band the idea of *Sunday Mornings*, how it would sound, the kind of instruments we would use."[306]

Adam was finally coming back to earth. He recommitted himself to his mental and physical health and put the Crows on notice. "I told everybody at the beginning of the record, it was my fault," he says. "I took off for the last few years, but there isn't any more free ride here. Everybody's ass is grass. We're going to be a great band or we're not going to be a band."[307] Adam began a punishing physical program, centered around running and boxing. He continued to work with his doctor to find medications that would enable him to function.

Reflecting his own experiences, Adam insisted that the follow-up to *Saturday* not be about healing or atonement. "*Sunday Mornings* isn't about being better. It's really about when a person has wrecked his life for so long and doesn't know how to fix it, but wants to do so."[308] He elaborated, "*Sunday Mornings* is not about redemption, but how you come out of degradation."[309]

Adam wanted a different sound for *Sunday Mornings*, a folksy Americana tenor that was not lightweight or restricted to acoustic instrumentation. He went on a listening tour of contemporary indie folk records, and producer Brian Deck's name appeared over and over again. Deck was best known for his work with Modest Mouse and Iron & Wine. Adam set up a meeting in his apartment.

Deck arrived, and Adam laid out his vision for *Sunday Mornings*. "Nowadays, people think of folk music and they think unplugged acoustic guitars. But folk music used to have these really interesting arrangements. [Carole King's] *Tapestry* is not an acoustic album. Nor are the Simon and Garfunkel albums. They have strings, they have some loud electric guitars."[310] Adam and Deck began collaborating right away, setting up a ProTools rig in the "garden" section of Adam's apartment and recording demos.

In early March 2007, Adam and the Crows gathered in Berkeley to record *Sunday Mornings* with Deck. "I didn't want to do it in New York," Adam explained. "I knew that *Saturday Nights* should be recorded in New York, and *Sunday Mornings* shouldn't. I thought it would be good to come to Berkeley. It was away from home for me, but it was still home. My parents still live there, I stayed with my mom and dad."[311]

With Deck at the helm, the Crows worked for twenty-five days straight throughout March and April, putting in long hours at Fantasy Studios. The sessions yielded nine songs, including "There Goes Everything" and "Sunday Morning L.A.," outtakes that appeared as bonus tracks on some editions of the finished album.

"I was less insane, so that was good, but it was really hard music to make," Adam recalled of the *Sunday* sessions. The singer added that *Sunday* was "even harder than *Saturday Nights* because we had no idea even how to make that kind of music. We sort of had to teach ourselves on the fly how to compose and play this whole 'reinvention' of our acoustic music."[312]

In an interview shortly after the *Sunday* sessions were complete, Adam summarized the difference between the two sides of the record. "This album is really starkly divided, not just musically but thematically," he said. "The first half is pretty dark stuff and *Sunday Mornings* is about sorrow and grief. Whether or not everyone else will like it or not, I don't know. It's not a normal Counting Crows record. It may turn some people off."[313]

Geffen was not enamored with Adam's concept, preferring that the Crows blend the best of the hard and soft material into a cohesive single disc. "I was surprised at how big the resistance to making this album the way we did was," Adam said. "Almost no one wanted to make it the way we did. I mean, our producers did, and so did the engineers and so did my publicists, but almost everybody wanted to get rid of the two records and thought that we were wedded to a concept. It's not like the concept had driven the album. It was the complete opposite; the songs had created the record."[314]

Adam added that it was important to keep making albums in an era when records were dying or at least changing radically to suit new technologies. "If the album is disappearing as an art form, we wanted to make one last great album. We had a chance to make a point now and make a real album, an album that really means something to us, and this is as real an album as any we've made."[315]

Rock 'N' Roll Triple Play

The Crows were a touring band that filled their calendar with gigs, even during the worst of times. "Touring is almost always a good idea," Adam said that summer. "You make fans on the radio with hits. You keep fans by playing live."[316]

The Rock 'N' Roll Triple Play Concert was a package consisting of the Crows, Live, and Collective Soul, performing at twenty-three minor league baseball parks around the country. "I love playing baseball stadiums," Adam said. "I love that it's a big, open field."[317]

For the umpteenth time, the Crows toured the U.S. on a package tour and mostly ignored playing new material. The critics who had given Adam and company a hard time over the years seemed to give up on the group completely, abandoning the notion that the Crows could ever return to the credibility of yesteryear. In the minds of the critics, they were fat, Coke-shilling, Sun City-playing corporate hacks who'd do anything for a buck. Even self-described devoted fans such as *Paste Magazine's* Kate Kiefer viewed the Triple Play Tour as a new low. "I tried to justify it but I eventually faced the facts: Opening for a washed-up grunge-pop band at the Blair County Ballpark in Altoona, Pa., can't really be construed as a good thing."[318]

Kiefer and others missed the Crows' revitalization that summer. Despite the odds, the Crows were playing better than they had in years. "We're really into it right now," Adam said as the tour progressed. "We're sound-checking every day, and we don't need to. The recording of the record was really inspiring to everybody, and we really love it."[319]

At an August 24th, 2007 show at McCoy Stadium in Pawtucket, Rhode Island, the Crows played "Hanging Tree" for the first time. The song was written about the 2004 Australia incident, focusing on how Adam's hectic lifestyle made long-term romance impossible. "It's about losing that girl," Adam explained. "It's a snapshot about when I am very much in love but I know I have to leave. I wasn't good at being caring. It was a lot to handle me. I was 10,000 miles away and I wasn't there for her."[320]

The revitalization of the Crows went beyond music. On September 9th, 2007, the group performed at Farm Aid, with Adam sporting a t-shirt with Kiss' *Destroyer* album and looking healthier than he had in ages. The singer had lost an astonishing sixty-two pounds in the first months of 2007. "I run, I box, I lift weights. I eat like an intelligent person," he explained. "But most of all, I'm taking the right medication now. What I was on before made it impossible for me to lose weight, but when that changed? Well, like everything else, just because it's possible doesn't mean it's going to happen. I made the decision, did the work, and lost the weight. Which is good, because, man, when the world's unreal to you and you're trying to recognize the guy in the mirror, it doesn't help if he weighs seventy pounds more than he's supposed to. But I feel great now. The work worked. I can feel all the time now. Life's like one big wonderful raw nerve."[321]

Delay of Game

On September 18th, 2007, the Crows played *August and Everything After* in its entirety at Town Hall, a venue in New York City. Earlier that day, Geffen had reissued the album with bonus tracks and a 1994 Paris concert. Adam penned extensive liner notes, which promised that *Saturday Nights & Sunday Mornings* was arriving in November. Like most record companies, Geffen was eager to cash in on the Christmas shopping season.

But on September 27th, Adam posted to the Crows website that the album would be delayed until sometime after the new year. "It was just a crazy busy summer. Between all the touring and the traveling and the mixing and mastering of the new album and putting together the package and writing all the essays for the *August* reissue, we just let some little things fall through the cracks. The record itself is finished but we just did the photo shoot a few weeks ago, the art and packaging deadlines were last week, and, even putting in twenty-hour days, it was just impossible to get it all done."

In his post, Adam conceded that Geffen was not thrilled with the delay. "It's a tough pill for our record company to swallow. Especially in this day and age, it's not easy to ask them to postpone a Counting Crows album that would have been on sale for fall and through the Xmas season … Luckily for us, the people we deal with at our label *are* music people and they know that our partnership with Geffen has been a marathon, not a sprint."

Crows manager Gary Gersh did a bit of damage control, explaining to a reporter from *Billboard* that, "Since the Counting

Crows don't release albums very often, we wanted to make sure we had all the relationships in place. You only get to deliver a record once. Our goal is to reach fans, not to create sponsorship deals."[322]

But the delayed release led to misunderstandings and online rumors: Geffen hated the record and refused to release it; the company forced the band to go back and rewrite the songs.

Saturday Nights & Sunday Mornings

Some of the contention with Geffen seemed to be over how to leverage technology in delivering the album to the public. Adam wanted to release some or even all of *Saturday Nights & Sunday Mornings* online for free, an idea that did not go over well with the bean counters at Geffen. Eventually, they reached a compromise. On January 12th, 2008, the Crows released a free digital single on their website. It featured a song from each side of the new album, "1492" and "When I Dream of Michelangelo." A music video for "1492" was created from clips of Adam and the band recording the song in a studio. The group also provided raw footage for fans to create their own "1492" videos, the best of which were featured on the Crows' YouTube channel.

At a February 10th performance at the 575-capacity Bowery Ballroom in New York, the Crows played ten favorites from the first four albums, followed by eleven of the fourteen *Saturday Nights & Sunday Mornings* tracks, performed in order. Adam was described as "looking fit and relaxed and often stopping to joke with the crowd."[323] In February, Geffen issued "You Can't

Count on Me" as a single. To promote the new album, the group performed acoustic sets at Apple retail stores in New York, Chicago, and San Francisco.

In a March 15th, 2008 interview, Crows manager Gary Gersh told *Billboard*, "There's a fire in this album that's been missing from the Crows for a long time. When you hear the breadth of the record, you'll hear Adam has something to say ... The band has made arguably one of the best records of their career and is completely focused and energized in a way that is really getting everybody excited."[324]

On March 24th, 2008, *Saturday Nights & Sunday Mornings* was released, with the Crows performing "You Can't Count on Me" on *The Late Show with David Letterman* that night. For the *Letterman* appearance, Adam sported blue jeans and an ill-advised sweater that zipped up the front. Better was the bunny costume he revived for an appearance on *The Howard Stern Show* on March 27th. *Saturday* entered *Billboard's* album charts at number three, the band's strongest opening since *Satellites* debuted at number one in 1996.

Adam was pleased but continued to insist that sales did not determine success or failure for him. "Odds are, your likelihood of selling millions of albums is small, but that's not up to you. What is up to you is putting everything you can into your music and being proud of the work you do. The music we make will outlive us all and what matters is that we've left these documents of ourselves behind for everyone to enjoy."[325]

There were no Crows other than Adam in the music video for "You Can't Count on Me," which featured the singer lip-syncing the song in an apartment, while scattering Polaroid photos about. It was the last time the singer appeared in a Counting Crows video. Going forward, Crows videos would feature actors playing out conceptual scenes. The song fared well on *Billboard's* AAA charts, eventually peaking at number one that spring.

On March 30th, the Crows performed four songs on the A&E television show *Private Sessions*, with Adam sitting for an interview between each. The program featured "Cowboys" and "Washington Square" from the new album, as well as "Round Here" and "Hard Candy."

A week later, on April 8th, 2008, the group appeared on *Soundstage*, a live performance TV show shot at WTTW Studios in Chicago. The band performed eleven of *Saturday's* fourteen tracks, as well as two unaired songs, "A Long December" and "Round Here." They also played around with a few lines from a multipart harmony acapella number titled "The Lone Wolf." On April 19th, 2008, Madonna released her eleventh studio album, titling it *Hard Candy*.

The Lonely Disease

In addition to numerous television appearances, Adam foregrounded his mental health struggles as part of the media campaign for *Saturday Nights & Sunday Mornings*. He even wrote an essay, "The Lonely Disease," that was published in the April 2008 issue of *Men's Health*. In the piece, Adam openly discussed his psychological and emotional troubles. "I have a form of dissociative disorder that makes the world seem like it's not real, as if things aren't taking place. It's hard to explain, but you feel untethered. And because nothing seems real, it's hard to connect with the world or the people in it because they're not there. You're not there."[326]

Adam added that for years he was ashamed to reveal his mental health issues to anyone. "I've been dealing with mental illness. But I didn't want to say anything for a long time. I went crazy. It was scary. Being crazy is bad. It's scary when the world isn't real to you. You come untethered. Everything seems imaginary. You look around the room and nothing seems real. You don't feel pain. I stopped letting myself feel."[327]

Adam revealed that things initially went downhill for him after his grandmother died in 2004. "That was the egg cracking. There wasn't much egg left anyway, but that just cracked me. After that, I just stopped. We played some gigs, but I was essentially done. I mean, we played. We still toured every summer. We did some gigs here and there, but I didn't want to make any more records. I knew I didn't know how to live anymore. I knew I had lost my mind."[328]

These issues were exacerbated by the media's focus on Adam's looks. "I endured ten years of fat jokes," he told a reporter from *Rolling Stone*. "My life looks perfect, and I've been whining about it for years. I could have said at the very beginning, 'I have lost my mind. I am mentally ill. I have to take all these medications that make me fat.'"[329]

Adam explained that, "A dissociative disorder worsens unless you take steps to fix it. First you treat it with medication, usually with mixed results. Then you learn to cope with it, which is a whole other challenge."[330]

Adam claimed that he had come to terms with these issues, that he accepted the fact that his disorder was permanent. "The world will never seem completely real to me, but I have to move on with my life. Beyond the music, I'm choosing to go out there and connect, be around people and work at relationships with my family, my friends and their kids. I'm making room for other things in my life besides the constant obsession with my career."[331]

Adam explained that the Crows' new album contained a full-blown chronicle of his mental health challenges. "*Saturday Nights & Sunday Mornings* is the double album that came out of my battle with dissociative disorder. Everything I went through is in there. The first part, *Saturday Nights*, is vicious and loud. *Sunday Mornings* is quieter—the day after. *Saturday* was recorded in New York City, *Sunday* in Berkeley. Two distinct sounds, two different coasts, two producers."[332]

Into the Grey

The critical response to *Saturday* was far more negative than any of the group's previous releases. To find a glowing review, one would have to track down a copy of *The Buchtelite*, a college newspaper from Akron, Ohio, that hailed it "the best Counting Crows' album since their debut."[333] Another college paper, *The Harvard Crimson*, offered faint praise for the overall effort, concluding that, "The more interesting part of the album is the *Sunday Mornings* portion, when the instrumentation doesn't compete with the lyrics for attention. Deck's influence as producer is evident in the delicate piano melodies and wailing harmonicas that provide a needed contrast to the loudness of the first half. The softer sound better showcases the deeply personal nature of Duritz's lyrics."[334] *Absolute Punk* had the opposite reaction: "After a relatively blistering six-song Saturday night, the next seven drag a bit in places as the relatively sparse arrangements quickly lose steam and leave us wishing for Monday to come."[335]

Paste weighed in with a lukewarm review, critiquing Adam's retreaded lyrical themes and calling *Saturday* a step down from the group's first four releases. "This is a fine record. But it's only fair to consider *Saturday Nights & Sunday Mornings* in the context of the rest of the Crows' catalog, and with that in mind—to borrow a phrase from Duritz—this one might fade into the grey."[336] Chicago writer Andrew Reilly knocked the album's "self-referential and continuously recycled lyrical motifs and the arrangements that at times sound more than a bit labored, as though the band feared each riff or melody may be the last one they ever write so they might as well squeeze as much as they can from it."[337]

Entertainment Weekly graded it a B-, opining that, "You're reminded of one thing that hasn't changed: Adam Duritz's pseudo-sensitive narcissism."[338] *PopMatters* rated the album five out of ten, noting that it, "directly challenges notions of what a Counting Crows record should sound like, but the most interesting moments come when each side takes a break from itself (ironically, resulting in songs that come closest to what we expect from the band) ... Somewhere in the middle of all that are the pieces of another great Counting Crows record. Maybe we'll get it next time around."[339]

Slant graded it two out of five stars: "Listening to the Crows' latest feels like being stuck in the past, when naming a song after Greenwich Village ('Washington Square') might've still been cool. That's because Duritz and his band more or less sound exactly the same: There are still the lame contemplative titles, the incessantly laidback beats, and Duritz's Hallmark observations about life."[340] *Music OMH* also gave it two out of five, snarking: "If your idea of a good Saturday night and Sunday morning is spending your time listening to Counting Crows, you need to get out more."[341] Finally, there was U.K. newspaper *The Guardian,* also scoring it two out of five stars, calling it a "trudging and effortful" effort that's "eking 15 songs out of 10 songs' worth of ideas ... Sodden trad-rock rarely gets less inviting."[342]

Those who dismissed *Saturday* overlooked the album's many strong points. "Sundays," an outtake from *This Desert Life,* retains that album's breezy atmosphere, and "Los Angeles," leftover from the *Hard Candy* sessions, sits nicely alongside sister songs like "Richard Manuel is Dead." The Crows attempt something ambitious with "Insignificant" and land on the right side of the equation. "Le Ballet d'Or" is marvelous, mysterious, and sounded even more dramatic in concert. "When I Dream of Michelangelo," a lilting ballad that took its title from "Angels of the Silences," is another standout.

Despite these and other highlights, *Saturday* lacked the high proportion of instant-classics that dominated the group's first four albums. There was no "Rain King" or "Hard Candy" or "Mrs. Potter's Lullaby" to be found. The closest contender, "Come Around," should have opened the record. It was recorded during the *Saturday* sessions and had a dose of the whimsy that made *Hard Candy*'s title track a perfect launching point. The song celebrated the band's commitment to performing live and promise to "come around" on tour year after year. There was even a stellar alternative version, eventually issued as a bonus track, that dialed back the electric guitars and allowed the tune's modest charms to shine. Instead of leading with his strongest number, Adam remained wedded to his concept, using "Come Around" as a closing statement and placing it at the end of a fourteen-track double album.

Saturday was dominated by previously recorded outtakes and castaways whose lyrical themes about the downsides of fame and the celebrity dating circuit sounded like retreads in 2008. At first glance, it seemed that Adam had little to say that he hadn't said before. Another mistake was to return wholeheartedly to *Satellite's* hard-rocking sound. The electric/acoustic concept had been used by the Crows on several occasions, including the two-disc *Across a Wire* live set and during many live concerts. Musically, the band had come full circle and seemed to have no more left turns to take. The album did not capitalize on the gains made from "Big Yellow Taxi" and "Accidentally in Love." These lighter numbers were significant hits, yet there was little on *Saturday* for listeners who discovered Crows through those songs.

Finally, by completing everything in the traditional studios that the group had spent their recorded history avoiding, *Saturday* lacked the vibe and consistency of the Crows' previous works. This shortage of cohesion was abetted by the departure of the septet's rhythm section.

Relationships

The critical backlash against the Crows had been building

for years, and Adam decided to take it on directly at this time. "For some reason, everyone decided we were a piece of shit," he told a reporter from *Rolling Stone* in April 2008. "I do something that people really don't like, [but] so much of our stuff got reviewed on people's judgment of me personally."[343]

The focus on Adam's romantic interests, rather than his music, was not only irksome, it was erroneous. "They don't report on my love life, they invent my love life," Adam said of the tabloid stories about his latest trysts.[344] He claimed, for example, that he barely knew Winona Ryder, let alone dated her, despite the actress' name regularly appearing on lists of Adam's supposed conquests. As for Jennifer Aniston, "We never even slept together."[345]

"It's always set up as, 'How does that fat fuck get all these women?'" Adam said.[346] In reality, "I'm 43, single and I sit at home a lot. That's not what I was supposed to accomplish in being a rock star," he told *Blender* in April 2008. But Adam was being coy, conceding that he had dated a long list of famous women. "Why should I have to pay for that? Why does that make me an asshole? Chris Martin marries Gwyneth Paltrow. Why is he not an asshole? I mean, I've met him, he's not an asshole. I don't understand it exactly, 'cause I'm really a nice person."

Adam said that his mental health issues destroyed any chance he might have of enjoying a traditional relationship. "This thing would happen to me with every person I'd ever gone out with—just like a shutdown where you can't feel anything. There was nothing I knew how to do that was going to fix my ability to have any kind of connection with another person."[347]

These relationships never worked out, Adam said. "I've been lucky in my life to have known and cared for some incredible women and some wonderful people—real people who were wonderful and I let slip by. We're all still friends. I never cheated. They want to see me married. They'd like to set me up."[348]

These friends included famous women but also the women Adam made famous through his songs. "I didn't mean to, but I used their real names—Anna, Elisabeth," he said. "I've got great songs, but not them. I've spent my life trading people for songs."[349]

Adam claimed that the mental health struggles he faced over the past four years took a toll on his love life. He was in and out of relationships constantly. Some lasted a month or two, some a day or two. Still, Adam insisted that he could envision a long-term, meaningful relationship. "I would have settled down a long time ago, but I wasn't healthy," he said. "I shouldn't have had children. I'm a normal guy. I want the same things people want."[350]

These revelations, Adam said, did not bring him peace or reduce his anxieties. "I am nervous about the future," he admitted. "I've never been this healthy before. Now I can have all the things I want. Though I'm not seeing anyone yet, I know I can stay with a woman now. I could see that person every day and be emotionally engaged. I could have kids (who would hopefully not be like me) and be there as they grow up. I have all these possibilities in front of me that were never there before."[351]

Adam even teased that overcoming his mental health

challenges made him consider quitting music altogether. As he did on "Come Around," however, Adam concluded that life was not perfect and he was not either, but the best thing he could do was hit the road with the band.

Marooned

The Crows spent May, June, and July performing throughout Europe, with a few dates in South Africa. "I'm still here because I put the work in," Adam insisted. "Even these last few years when I was losing my mind and it kicked my ass. I appreciate it and I never take it for granted. I'm not pissing it away."[352] The singer added that he had no plans to retire, either. "Me, I don't really do anything else, so I'll be doing this for the next twenty, thirty years."[353]

On July 22nd, Geffen released a digital album, *iTunes Live From SoHo*, capturing the Crows' March 27th performance at the Apple store in New York. *iTunes* was part of a series of live albums that featured musicians performing in Apple stores. The series, which ran from 2008-2011, featured Taylor Swift, Kings of Leon, Maroon 5, and others. The Crows' eleven-song set included six tunes from *Saturday* as well as a selection of hits from the previous records. Given that it was the their second live album in two years, the release seemed entirely superfluous and, once again, inserted the name of a corporate product into a Crows album. It barely registered on the *Billboard* charts for a week at number sixty-six before disappearing.

Maroon 5 and the Crows paired up in August for a co-headlining tour of American amphitheaters. Critics bashed *Saturday* but were more positive in their assessment of the band's live show. "Duritz, obviously healthier these days, was far more animated than during the group's 2006 Verizon appearance alongside Goo Goo Dolls. He constantly jumped in the air, wildly danced around and actually seemed glad to be there."[354]

Adam would be the first to agree. "I love playing gigs," he said. "I don't like touring. I tour because we have to tour—because it's magic."[355] In July, Geffen issued "Come Around" as a single, which topped *Billboard's* AAA charts on September 27th. Adam was always happy to add a new hit to the Crows' arsenal but emphasized the importance of performing those songs in front of audiences. "I really truly believe that the impression you make on someone on the radio at one given moment is very fleeting. But the impression you make on a given evening when it's you and them and you make a real connection with an audience, that can last forever—and does."[356]

The Crows took November off, with Adam appearing in *Variety* to announce his involvement in a comedy film, *Freeloaders*. The plot revolves around a group of slackers who live in Adam Duritz's L.A. mansion and are threatened when he announces plans to sell the place. Adam would play himself and co-produce the film, which featured members of Broken Lizard, the comedy troupe behind the 2001 hit *Super Troopers*. It was not the first time Adam had been in a movie. In 2007, he made a brief voice appearance in the animated direct-to-video spoof, *Farce of the Penguins*, produced by Adam's friend Bob Saget.

The *Freeloaders* script was co-written by Gigolo Aunts leader Dave Gibbs. "Two friends of mine wrote it and I wanted to make sure they got to be able to make it and one of them got to direct it," Adam explained. "So I took over the option and me and a couple of partners raised all of the finance for it ourselves. And Broken Lizard [partnered] with us, which was great. They're getting ready to do the first screening in a week or so. I think we made a hysterical indie comedy. It's very funny and very vulgar."[357]

Split with Geffen

In December 2008, the Crows played a month of European dates, followed by a rare lull in activity for the first three months of 2009. Geffen issued "When I Dream of Michelangelo" as a single on January 31st, with the song peaking at number seven on *Billboard's* AAA charts in March.

Any success the single might have enjoyed was overshadowed by Adam's announcement on March 17th that the Crows had split with Geffen. In a post to the Crows' website, the singer wrote, "When Counting Crows signed our first record contract, we were an unknown band signed to DGC, the cool indie-flavored boutique label of Geffen Records … A lot of things changed in seventeen years. DGC disappeared except as a logo on our records, and Geffen became one of many labels of a much larger conglomerate. Still, Geffen and Counting Crows never stopped working together and never stopped succeeding together. We made great music and together we sold a lot of records. We're still here."

Adam indicated that he and Geffen struggled over how to distribute the Crows' music online. "The internet opens a world of limitless possibility, where the only boundaries are the boundaries of your own imagination. We want a chance to push those boundaries back as far as we can. Unfortunately, the directions we want to go and the opportunities we want to pursue are often things that our label is simply not allowed to do. We all want what's best for everyone which is why we've decided to part ways."

Adam clarified himself in an interview with *Entertainment Weekly*. "The record companies aren't owned by the David Geffens anymore," he said. "They're owned by a guy who just works at a large corporation. And his job is to see the bottom line. And when someone comes to him and says, 'We'd like to give something away free,' I imagine that's something his superiors don't want him to say ... It doesn't matter whether you are artist-friendly or not, there are rules about proprietary uses of music, and those rules come from on high and you are just not allowed to do things."[358]

Adam spun this as a positive move, but it was likely that Geffen had declined to renew the Crows' original six-album deal. When pressed for details, the singer refused to elaborate. "Understand that I was there for eighteen years. A long time. And they did not have to let us go. So, I'd rather not get into specific things."

Adam concluded his announcement of the Geffen split by giving away a free download of the Crows covering Madonna's "Borderline," taped at a recent show at the Royal Albert Hall in London. "In the spirit of this new frontier we're entering, we offer you our homage to a certain lady who honored us last year by expressing her longtime deep and abiding worship of our band by naming her entire album after one of ours."

When Adam and Geffen parted ways in 2009, there was no turning back. That seemed to be the point where he gave up on trying to be a rock star at the center of the media hurricane and transformed into a beloved cult figure, a dreadlocked Buddha for the 1990s alt-rock nostalgia set.

The singer was not concerned about the Crows' ability to keep recording and releasing albums. The group had purchased a lot of studio equipment over the years, and Bryson could always step in to produce. Adam expressed enthusiasm over the internet's potential, not only to get his music to fans but to connect with his audience on a personal level. "The internet is the greatest thing in the world for a band. It looked like it was going to be the death of all of us, but I don't think it is. It's a pipeline, a conduit, an instant way to reach everywhere. It's a way to communicate to fans, a way for me to express myself, which is kind of what my life is all about."[359]

When asked about a new album, Adam replied, "I don't have one bursting out of me right now."[360] Instead, he and the Crows did what they always did, hit the road. In March 2009, the group launched a tour of New Zealand, Australia, and an extensive trek across Europe that went through the beginning of June.

While in London, the group was interviewed and filmed at the famed Abbey Road Studios. The footage was shot for the third season of *Live from Abbey Road*, a series where musicians such as Paul Simon and Sheryl Crow perform Beatles songs in the renowned recording studio. Adam chose to play part of the medley that closes the second side of *Abbey Road*, which blends several short songs together into one extended piece. The finished episode featured the Crows tackling "Carry That Weight," "Golden Slumbers," and "The End." It aired on the

Sundance Channel in the U.S. in late 2009.

Traveling Circus

On August 27th, 2009, Adam, accompanied by David Immerglück, Dan Vickrey, and Augustana frontman Dan Layus, performed "Washington Square" at *WSJ Cafe*, an arts program sponsored by *The Wall Street Journal*. "We're on this tour right now called the Saturday Night Rebel Rockers Traveling Circus and Medicine Show," Adam said by way of introduction. "It involves three bands pretty much playing together off and on all night."

The Saturday Night Rebel Rockers Traveling Circus and Medicine Show starred Counting Crows, supported by roots rockers Augustana and former Disposable Heroes of Hiphoprisy leader Michael Franti's new reggae group, Spearhead. The Medicine Show was inspired by Bob Dylan's Rolling Thunder Revue tour of 1975-1976, which featured Dylan sharing the stage with Joan Baez, the Band, and others. Rather than following the standard opening-act/headliner format, the three acts would mix and match musicians and trade songs throughout a three-hour jamboree. The night opened with everyone performing Van Morrison's "Caravan" and closed with the full lineup's take on Woody Guthrie's "This Land is Your Land." Throughout the show, Crows songs were reconfigured and heavily represented.

Reviewers were charmed by the hootenanny concept. "If last night's show was a circus, Adam was both ringleader and lovable clown. Singing lead, background or duet, depending on the song, he rarely left the stage," enthused the *Baltimore*

Sun."[361] Adam seemed relieved to cede the spotlight to others, to hide out on a stage filled with nineteen musicians. The Crows would spend the next several years touring under a similar conceit. "It's three bands, but I think as you've seen tonight, it's one band," Adam told the audience in Baltimore at the end of the show. "For the first time in a long time, I remember what it's like to deeply love music."

At a few concerts, the musicians were joined by actress Emmy Rossum, Adam's latest girlfriend. The mainstream media's interest in Adam's love life continued unabated. In October, *People* ran a feature story about the pair titled "What's the Secret of Adam Duritz's Sex Appeal?" The story listed a number of Adam's exes—Jennifer Aniston, Courteney Cox, Mary Louise Parker—and noted that, "The singer seems to be enjoying his time with Rossum. The two have been spotted on both coasts, having lunch in Beverly Hills Sept. 24—two weeks after a dinner date at Dos Caminos in New York City."[362]

After the Medicine Show tour concluded, the Crows went on hiatus, cropping up in December to perform as part of the Warren Haynes Christmas Jam 2009. The group mostly stayed off the road for the first half of 2010, playing the usual round of festivals and amphitheaters that summer under the Medicine Show concept. The 2010 version was a repeat of the previous year, but Spearhead was replaced by Notar, a Connecticut rapper signed to Adam's Tyrannosaurus Records. In 2010, the label issued a Notar EP that included "Stranger," a song featuring backup vocals from Adam.

PopMatters praised the second of a two-night stand at the Wellmont Theater in Montclair, New Jersey: "Adam Duritz, wearer of many hats and also many t-shirts throughout the night, was definitely a sight. Duritz made great use of the stage, perambulating from one side to the other, checking out all of the band members as they showed the crowd that they are in fact, masters of their craft. The near sold-out audience was equally as energetic, singing along and dancing."[363]

In an interview at the onset of the summer 2010 dates, David Immerglück hinted that the Crows planned to record a new album soon. "We've got a backlog of unfinished business that I expect we'll be getting to sometime after the tour is over," he said.[364] By mid-tour, however, Immerglück had changed his tune. "I can't, I'm not going to tell you when," he said of a new album. "I'd just wind up stepping in my own mess there ... I refrain from answering that question. I'm not at liberty to discuss that."[365]

In July, Adam told a reporter from the *Baltimore Sun* that he had not been writing any new Crows music. Rather he was working on smaller projects, including a pop culture website called underwatersunshine.com. Adam explained, "What I've been doing is getting my life together. I realized I'm turning my life around and getting somewhere."[366]

Chapter 7

Somewhere Under Wonderland

In early February 2011, Adam and his most recent girlfriend broke up. Rather than sitting on the couch moping, the singer announced on social media that he would learn and record a new love song each day for the week leading up to Valentine's Day. He posted the first number, recorded late at night in his apartment, which featured Adam playing piano and singing "Valentine's Day" by Steve Earle. For the next week, he followed this with covers of Ryan Adams, Tom Waits, Bob Dylan, and the jazz classic, "On the Sunny Side of the Street." Adam said that he barely slept the entire seven days. The singer received the most attention for his mournful take on the Cars' "You Might Think," rendered, like the other numbers, on a stark piano accompanied by plaintive vocals. To accompany each song, he would post a one or two-sentence explanation, ranging from whimsical to cryptic. "It was the most accidental, DIY thing I'd ever done," Adam told a reporter from *The Wall Street Journal* not long after the release.[367]

Once the seven tracks were posted, Adam named the collection *All My Bloody Valentines*, a title that combined the *Desert Life* song "All My Friends" with the 1980s Irish-English rock band,

My Bloody Valentine. He held an online cover design contest, with fans uploading a total of about 1,300 entries and voting on their favorites. Adam picked two images he liked, printed 500 vinyl copies of each record, and gave them to friends and fans.

The Crows' first show of 2011 was a benefit for Dare 2 Dream, a philanthropic organization that paired musicians with charitable causes. The sold-out concert took place April 21st at the House of Blues in Chicago. Adam appeared visibly heavier, with his dreadlocks exploding out in all directions as the group cranked through a sixteen-song set.

Black Sun

It was one of only a few Crows concerts in 2011. Adam spent a good portion of the year working on *Black Sun*, a stage musical he co-wrote with playwright Stephen Belber. Belber, best known for his work on *The Laramie Project*, handled the plot points, while Adam composed the songs. Never one to let an old tune go to waste, Adam resurrected a couple of *Satellites* leftovers for use in the play: "Chelsea," issued on the live *Wire* CD, and the piano ballad, "Good Luck."

Adam drafted several new songs, too, and said the experience opened up new avenues for his writing. "I had never written any songs for anybody else," he explained. "I've also never taught anyone to sing one of my songs—that's always been something I did myself, so I wasn't sure how that was going to be. I'd never written for women's voices and I did that on this one too. And I had never written for a musical, or for a voice that wasn't my own. And doing all these things, I wasn't really sure how any of it was going to go."[368]

As it turned out, Adam enjoyed the experience of writing for someone else, of not having to sing his own lyrics. For once, his focus was directed somewhere other than on himself. "It was really liberating to do that for me, to take it out of myself, but also it showed me about how much it is possible to make a song really personal and talk about things that are really important to you without it being first person singular."[369]

Black Sun remained a work in progress. Belber was still hammering out the plot details, while Adam reported that he had "about ten songs ready with five more that [he] just need[ed] to know a little more about the play to finish."[370]

The two met regularly to discuss the musical, but progress was slowed by Belber's ascendant career in theater. With his prominence rising, the playwright was suddenly being asked to transform his earlier plays such as "Match" into feature films. Adam did not want to attempt writing a new Crows album while enmeshed in work on *Black Sun*. He decided that this would be the ideal time to revive the Crows' long-dormant album of cover songs. "It was hard for me to split my focus between songwriting for the play and the band," the singer explained.[371] "The covers album was meant for me to be able to work with the band while still writing for the play. That was the main reason to do that."[372]

Recording Sunshine

With three years since their last studio release and little sign of a new record on the horizon, a covers album would keep the Crows' name in the spotlight. For years, the group had recorded covers while making their albums, with the intent of someday releasing them as a collection.

Adam explained, "I really like the idea of interpreting other people's music. As a musician, it's a very satisfying thing to do and it's a big part of musical tradition. We're not just writers; we're also musicians. It's not all about my life every day. There's something really nice about other people's ways of looking at the world."[373]

Cover songs enabled Adam to get into the mind of another songwriter, speaking in their voice, using their words. It allowed him to experience chord progressions and rhythmic patterns that would never have occurred to him. For Adam, playing someone else's song was almost like collaborating with that artist. "Once you work with all those different songwriters you realize how limiting it is to work with one songwriter your whole life, even if that songwriter is me ... It's nice to spend time as a singer and an arranger without having quite as much invested personally, or the need to make it be the be-all, end-all statement."[374]

Adam and the band spent a week in April 2011 and another in June recording songs for the covers album. They worked from Ocean Studios and Glenwood Place Studios, two facilities located in Burbank, a suburb of Los Angeles. Shawn Dealey handled production duties. At the onset of the April sessions, Adam was taking seven different prescription medications. He reduced his dosage, cutting back to the point where he began to encounter withdrawal symptoms.

While recording Coby Brown's song "Hospital," Adam was overcome with shakes that were audible on the final vocal take. "I'm just literally vibrating around the room trying to just stand still and I couldn't do it," the singer recalled.[375] "Strangely enough, there's a line in there about these 'pills I shouldn't take,' and I was going through this twitching, shaking thing while we were recording. And you can hear me actually vibrating on that one song — I just couldn't stop shaking."[376] The singer concluded, "My guts are all over these songs."[377]

In June, 2011, Adam posted an open message about his struggles with prescription medications on the Crows' website. "The withdrawal symptoms aren't helping the recording of the new album," he wrote. "I stopped dropping the meds dosages for recording. Couldn't shake uncontrollably and sing at the same time. Forgivable. But I got home. Docs Friday instructions: cut Lithium dose in half. Fuck me—not so good now. Gotta keep pushing/get off this shit. Going faster than I should but it still takes too long. All my friends say how clear and present I am. 'Clear and present.' Horror. Not mutually exclusive. These are not drug addiction problems. I was fucking crazy. I needed meds."[378]

With the help of his doctors, Adam reduced his dosage slowly, weaning himself off of five of the seven medications over a period of nearly seven months. "It was pretty brutal," he recalled.[379] Adam described this period as characterized by "horrific drug withdrawals, both physical and mental. Tough going while I was making a record and working on a play—it was like being stoned for an entire year." Adam added, "A hundred years ago, they just locked people up forever in my situation. So I'm really lucky to be a part of modern medicine."[380]

As always, Adam continued performing through the haze.

Ojai August

With about half of *Black Sun* and its accompanying songs complete, Adam and Belber held a reading of the work at the Ojai Playwrights Conference on August 11th, 2011. The play was voiced by a cast that included Evan Rachel Wood and Rob Morrow. "The playwright conference at Ojai is pretty high-level playwriting," Adam said. "We were the only musical there and we were very unformed, but I found that I really loved it. I was very nervous the day it went up but I also just had the best time watching it."[381]

Adam was blown away by the positive reception to *Black Sun* at Ojai. "We put on about half a play and we really loved it and the audience kind of went crazy—it got quite a response. It's a long way from being done. Would I love to see it as a Broadway show? I mean, yes, but I'd love to go to the moon too! I'd be happy just seeing it Off-Broadway really, that would be just thrilling. And if it got to Broadway, that would be really cool."[382]

Adam said that he and Belber had recently met to discuss their progress, but that everyone was waiting to see if the playwright would take a new directing gig. "Right now I feel like my mind is stuck on the play," Adam said. "If we don't do that I have to get it out of my mind and … go write a record for the band."[383]

On August 29th, 2011, the Crows issued a concert DVD, *August and Everything Live at Town Hall*. The footage, shot in 2007, was four years old. An accompanying CD release entered the *Billboard* charts at number seventy-three before falling off the charts the next week. The release was largely ignored by everyone except the diehards, who had been waiting eons for an official live video. A review in *PopMatters* was dismissive, accusing the group of performing "the same covers and alternates they've done for years ... It's like they're recreating a set from 1997 minus the hunger that made those early sets so powerful, adding neither to the standalone beauty of *August and Everything After* nor to the well-documented Counting Crow live experience."[384]

For his part, Adam claimed to be finished excavating the *August* sessions for demos, outtakes, or other rarities. "At this point, there's nothing more to reveal about *August and Everything After*. There's no more unreleased material. Also, everybody's either got that record, or they're not going to get it."[385]

This was not strictly true; most of the Crows' original fifteen-track demo remained unreleased, including the demos of some of the group's most iconic songs. Also in the vault were several numbers that they had performed live prior to *August's* release, but had not recorded. Yet Adam was firm that he had no plans to reissue *August* for its twenty-year anniversary in 2013. "Honestly, a group of years seems like a particularly lame reason to revisit a record," he said. "It would be like just taking money from the fans. We just did that live album and DVD, which I think is great. I'd be hard-pressed to think of a better testament to that album than that."[386]

Adam showed more interest in revisiting *Recovering the Satellites* for an anniversary edition. "That's a truly great album a lot of people missed," the singer said. "I don't think it necessarily got the credit it deserves 'cause there was a bit of backlash after *August*. It was a huge step forward for the band to go from

August and Everything After, which was pretty contained, to *Satellites*, which is a much more sprawling record."[387]

According to Adam, a *Satellites* anniversary edition would make use of the wealth of video footage the group commissioned around that time. It included the tapes from *Live at the 10 Spot* and *VH1 Storytellers*, as well as the making-of documentary shot by Jonathan Dayton and Valerie Faris (*Little Miss Sunshine*).

As for the recordings themselves, Adam claimed that Geffen had misplaced the original master tapes to the album and its attendant sessions. "Geffen lost all the tapes," Adam reported. "What exists is the digital tapes that they transferred to do the mix; those still exist, but it's only the songs mixed for that record. Anything not mixed for the record is gone. We tried to find some stuff a few years ago for something else we were doing, and Geffen has no idea where they are. 'A Long December,' all the songs, the actual two-inch tapes are gone. It's disgusting, just so frustrating."[388]

In October, Adam hosted a showcase of up-and-coming bands at Arlene's Grocery as part of the annual CMJ music festival, held in New York City. Adam hand-selected artists he liked and called the event the Outlaw Roadshow. At the shows, he was known to emcee and even hop on stage to sing backup from time to time. Adam had so much fun that he held another one during the South by Southwest music festival in Austin. In 2012, he teamed with blogger Ryan Spaulding and made the two showcases an annual event.

Underwater Sunshine

On March 9th, 2012, the Crows played a warmup show at Slim's in San Francisco, followed by a second gig at the Great American Music Hall the next night. The encores at both performances included the Beatles trilogy of "Golden Slumbers," "Carry That Weight," and "The End." A week later, the Crows played South by Southwest, where they showcased six songs from their new album, four from *August* and two apiece from *Satellites*, *Desert Life*, and *Candy*. Adam only called for one number, "Washington Square," from the Crows' most recent studio effort.

On April 10th, 2012, the Crows released their covers album, *Underwater Sunshine (or What We Did on Our Summer Vacation)*. The record was issued on CD and vinyl by Collective Sounds, an independent label based in Beverly Hills. *Sunshine* entered the *Billboard* charts at number eleven, the highest position it would reach.

PopMatters praised the release, writing, "Several alt-country snoozes aside, these are smart choices."[389] *The Guardian* rated it three out of five stars, asserting that the songs on *Sunshine* were "still other people's material, and it seems a waste of energy for the Crows to have turned their weatherbeaten attention to them."[390]

Perhaps the best example of what Adam hoped for with *Sunshine* is found on its opening track, "Untitled (Love Song)" by an unknown California outfit, The Romany Rye. Adam caught the group at South by Southwest in 2011. On *Sunshine*, the Crows utterly inhabit Rye's tune, and the song's obscurity makes it sound more like an original than a cover.

"This has got to be the most obscure covers album ever made," the singer said.[391] "We tend to look for great songs that people don't know, that we can come up with our own versions of."[392] He added, "We didn't just do singalong songs that everybody knows. It's a covers album that comes off like an original album."[393]

Outlaw Roadshow

Three days after the release of *Sunshine*, the Crows launched their latest tour from Seattle, with setlists that drew heavily from the covers album. "The set gets to feeling one note-y," *PopMatters* wrote of their April 16th, 2012 show at the Fox Theater in Oakland. The reviewer was put off by the inclusion of eight cover songs from *Sunshine* and the lack of tunes from the first two albums. "It may be that the heavy inclusion of other people's material keeps them from playing to their strengths, but too many of the songs lack any kind of real dynamic range and it causes the set to start feeling like a flat line."

"Only Bruce Springsteen or Neil Young can get away with doing so many unfamiliar new songs in one night because they are such compelling performers," the *Star Tribune* griped of the band's *Sunshine*-heavy April 21st show at the State Theater in Minneapolis. "Adam Duritz has long been an indulgent performer. In concert, he performs for himself. And sometimes the audience comes along for the ride with him."[394]

Adam, who handcrafted the Crows' setlists, claimed that playing the cover songs live was transformative and would influence the group's next studio release. "It's already had a huge impact," the singer said that fall. "There's something liberating about doing someone else's songs. Everybody loosened up and played free but still listened to each other. It's just transformed the band live; we've turned into a way better band live, and I think that will come out even more on our next record. So when the songs start to come out, we'll see what the record's about. I'm not sure where we're going just yet."[395]

Adam prided himself on adjusting the setlists each night, so that no two concerts were ever the same. The lineup was always decided the day of the show; the only song to regularly make it was "A Long December." Otherwise, all bets were off. Adam would solicit requests from the Crows, the opening act, and the road crew after sound check was complete. Scrambling the setlist each night and drawing deeply from his entire catalog, enabled the singer to engage with his songs, rather than going through the motions and burning out on his own material. "I've never wanted our songs to turn into an obligation," he explained. "I want to play them because I really want to play them. I think that keeps the songs fresh."[396]

Singing night after night had taken its toll on Adam's voice over many years of relentless touring. At one point, he took steroids for his throat but did not like the side effects. Adam had always been a hard partying carouser on tour, but these days, he tended to keep to himself in order to preserve his vocal cords. "I've had a lot of problems with my voice over the years because I sing really hard and it doesn't recover really well," he explained. "It's gotten really beat up over the years of touring … I'm kind of like a monk on the road now. Nowadays I can't go out and mess around in bars and stuff."

As for other substances, Adam claimed that he had scaled

back considerably. "It's been hard to find the right medications and I probably shouldn't be existing so unmedicated. It's a little bit of a raw world. I spent a lot of years wrapped in a weird, creepy gauze. It's pretty raw out here without anything."[397]

Black Sun Stalled

On December 18th, 2012, *Freeloaders*, Adam's film project with Broken Lizard, was released to minimal fanfare. Adam claimed that the movie's plot was loosely based on the truth. "These guys lived in my house and they wrote a story about it. It's what happens when I'm out of town. At the time I had about twenty people living in my house. I lived in L.A. and a lot of my friends came to town trying to be actors or writers or musicians so I let them stay in my house."[398]

A review of *Freeloaders* on the website Blu-Ray.com called it a "crude and clueless comedy." Writing specifically about Adam, the review went on: "The unironic use of Adam Duritz as the rich and powerful celebrity of the story is strange ... Duritz isn't much of an actor, and his blinding fame died down a long time ago, contributing to the stale atmosphere of the feature. The role seems ripe for a lunatic cameo from a cult film star, someone capable of making an impression without actually participating in the picture. Duritz certainly isn't that guy."[399]

Freeloaders had taken years to come together, yet the artistic and financial payoff were minimal. Seemingly, Adam wanted to put the entire movie-making endeavor behind him. "It took me away from the band a lot," he said of *Freeloaders* a few months before it was released. "It's really funny. In films I like doing silly comedy. I'm a huge movie buff but if I'm going to work on one, I just want to laugh. I think if I could choose anything to do right now, I really want to do more plays. My play is called *Black Sun* at the moment and it's really cool to write music for other people."[400]

Adam was frustrated by the lack of progress on *Black Sun*, the musical he was writing with Stephen Belber. "We never have much time to work together. It was pretty cool but I don't know when we'll get a chance to finish it."[401] The project was "just sort of sitting right now" while Belber worked on the film adaptation of his 2004 play *Match*. Coordinating their schedules proved challenging. "Listen, when you have the opportunity to make a movie, you need to do that. I totally understand," said Adam, who was basically giving up and re-focusing on music. "I wanted to shift to doing something for the band, which is good. It's about time for that, anyway. I felt with the play I was letting that slip, so it feels good to be back in that (band) frame of mind again."[402]

Adam built a career out of oversharing. He admitted that after the play and the covers album, he found it difficult to write from a first-person perspective. "It was hard to drag myself back to writing about myself. There was a part of me that sort of felt like, 'I have shared enough—I don't want to write about me anymore.'"[403]

As it turned out, he did not have to. In autumn 2013, Adam's bandmates traveled from their West Coast homes to the singer's Manhattan apartment to get back to work. They wrote five songs in six days. "It was pouring out," the singer remembers.[404]

Echoes from the Outlaw Roadshow

On April 8th, 2013, the Crows issued their fifth live collection, *Echoes from the Outlaw Roadshow,* featuring highlights from the 2012 summer tour. The album sold so few copies that it did not make the *Billboard* charts. Adam thought the release captured the Crows at a particularly good juncture. "Something about making the *Underwater Sunshine* record really woke the band up. We played the best live shows of our career last year and it just seems to be getting better and better," he explained.[405] "Recording songs by other people was really good for us. Everything got way better because of the experience of making this record."[406]

Echoes from the Outlaw Roadshow differed from the group's previous live releases. *Across a Wire, Live at Town Hall,* and *iTunes Live* chronicled one-time performances, and *Heineken Hall* consisted of tracks recorded over three nights at the same venue. *Echoes* was the first live Crows album to cull material from an entire tour. "It had been such a good year for playing gigs and there were probably some great single gigs, but there were also great tracks from all different places," Adam explained. "Somehow we chopped it into an album."[407]

Echoes, bookended by songs made famous by Bob Dylan, heavily featured covers from *Sunshine*. "It was important to get the songs we thought were really good," Adam said. "That's the only thing we are thinking about when we make a record — does the record hold together and is it the best collection of songs? There are a lot of takes of 'Start Again' to choose from; we play it a lot of nights, 'Untitled (Love Song)' we play a lot of nights, and some of those versions are pretty stellar, so we wanted to find one of those and put it on the record."[408]

Adam believed the resulting album captured something special. "I was onstage for almost every set of every band all summer. It was really fun. It just seemed like the place to be was onstage. That was where I wanted to be and that was where it was all happening. It was a hot summer too, it was over a hundred degrees [some nights] and with all of those lights onstage, I'd get onstage and go, 'Whoa, I'm a little out of it now.' But there was something really great about it too. It was one of the most enjoyable summers I've ever had."[409]

Wallflowers

That spring, the Crows returned to Australia and then to Europe. Summer was on the horizon, and Adam had no intention of sitting at home. "I actually do better on the road these days than I do at home. At least I know what I'm supposed to do every day on tour. Sometimes I get home and just sit in my apartment trying to remember people I know so I can get out of the house."[410]

For Adam, being on the road increasingly meant staying sober most of the time. "I rarely drink. It just takes too heavy a toll over the course of an entire tour. I can't do that and keep my voice together. It's funny though: I read a lot of stories about how I was wasted at a show but it's almost never the case on tour. This is not to say that I don't like drinking and playing music. I *love* drinking and playing music. I just can't do it very often."[411]

Sticking to a routine and staying sober went a long way towards keeping Adam happy and sane. "I wouldn't say I'm fully healthy," he explained. "My brain is still a mess, but I don't feel like I'm dying and I feel like I'm doing really well and playing and that's kind of nice. It's full of possibilities."[412]

Beginning in mid-June, 2013, the Crows hit the road with the Wallflowers opening, a repeat of the feted tour of 1997, when both groups were far more famous. Fans who bought tickets that summer received a free download of *Echoes from the Outlaw Roadshow*.

"The night as a whole had a real '90s vibe with the Wallflowers as the opening act," wrote a reviewer for *The Los Angeles Times*, after catching the final date of the tour, held at the Orange County Fair.[413] The reviewer was disappointed that Adam never joined the Wallflowers for "6th Avenue Heartache," but the Crows singer did not want to spend another summer staying onstage all night. After several years of traveling medicine shows and outlaw circuses, Adam was relieved to be back on tour with an established opening act that could stand on their own. Adam wanted to avoid distractions on the road, so that he could focus on a new Crows album. "It took me a while to shift back to writing for Counting Crows, in that vein, but now I'm there," he said.[414]

Adam typically did not compose new material on the road. This summer, he wanted to use the tour as a chance to write and try out new ideas. "I want to concentrate on writing songs right now, working on songs during the tour, soundchecking and working on stuff and then getting ready to record in the fall," he said. "I really wanted less distraction this time. I just wanted to clear my mind and get ready to make a record."[415]

Adam said that ideas for the new record were just

formulating, but that he had been amassing fragments of songs. "There are four or five songs I've been working on. We've been playing them with the band in sound checks on the last tour, down in Australia. We had a little time to work on them and the band really liked them. I just have to finish writing them now and get some more going and then get us back in the studio."[416] Adam added, "Maybe when it's done, I can look back on it and say 'Well, that was kind of influenced by this,' but there's just no way to see it ahead of time. I have no idea. I'm excited to make the record, though."[417]

Writing Wonderland

Adam knew one thing going into the new Counting Crows album: it was time for a change. "I really reached a dead end in a lot of ways with *Saturday Nights & Sunday Mornings*. I'm not sure I had much more to share on that subject, in the way I was doing it."[418] He elaborated, "I felt a bit shared out. At some point, is there anything else that you have left to [share]? That album was such a gut-emptying thing that afterwards I was like, 'Geez, I don't know what to say now.'"[419]

Adam was tired of writing from an autobiographical perspective. "People start to expect a certain plot arc from you, and while you can write as well as you can write, you can't change the actual plot of your life. I felt like I was not only trying to live my life to get my life together, but trying to live my life so I have a more interesting plot arc for the records . . . I was kind of tired of just talking about being crazy. It's not all there is to me."[420]

For most of his career, Adam wrote new songs in single, inspired sessions. He would sit down at the piano with the germ of an idea and, by the time he got up, he would have produced a mostly finished song. He would bring it to the band, who would flesh it out and add their instrumental flourishes. For the past couple of years, however, Adam had not finished anything. He would come up with ideas, but they never resulted in complete songs. Normally, he would discard bits and pieces that went nowhere, assuming they were not good enough to keep. "I had all these ideas, and they just didn't seem like the kinds of things I wrote about. I kept throwing them out," Adam explained.[421] "When you're used to, say, blue being quality, and all of a sudden things are coming out green? It's hard to judge it, initially."[422]

Rather than throwing away new ideas that didn't seem to go anywhere, Adam began collecting song fragments on his phone for potential use later. On July 30th, 2013, he posted a message to the Crows website: "As for a new album, I'm busy writing right now and we're going to start recording late this fall. Millard and Dan are coming to my house tomorrow to start woodshedding ideas."[423] In August 2013, Powers and Vickrey traveled to New York and spent a week working with Adam at his apartment. "I started to pull these things out, and they were flipping out over them. They loved them."[424]

That week, the trio completed a new song, "God of Ocean Tides," and made progress on several others. Adam told reporters on several occasions that composing songs for *Black Sun* and recording the covers album influenced him in unexpected ways. "I was writing for other people, so I kind of got out of that first-person confessional mode that I've been writing in my whole life," he explained. "And then seeing all the different ways those other people wrote in *Underwater Sunshine*. It was like collaborating with fifteen people who weren't there."[425]

Adam said that this process turned him away from strictly autobiographical songs and towards writing about other people and their experiences. It was composing for *Black Sun*, he said, that shifted his thinking in this regard. "That really opened up a huge vista for me, a much broader palette to write from. I was being chained to the plot of my own life. The important thing isn't really that you write about what you did today; it's that you write about how you feel today. There's a lot more range in that."[426]

In September 2013, Powers and Vickrey returned to Adam's apartment, this time with Immerglück and Bryson in tow. In a six-day whirlwind session, Adam and his bandmates cooked up five new tunes: "Earthquake Driver," "'Scarecrow," "Cover Up the Sun," "Dislocation," and "Elvis Went to Hollywood." Everyone contributed to the music, while Adam continued to write all of the lyrics.

"Elvis," which imagines Elvis Presley triggering the end of Western civilization via an alien invasion, began as a song fragment that Adam was going to throw away. He thought it was clever but not emotionally moving. "I wasn't used to being humorous in a song," he said, recalling that "Einstein on the Beach" was a somewhat funny tune that he and the band never liked. "'Elvis Went to Hollywood' could have turned out to be that kind of song, too. It's sort of a silly idea. I mistook it for that kind of thing at first when I started it, but then I got a lot of really positive responses from the guys when I was playing the first verse for them. That got me to start taking it a little more seriously."[427] He added, "I allowed myself to work with some absurdity."[428]

Adam and his bandmates reconvened for another week in October 2013. "I love the songs we've been writing," he told a journalist the following month. "It's been a totally different process for me—I've had a lot of doubts about these songs when I started working on them, but the guys have been flipping out. Immy thinks it's the best lyrics I've ever written. They're really different. There's a lot more imagery. I didn't have a lot of faith in it at first, but as I finish them, I really love the new songs."[429]

The October session yielded "Palisades Park," which clocked in at over eight minutes and became the Crows longest and most ambitious song to date. "Palisades" takes place in New York in the late 1970s, and tells the story of two young friends, setting out to conquer the world. Adam said that the song celebrated "being on the fringes, wanting to try on the wrong sex's clothing, and wanting to try PCP, which is a bad idea. But it's about that experimentation."[430] The ambitious "Palisades" drew inspiration from the band's storied live interpretations of numbers such "Round Here" and "Rain King," where Adam would incorporate the lyrics of other songs into the middle section. Adam thought it was the best piece he had ever written and decided it would have to be the first track on the new album.

"I've always wanted to write a song like that, where it's part of the song itself," he explained. "I've never fully been able to do that, to recreate the kinds of things we do improvisationally in a song on a record until this record. 'Palisades Park' goes through a bunch of different movements before coming back to where it was in the beginning, and it really does take you on this same kind of trip you get at our live concerts."[431]

The idea for "Possibility Days" came from "Sunday in the Park with George," a Stephen Sondheim play about the painter Georges Seurat. The play's final line, that Seurat loves blank canvases due to their infinite possibilities, inspired Adam to pursue the subject in a song. He thought of how there was a silver lining of hope in every failed relationship. "It's trying to be an optimistic song in a way about something pessimistic that happens," he explained. "There are always possibilities. It took me a while to realize that in life. Things are possible. Blank canvases mean that you can paint on them."

Adam believed that this philosophy applied not only to relationships, but to his own challenges with mental illness. "A few years ago I realized I wasn't maybe ever going to be cured. I'm not sure you can get cured from stuff like that. That kind of sent me off the deep end at a certain point. I guess what I realized is even falling off that deep end didn't kill me."

Adam says that this perspective gave him a sense that he could have mental illness but that a rewarding life was possible. "It's sort of like a disability in a way, but it's not the same as being doomed, either. It's just different. You have to reset your sights. I was feeling so depressed about that a few years ago that I let it halt everything in my life. I realized maybe I have to lower my expectations. I could still write. I could still make music. The band is really good. It's kind of a mixed bag, but that song looks at something going wrong and how it's not the end of the world."[432]

Comfortable

Most of *Somewhere Under Wonderland* was recorded at Fantasy Studios in Berkeley during a three-week session in December 2013. Follow-up work at Fantasy took place in February 2014. "Making albums is hard," Adam said. "It's not necessarily something you look back on thinking it was fun. It's really difficult, but it's very satisfying."[433] In May, Adam announced that the band's sixth album of original material, *Somewhere Under Wonderland,* would be released that fall as part of a one-time partnership with Capitol Records. "Just like the Beatles!" Adam tweeted.

The group put together a summer tour with Toad the Wet Sprocket opening. Adam had no plans to release *Wonderland* until that fall. "Summer is not a good time to put out a record," he said. "You want to give something plenty of set-up time. It usually takes three or four months to put out a record once it's done."[434]

That did not stop the singer from calling for "Palisades Park" at most of the concerts. "We played an entire summer of shows with an eight-and-a-half-minute song that nobody knew as the opening song of the encore, which is kind of crazy. We had the confidence to do it."[435]

Not everyone agreed. *Indy Week* called the group's Raleigh stop, a "low-energy waltz of fumbled steps and modest ambitions. The band shuffled behind the seven-part harmonies like they'd just finished a collective backstage nap. That feeling never really left, despite the overabundance of onstage strobe lights or the upbeat and thoroughly uninspired new songs."[436]

The critic noted that Adam's voice was in rough shape,

possibly from laryngitis. Around this time, Adam postponed an interview with a journalist more than once due to vocal issues. "The voice is okay now," the singer explained when they finally talked. "It just gets a little worn down. We have been playing full, two hour shows every night and that takes its toll. It is nothing serious but I have to be careful. If I want to play two hour shows every night I have pretty much got to be a mute the rest of the time. That does not come naturally to me."[437]

Adam said that being on the road still topped sitting at home alone, vocal problems or not. The daily routine and steady rhythms of touring had become the norm. "At this point in my life I'm almost more comfortable when I'm on tour and there's a schedule to follow. I've got a lot of my shit together in the last couple of years and I'm very functional. I work well now, but I still don't know exactly what to do with myself when I don't have a set amount of things to."[438]

Adam added that the band had a fun summer, trying out songs from the forthcoming record and playing their hearts out. "We had a great tour this summer. The record wasn't out, but we were playing all of the songs anyway because we wanted to get good at playing them before it was time to tour the record."[439]

As the Crows' tour was wrapping up, Adam made headlines when it was revealed that he had posted a profile on Tinder, the online dating service. The media was unable to resist the story of a rich and famous rock star reduced to begging for dates online. They pounced, trotting out the usual list of famous actresses Adam supposedly dated and ridiculing him without mercy. "Will Someone Please Right Swipe Adam Duritz on

Tinder?" ran the headline in *Stereogum*, while *Spin* called his Tinder page "the saddest online dating profile music fans have ever seen."[440]

Adam did not deny having a Tinder profile or take his down. Instead, the singer posted a screen shot of his Tinder profile on Instagram with the caption, "Seriously? Is there anyone who's *not* on Tinder? It's my favorite video game." Adam was asked about Tinder continually during the promotional interviews for the Crows new album, but shrugged off any controversy. "Everybody is on Tinder. My married friends are on Tinder. Seriously, there is nobody who is not on Tinder at this point. It's a video game. My married publicist who told me not to go on Tinder is on Tinder, and so is her husband."[441]

The focus on Adam's love life was a distraction from a major change that occurred around this time, the band's separation from longtime manager Gary Gersh. Neither Adam nor Gersh commented publicly on the split, and the Crows signed with mega-firm Red Light Management, whose roster included more than 250 major acts.

Somewhere Under Wonderland

On September 2nd, 2014, Capitol Records issued *Somewhere Under Wonderland*, the Crows' first new album of original material in six years. *Wonderland* entered the *Billboard* charts at number six, a strong showing for a band in their third decade. A single for the song "Scarecrow" reached number seven on *Billboard's* AAA charts on September 27th. "I never know what's going to be a hit," Adam said. "I don't pay attention to that. Some of the most popular songs we've ever written were never singles, like 'Holiday in Spain,' 'Anna Begins,' 'Omaha,' and 'Colorblind.' But they were used in movies and other things and audiences love them."[442]

Reviews of *Wonderland* were largely positive. The fact that the Crows still existed and continued to make music seemed to be enough to win accolades in an era where few 1990s rockers were still around.

U.K. newspaper *The Telegraph* called *Wonderland* Adam's best work since *August*. "At 50, the wild-haired front man is still finding exhilaration in heartbreak, loneliness in fame and adventure in everyday America."[443] *PopMatters* praised *Wonderland*, asserting, "They are still finding ways to win the battle against irrelevancy. What other early '90s alt-pop-rock band can say that?"[444] *Consequence* graded *Wonderland* a B, writing that the album allows the Crows to "find their footing as a middle-aged band. Sure, Duritz's normal hang-ups still emerge, but they come in a warmer, more emotionally rounded context these days."[445] *Rolling Stone* scored it three out of five stars, writing that Adam "barrels through a buoyantly alienated set that only occasionally gets bogged down in meditative goop."[446] A review in *The New York Times* was lukewarm, praising "Possibility Days," but asserting that *Wonderland* "teems with lyrics full of rambling travelogue and mystical gobbledygook. Mr. Duritz sings them confidently, in a voice that's not as laden with meaning as he seems to think."[447]

Adam was pleased with *Wonderland*, which he believed advanced his writing in important new directions. "The songs are different lyrically, and I feel like they're a step forward, for me, as a writer. There's less first person, though they still feel personal," he explained.[448] "These songs are much more vivid, they're much more stories about things. Not just about what happened to me last week. They're much more wider-ranging than that."[449]

Despite the singer's proclamations about third-person writing, *Wonderland* is very much a Counting Crows album. On "Earthquake Driver," the singer ruminates about the isolating effects of celebrity over a snappy backdrop, and he sings about being born in Baltimore on "Dislocation." "John Appleseed's Lament" features an appearance from Maria and a lover calling out to a guy named Adam. "Cover Up the Sun" is another way of saying daylight fading, and the countrified rambler resembles the band's previous hitting-the-road-and-leaving-the-girl-behind anthems. There are circuses, sunsets, falling, and people who move from Los Angeles to New York City. And there is "Possibility Days," as personal and heartfelt a song as Adam ever wrote.

Despite whatever criticisms have come their way, Adam said that he loved every one of the Crows albums and would not change a thing. "I'm absolutely satisfied with every record. I think that's the point of them in a way. Like them or hate them, that's what we meant for them to be. For the most part, they're exactly how we wanted them to be … They are very much statements of where we were at for those different points in our lives. They're perfect in that way to me."[450]

Legacy

The Crows mostly stayed on the road through the end of 2014, traversing Europe in the fall and closing out the year with two weeks in the Midwest. Material from *Wonderland* featured heavily in the setlists, but the group continued to change it up for every concert, featuring songs from each of their albums. "There's nothing that's sacred, that has to be played," Adam said. "I love 'Mr. Jones,' but I do not play it every night. The way we look at it, we've got all these songs now from making these records, so we want to play all the songs."[451]

Adam explained that this strategy was long-term, intended to keep the Crows together and working. His career-spanning focus on unique and engaging live concerts yielded a devoted fanbase that continued to buy tickets year after year. "People are still coming. We're not the center of culture, but a lot of those bands that were the center of culture for five seconds aren't even existing anymore.[452]

After decades of personal turmoil and instability, Adam finally discovered a routine that worked. Every year, from late spring to early fall, he hit the road with the Crows, where he found consistency and companionship. As much as the singer enjoyed the rock-star lifestyle, he envied those who found happiness through marriage and children. "Clearly there is something about being in love and having a family that is very rewarding and wonderful," he said. "I have put my whole head and heart into the band for so long, I couldn't figure out how to do this other thing."[453]

Adam realized that living life on the road meant never settling down, getting married, having children, or other traditional hallmarks of adulthood. "Part of the fallout of having the success that I do have means there are other areas in my life that I left unattended," he explained. "Relationships, families, those were things I didn't have. Maybe I would have moved toward that earlier if it was a priority. But then, maybe I wouldn't have done this."[454]

Yet, the singer continued to be inspired by music and drawn to creating it, in the studio and on stage. "I still like it," he enthused. "I like collaborating. I like going in the studio and working on arrangements. Taking something that is like this skeleton of some music that I came up with on the piano, going in and working with a producer and turning that into a song. Writing harmonies together. All the shit we do. And then going out and doing it every night. I dig that."[455]

The Crows operated like a well-oiled machine, with a largely stable lineup that included day-one members like Bryson, Immerglück, and Gillingham. Adam cautioned that his fellow musicians were not his best friends. "Some of us have been playing together for twenty-seven years, so it's probably more like siblings, more like brothers and sisters. It's friendly, but not like best friends. After all, we're working—it's a job."[456] And there was no question about who was running the show. "There's got to be someone in charge, and that's been me, and sometimes that stifles other people," Adam insisted. "It's not my intention. But it does happen."[457]

Adam felt responsible for keeping everyone in the Crows organization working, from his bandmates to the road crew, many of whom had stuck by him for three decades. "There are a lot of people whose lives are entwined in my being a responsible adult," he said. "I can't walk away from this, there is just too much responsibility tied up in it. And I don't really want to … Counting Crows is my life."[458]

For that reason, Adam thought the group maintained a sense of credibility, despite whatever snobbish rock critics believed. "There's no way to know what you're doing is the right thing a lot of the time," he conceded. "I pissed a lot of people off sometimes. But, you know, I feel pretty clean about things, too. I may have made the wrong decisions occasionally, but I think I made them for the right reasons."[459] Adam believed this helped the Crows stay intact over three decades of music making. "Part of what destroys bands and pulls them apart is they look back on things and they don't feel clean about it. There were things we probably could have done to make us sell more records, but we were never really interested in that."[460]

As for the Crows' place in music history, Adam was unconcerned about his legacy. "Do we get the respect we deserve? I don't know what we fucking deserve. I think there are always going to be bands that are critical darlings ... I started off my career playing at the Rock and Roll Hall of Fame as an unknown band. I don't know that I would even show up if we got into it now."[461]

Come Around

In 2015, the Crows toured from April to October. In 2016, it was May to October, and in 2017 and 2018, late June to October. Adam seemed uninterested in writing new songs and recording new albums. "I've got a lot of pieces and ideas, I just haven't put them together in songs," he said in 2018, four years after the Crows' last studio album was issued. "I just haven't had the urge to do that part of it. But I've got five million pieces recorded."[462]

A new Crows album wasn't all that important. Making records was time-consuming and expensive. Besides, most of the concertgoers preferred the old songs anyway. "I don't think we're the center of pop culture by any means, but we're going to sell about 15,000 or 16,000 tickets in the New York City area this summer," Adam said. "When we were in the mainstream, it was very profitable, but in a lot of ways, annoying too. We're still making money and supporting everybody."[463]

The Crows only played a handful of shows in 2019, but Adam made international headlines when he shaved his signature dreadlocks that August, around the time of his fifty-fifth birthday. "I'd been thinking about it for a while," Adam said, explaining that he was getting tired of the dreadlocks. "It's weird because I have accomplished a lot in my life, and every single bit of it was done with those on my head. Previous to that I was a kid or a bum—those are the two choices from my childhood and my twenties."[464]

The Crows spent 2020 at home, the first year since their inception that they did not play any shows. Adam used the pandemic to launch an Instagram cooking show. In 2021 and 2022, the group resumed their May-to-October touring schedule, stopping to release a four-song EP, *Butter Miracle, Suite One* in 2021. It was the first new material they had issued in the seven years since *Wonderland*.

In 2022, Counting Crows once again paired with the Wallflowers for a cross-country trek. The two bands, who first toured together in 1997, had remained in the studio and on the road for the past twenty-five years, playing to diminishing audiences of diehards amidst the summer festival and shed-tour revelers.

But those crowds still showed up, as they did at the Minnesota State Fair, where the Crows and the Wallflowers drew an audience of 10,000. "Duritz, 58, remains a compelling charismatic original, a poetic storyteller whose songs are filled with vivid characters," opined the *Star Tribune*. On stage, "He's very in the moment, open and unpretentious even if his songs often strive for profundity."[465]

The signature dreadlocks and beard were gone, but Adam Duritz remained one of rock's most captivating live performers, delivering those same intimate songs with passion and conviction. And so long as fans are there to listen, he will come around.

Discography

August and Everything After	1993
Recovering the Satellites	1996
Across a Wire: Live in New York City	1998
This Desert Life	1999
Hard Candy	2002
New Amsterdam: Live at Heineken Music Hall	2006
Saturday Nights & Sunday Mornings	2008
iTunes: Live From Soho	2008
August and Everything After: Live at Town Hall	2011
Underwater Sunshine (or What We Did on Our Summer Vacation)	2012
Echoes of the Outlaw Roadshow	2013
Somewhere Under Wonderland	2014
Butter Miracle, Suite One (EP)	2021

Videography

"Mr. Jones"	1994
"Round Here"	1994
"Angels of the Silences"	1996
"A Long December"	1996
"Daylight Fading"	1997
"Hanginaround"	1999
"Mrs. Potter's Lullaby"	2000
"American Girls"	2002
"Big Yellow Taxi"	2002
"If I Could Give All My Love (Richard Manuel is Dead)"	2003
"She Don't Want Nobody Near"	2003
"Accidentally in Love"	2004
"1492"	2008
"You Can't Count on Me"	2008
"Palisades Park"	2014
"Scarecrow"	2014
"Earthquake Driver"	2014
"Butter Miracle Suite One"	2021

Acknowledgements

First and foremost, thank you to Adam Duritz and the members of Counting Crows past and present. I am grateful for the songs, the shows, and a lifetime of incredible memories.

Writing books can be a solitary process, but it is always a collective one. My thanks go to Kaitlin Travis for fastidious copyediting and Penny Brucker for assistance with design, layout, formatting, and just all-around genius.

Many thanks to Kelsyn Rooks, Scott Woermann, and everyone at the Center for Recorded Music. I dig what c4rm does and the people who do it. Thanks for making me a welcome member of the team!

I am grateful for my colleagues at Rhode Island College: Mikaila Mariel Lemonik Arthur, Alessandra Bazo Vienrich, Tanni Chaudhuri, Desirée Ciambrone, Roger Clark, Jill Harrison, Pam Jackson, Darek Niklas, and Carse Ramos. Thanks also to colleagues elsewhere: Bob Antonio, Pat Bass, Michaela DeSoucey, Gary Fine, Anthony Kwame Harrison, Charis Kubrin, Steve Leonard, Matthew Oware, Tim Pippert, and David Smith.

Special thanks to the Amor, Harkness, Maxfield, and Taylor families, and to my friends Greg Douros, Kathryn Kollet, Doug Lerner, Paul Marinescu, Jon Niccum, Ken Perreault, Eliott Reeder, Jeff Roos, and Spencer Wright. So many of my favorite Counting Crows memories involve one or more of you. Here's to friends who feel like family!

I am lucky to be called "Dad" by the two most amazing kids a guy could ask for. Ben and Emma, I love you so very much and am proud of your many accomplishments. I know you will make a positive contribution to the world and I am glad to have a front-row seat. Laura, L-Train, Mom Harkness, you already know. I do it all for you. I love you, babe, now and forever.

Notes

[1] Geoff Harkness. "Counting Crows." *Lawrence Journal-World*, July 27, 2000.

[2] Leslie Michele Dreeouigh. "Adam Duritz of Counting Crows." *Glide Magazine*, June 12, 2014.

[3] Ibid.

[4] David Wild. "Counting Crows: Bird on a Wire." *Rolling Stone*, June 30, 1994.

[5] Bruce Adams. "Golden Bear Athletes Can Count on Rock Star's Support." *SF Gate*, December 26, 2003.

[6] Nick Hasted. "Counting Crows: Alive in Wonderland." *Louder*, December 17, 2014.

[7] "Adam Duritz of Counting Crows." *Hartford Courant*, August 29, 2009.

[8] Pete Crooks. "Long Play Version: An Interview with Adam Duritz of Counting Crows." *Diablo Magazine*, March 9, 2008.

[9] David Wild. "Counting Crows: Birds on a Wire." *Rolling Stone*, June 30, 1994.

[10] "Counting Crows' Frontman Adam Duritz." *Dark Horse Sessions*, Episode #55, April 13, 2019.

[11] David Brinn. "Counting Crows Coming to Holy Land." *Jerusalem Post*, July 11, 2022.

[12] Yulia Karra. "Counting Crows' Adam Duritz Talks Working on Kibbutz and Surprising Origins of 'Mr. Jones.'" *YNet News*, September 4, 2022.

[13] "Counting Crows' Frontman Adam Duritz." *Dark Horse Sessions*, Episode #55, April 13, 2019.

[14] Allison Kaplan Sommer. "Counting Crows Are Coming to Israel. For Their Lead Singer, It's a Trip Down Memory Lane." *Haaretz*, September 7, 2022.

[15] Julie Rubenstein. "Crows Fly High." *Washington Post*, May 14, 1994.

[16] "Notable Sigma Nu Members." *Sigma Nu Fraternity*. www.sigmanu.org.

[17] Marc P. Resteghini. "Favoring Respect, Intimacy Over Popularity." *Harvard Crimson*, November 7, 1997.

[18] "Counting Crows." *A&E Private Sessions*, March 30, 2008.

[19] Leslie Michele Derrough. "Adam Duritz of Counting Crows." *Glide Magazine*, June 12, 2014

[20] "Adam Duritz, Counting Crows." *Little Known Facts with Ilana Levine*, March 2, 2022.

[21] "Mod-l Society." *ETree DB*. etreedb.org.

[22] Reid Genauer. "Chapter 7: Danny Eisenberg." *Your Lore*, March 13, 2019.

[23] "Counting Crows." *A&E Private Sessions*. March 30, 2008.

[24] Evan Schlansky. "Hangin' Around with Adam Duritz." *Rolling Stone*, July 12, 2002.

[25] David Wild. "Counting Crows: Birds on a Wire." *Rolling Stone*, June 30, 1994.

[26] Ibid.

[27] Marc P. Resteghini. "Favoring Respect, Intimacy Over Popularity." *The Harvard Crimson*, November 7, 1997.

[28] Sason Bishope Parry. "Artist Spotlight: Tobias Hawkins." *FSHN*, February 9, 2016.

[29] "Counting Crows." *A&E Private Sessions*. March 30, 2008.

[30] David Wild. "Counting Crows: Birds on a Wire." *Rolling Stone*, June 30, 1994.

[31] Grant Walters. "Counting Crows' Debut Album 'August and Everything After' Turns 25." *Albumism*, September 14, 2018.

[32] Heather Browne. "The Himalayans: She Likes the Weather." *Fuel Friends Blog*, March 9, 2007.

[33] Ibid.

[34] "In Depth with Adam Duritz and Charlie Gillingham." *Counting Crows August and Everything After Live at Town Hall*. Eagle Rock Entertainment, 2011.

[35] Brian Hiatt, "Adam Duritz: 1991 and Everything After." *Rolling Stone*, August 28, 2012.

[36] David Wild. "Counting Crows: Birds on a Wire." *Rolling Stone*, June 30, 1994.

[37] Ibid.

[38] Nick Hasted. "Counting Crows: Alive in Wonderland." *Louder*, December 17, 2014.

[39] Joel Selvin. "Anatomy of a Hit." *San Francisco Chronicle*, April 10, 1994.

[40] "Matt Malley: Life as a Counting Crow." *DIY Musician Podcast*, #57, April 27, 2009.

[41] Nick Hasted. "Counting Crows: Alive in Wonderland." *Louder*, December 17, 2014.

[42] Jean Rosenbluth. "Down-Home Benefit for Ailing Singer." *Los Angeles Times*, June 18, 1992.

[43] "Matt Malley: Life as a Counting Crow." *DIY Musician Podcast*, #57, April 27, 2009.

[44] Joel Selvin. "Anatomy of a Hit." *San Francisco Chronicle*, April 10, 1994.

[45] Ibid.

[46] Cary Tennis. "Start Counting: Counting Crows Begin their Ascension." *Soma*, Fall 1993.

[47] Joel Selvin. "Anatomy of a Hit." *San Francisco Chronicle*, April 10, 1994.

[48] David Wild. "Counting Crows: Birds on a Wire." *Rolling Stone*, June 30, 1994.

[49] Grant Walters. "Counting Crows' Debut Album, 'August and Everything After' Turns 25." *Albumism*, September 14, 2018.

[50] Julie Rubenstein. "Crows Fly High." *The Washington Post*, May 14, 1994.

[51] Bill Flanagan. "Counting Crows Learn to Fly." *Musician*, May 1994.

[52] Grant Walters. "Counting Crows' Debut Album, 'August and Everything After' Turns 25." *Albumism*, September 14, 2018.

[53] "Drumwise Meets Steve Bowman." https://youtu.be/B0DFYmbtL6U

[54] Joel Selvin. "Anatomy of a Hit." *San Francisco Chronicle*, April 10, 1994.

[55] Larry Fitzmaurice. "We Got a File on You: Adam Duritz." *Stereogum*, May 21, 2021.

[56] Chris Willman. "Another Feather in Their Caps." *Los Angeles Times*, December 17, 1993

[57] David Wild. "Counting Crows: Birds on a Wire." *Rolling Stone*, June 30, 1994.

[58] Joel Selvin. "Anatomy of a Hit." *San Francisco Chronicle*, April 10, 1994.

[59] David Wild. "Counting Crows: Bird on a Wire." *Rolling Stone*, June 30, 1994.

[60] Stephen Jacques. "Suede, Cranberries, and Counting Crows at Avalon." *The Heights*. October 18, 1993.

[61] Jon Pareles. "Pop and Jazz Review: Counting Crows." *The New York Times*. November 18, 1993.

[62] "Chart History, Counting Crows." *Billboard.com*

[63] "Fear of Flying." *Entertainment Weekly*, February 18, 1994.

[64] Ibid.

[65] Bill Flanagan. "Counting Crows Learn to Fly." *Musician*, May 1994.

[66] Joel Selvin. "Anatomy of a Hit." *San Francisco Chronicle*, April 10, 1994.

[67] Julie Rubenstein. "Crows Fly High." *Washington Post*, May 14, 1994.

[68] Bill Flanagan. "Counting Crows Learn to Fly." *Musician*, May 1994.

[69] Thom Jurek. "August and Everything After." *Rolling Stone*. October 28, 1993.

[70] David Wild. "Counting Crows: Birds on a Wire." *Rolling Stone*, June 30, 1994.

[71] Bill Flanagan. "Counting Crows Learn to Fly." *Musician*, May 1994.

[72] David Wild. "Counting Crows: Birds on a Wire." *Rolling Stone*, June 30, 1994.

[73] "Matt Malley: Life as a Counting Crow." *DIY Musician Podcast*, #57, April 27, 2009.

[74] David Browne. "August and Everything After." *Entertainment Weekly*, February 18, 1994.

[75] Robert Christgau. "Consumer Guide." *Village Voice*, July 26, 1994.

[76] Christopher John Farley. "First Class Flyers." *Time*, October 21, 1996.

[77] Ibid.

[78] Craig Shapiro. "Crows Drummer Says It's the Music That Matters, Not Personalities." *The Virginian-Pilot*, February 15, 1997.

[79] Dan Kening. "Counting Crows Concert Short, Sweet, Bewildering." *Chicago Tribune*, July 10, 1994.

[80] Ibid.

[81] "No One's Listening to Rejection." *No One's Listening Podcast*, September 18, 2011.

[82] "DrumWise Meets Steve Bowman." *DrumWise Drum Tuition*, March 20, 2021.

[83] Logan Neill. "On Top and On the Way Up." *Tampa Bay Times*. August 15, 1997.

[84] Craig Rosen. "Geffen Records Enjoys Best Year." *Billboard*. January 21, 1995.

[85] Natalie Nichols. "As the Crows Flew." *Los Angeles Times*, October 13, 1996.

[86] Joe Jackson. "Adam's Angst." *The Irish Times*, November 8, 1996.

[87] Christopher John Farley. "First Class Flyers." *Time*, October 21, 1996.

[88] Ibid.

[89] Ibid.

[90] Joe Jackson. "Adam's Angst." *The Irish Times*, November 8, 1996.

[91] "Counting Crows." *Much Music Spotlight*, September 1996.

[92] Natalie Nichols. "As the Crows Flew." *Los Angeles Times*, October 13, 1996.

[93] "Counting Crows Debut New Material." *MTV.com*, November 21, 1995.

[94] David John Farinella. "Counting Crows Rock the House." *Mix*, February 1997.

[95] Joe Bosso. "Production Legend Gil Norton on 16 Career-Defining Records." *Music Radar*, December 1, 2014.

[96] Rebecca Thomas. "Counting Crows Survives Success." *Orlando Sentinel*, January 30, 1997.

[97] "Counting Crows." *Much Music Spotlight*, 1996.

[98] David John Farinella. "Counting Crows Rock the House." *Mix*, February 1997.

Notes

[99] Natalie Nichols. "As the Crows Flew." *Los Angeles Times*, October 13, 1996.

[100] Ibid.

[101] "Counting Crows Count Down to Next Album." *MTV.com*, January 4, 1996.

[102] Joe Bosso. "Production Legend Gil Norton on 16 Career-Defining Records." Music Radar, December 1, 2014.

[103] Ibid.

[104] Natalie Nichols. "As the Crows Flew." *Los Angeles Times*, October 13, 1996.

[105] Julian Rubinstein. "When Fame Glows Bright, It's Hard to be Tortured." *The New York Times*, December 1, 1996.

[106] David John Farinella. "Counting Crows Rock the House." *Mix*, February 1997.

[107] Natalie Nichols. "As the Crows Flew." *Los Angeles Times*, October 13, 1996.

[108] "Counting Crows Leader Adam Duritz's New Friend." *MTV.com*, March 9, 1996.

[109] Jane Ganahl. "As the Crows Fly." *SF Gate*, September 6, 1998.

[110] Jane Ganahl. "Counting Crows' Duritz Finds Emotional Balance." *SF Gate*, December 9, 1999.

[111] Joe Jackson. "Adam's Angst." *The Irish Times*, November 8, 1996.

[112] Jane Ganahl. "As the Crows Fly." *SF Gate*, September 6, 1998.

[113] Ibid.

[114] "Counting Crows – This Desert Life." *Throwback Podcast*, February 9, 2022.

[115] Joel Selvin. "Counting Crows Try Out Wings." *San Francisco Chronicle*, September 6, 1996.

[116] Jane Ganahl. "Crows Prove That They're the Real Thing." *San Francisco Examiner*, October 16, 1996.

[117] Anthony DeCurtis. "Recovering the Satellites." *Rolling Stone*, November 4, 1996.

[118] Michael Goldberg. "Counting Crows Shoot for the Stars." *MTV.com*, November 4, 1998.

[119] Neil Strauss. "Stars Come Out From Under." *The New York Times*, October 15, 1996.

[120] Ken Tucker. "Recovering the Satellites." *Entertainment Weekly*, October 25, 1996.

[121] David Schonfeld. "For Counting Crows, Everything After 'August' Fails to Recover Early Magic." *The Daily Collegian*, October 18, 1996.

[122] Andy Gill. "Counting Crows Recovering the Satellites." *The Independent*, October 10, 1996.

[123] Yale College. "College Teas." https://gracehopper.yalecollege.yale.edu/college/college-teas

[124] Julian Rubinstein. "When Fame Glows Bright, It's Hard to be Tortured." *The New York Times*, December 1, 1996.

[125] Ibid.

[126] Jon Parales. "Something to Whine About." *The New York Times*, December 5, 1996.

[127] Julian Rubinstein. "When Fame Glows Bright, It's Hard to be Tortured." *The New York Times*, December 1, 1996.

[128] Phil Gallo. "Counting Crows." *Variety*, December 18, 1996.

[129] Matt Wardlaw. "Counting Crows Recovering the Satellites." *Diffuser*. October 14, 2016.

[130] Patrick Macdonald. "Bitter, Sweet Success for Crows." *The Seattle Times*, March 27, 1997.

[131] Craigh Marine. "Duritz's Soul, Sincerity Set Crows Apart." *SF Gate*, April 6, 1997.

[132] John Roos. "Adam Duritz: Counting Woes." *Los Angeles Times*, April 7, 1997.

[133] Logan Neill. "On Top and On the Way Up." *Tampa Bay Times*. August 15, 1997.

[134] *Much Music Spotlight*, September 1996.

[135] "Crows Cancel Shows; Duritz OK?" *Rolling Stone*, July 24, 1997.

[136] "Counting Crows Counted In." *MTV.com*, July 25, 1997.

[137] Katy Daigle. "Counting This Concert Gives Meadows a Thing to Crow About." *Hartford Courant*, July 30, 1997.

[138] Matt Melucci. "Counting Crows Make Plans for Third Album." *MTV.com*, October 27, 1997.

[139] Melissa Schorr. "Rockers Sing the Blues at Concert." *Las Vegas Sun*, September 19, 1997.

[140] Natasha Stovall. "Counting on Lead Singers." *SF Gate*, September 23, 1997.

[141] Marc P. Resteghini. "Favoring Respect, Intimacy Over Popularity." *The Harvard Crimson*, November 7, 1997.

[142] Jane Ganahl. "As the Crows Fly." *SF Gate*, September 6, 1998.

[143] Colin Devinish. "Counting Crows Unveil New Music at Secret Shows." *MTV.com*, April 22, 1998.

[144] Ibid.

[145] Stephen Segerman. "Across a Wire (Live in NYC)." *Amuzine*, 1998.

[146] Stephen Thomas Erlewine. "Across a Wire: Live in New York City." *All Music*, 1998.

[147] Greg Kot. "Counting Crows Across a Wire: Live in New York City." *Rolling Stone*, July 9, 1998.

[148] Gavin McNett. "Across a Wire." *Salon*, July 22, 1998.

[149] Gil Kauffman. "Cracker Leader to Co-Produce Counting Crows Album." *MTV.com*, June 4, 1998.

[150] Jane Ganahl. "As the Crows Fly." *SF Gate*, September 6, 1998.

[151] Ibid.

[152] Jane Ganahl. "Counting Crows' Duritz Finds Emotional Balance." *SF Gate*, December 9, 1999.

[153] Ibid.

[154] Gil Kauffman. "Counting Crows' Adam Duritz Describes Experimental New Album." *MTV.com*, August 12, 1999.

[155] Geoff Harkness. "Counting Crows." *Lawrence Journal-World*, July 27, 2000.

[156] Dan Aquilante. "Plenty to Crow About." *New York Post*, August 11, 2000.

[157] David Basham. "Counting Crows Line Up Fall Tour, Talk 'Strange' New Album." *MTV.com*, October 1, 1999.

[158] Jane Ganahl. "Counting Crows' Duritz Finds Emotional Balance." *SF Gate*, December 9, 1999.

[159] Jane Ganahl. "As the Crows Fly." *SF Gate*, September 6, 1998.

[160] Gil Kaufman. "Counting Crows Return to Road for New Album." *MTV.com*, September 30, 1999.

[161] Jon Parales. "The Stars Give a Party for a Global Web Site." *The New York Times*, October 11, 1999.

[162] Jane Ganahl. "Counting Crows' Duritz Finds Emotional Balance." *SF Gate*, December 9, 1999.

[163] "This Desert Life. *College Music Journal*, November 8, 1999.

[164] Jane Ganahl. "Playlist." *SF Gate*, November 1, 1999.

[165] Marc Weinroth, "Crows Soar Again with This Desert Life." *South Florida Sun-Sentinel*, October 28, 1999.

[166] James Hunter. "This Desert Life." *Rolling Stone*, November 25, 1999.

[167] Michael Tortorello. "This Desert Life." *Spin*, December 1999.

Notes

[168] Marc Weingarten. "Some Endearing Melodies Mix with Duritz's Whine on 'Life.'" *Los Angeles Times,* October 30, 1999.

[169] Mark Bautz. "This Desert Life." *Entertainment Weekly,* November 5, 1999.

[170] Gil Kauffman. "Counting Crows' Adam Duritz Describes Experimental New Album." *MTV.com,* August 12, 1999.

[171] Neva Chonin. "Crows Turn Up the Volume but Don't Alter the Message." *SF Gate,* December 14, 1999.

[172] Jane Ganahl. "Counting Crows' Duritz Finds Emotional Balance." *SF Gate,* December 9, 1999.

[173] Daniel Durchholz. "Counting Crows, Live, and Galactic." *Riverfront Times,* July 26, 2000.

[174] Melinda Newman. "Live, Counting Crows to Inspire Each Other on Tour." *Billboard,* April 29, 2000.

[175] Matt Diehl. "Counting Crows/Live." *Rolling Stone,* October 12, 2000.

[176] Melinda Newman. "Live, Counting Crows to Inspire Each Other on Tour." *Billboard,* April 29, 2000.

[177] Ibid.

[178] Ibid.

[179] Ibid.

[180] Matt Diehl. "Counting Crows/Live." *Rolling Stone,* October 12, 2000.

[181] Geoff Harkness. "Counting Crows Plays to Dull Crowd." *Lawrence Journal-World,* July 31, 2000.

[182] Daniel Durchholz. "Counting Crows, Live, and Galactic." *Riverfront Times,* July 26, 2000.

[183] Dan Aquilante. "Plenty to Crow About." *New York Post,* August 11, 2000.

[184] Ibid.

[185] Melinda Newman. "The Beat." *Billboard,* April 14, 2001.

[186] Brandon Autrey. "Counting Crows Coming to Johnson Coliseum." *Sam Houston State University Office of Public Relations*, July 23, 2001.

[187] Maya Schecter. "Counting Crows to Play Centennial Dead Day Eve." *Arizona Daily Wildcat*, April 16, 2001.

[188] Ibid.

[189] Louise Story. "Counting Crows to Headline Final Tercentennial Weekend." *Yale Daily News*, July 6, 2001.

[190] Gene Stout. "Counting Crows in Party Mood at Winery." *Seattle Post-Intelligencer*, July 19, 2001.

[191] Ibid.

[192] "Counting Crows to Tour into November." *Billboard*, August 9, 2001.

[193] Julie Burrell. "Counting Crows ... They've Been Hangin Around Smith." *Massachusetts Daily Collegian*, October 21, 2001.

[194] James Campion. "Intimate Whispers." *Aquarian Weekly*, October 31, 2001.

[195] Geoff Harkness. "Counting Crows." *Lawrence Journal-World*, July 27, 2000.

[196] Matthew Despres. "Hangin' Around with Adam Duritz." *Massachusetts Daily Collegian*, October 4, 2002.

[197] Evan Schlansky. "Hangin' Around With Adam Duritz." *Rolling Stone*, July 12, 2002.

[198] Fabio Alcini. "Adam Duritz Talks About Hard Candy." *Rockstar*, July 2002.

[199] Evan Schlansky. "Hangin' Around With Adam Duritz." *Rolling Stone*, July 12, 2002.

[200] Matthew Despres. "Hangin' Around with Adam Duritz." *Massachusetts Daily Collegian*, October 4, 2002.

[201] Davide Poliani. "Interviews - Counting Crows." *Rockol*, July 29, 2002.

Notes

[202] Evan Schlansky. "Hangin' Around with Adam Duritz." *Rolling Stone*, July 12, 2002.

[203] Mike Seely. "Sensitive Swordsman." *Riverfront Times*, November 27, 2002.

[204] Evan Schlansky. "Hangin' Around With Adam Duritz." *Rolling Stone*, July 12, 2002.

[205] Billboard Staff. "Counting Crows Content in 'Candy' Land." *Billboard*, March 15, 2002.

[206] Alan Tular. "Counting Crows Getting a High Profile Ride on 'Big Yellow Taxi.'" *The Morning Call*, April 26, 2003.

[207] Evan Schlansky. "Hangin' Around with Adam Duritz." *Rolling Stone*, July 12, 2002.

[208] Matthew Despres. "Hangin' Around with Adam Duritz." *Massachusetts Daily Collegian*, October 4, 2002.

[209] Evan Schlansky. "Hangin' Around With Adam Duritz." *Rolling Stone*, July 12, 2002.

[210] Fabio Alcini. "Adam Duritz Talks About Hard Candy." *Rockstar*, July 2002.

[211] Davide Poliani. "Interviews - Counting Crows." *Rockol*, July 29, 2002.

[212] Evan Schlansky. "Hangin' Around With Adam Duritz." *Rolling Stone*, July 12, 2002.

[213] Ibid.

[214] Mike Seely. "Sensitive Swordsman." *Riverfront Times*, November 27, 2002.

[215] Evan Schlansky. "Hangin' Around with Adam Duritz." *Rolling Stone*, July 12, 2002.

[216] Ibid.

[217] Pete Crooks. "Long Play Version: An Interview with Adam Duritz of Counting Crows." *Diablo Magazine*, March 9, 2008.

[218] Billboard Staff. "Counting Crows Content in 'Candy' Land." *Billboard*, March 15, 2002.

[219] Alan Tular. "Counting Crows Getting a High-Profile Ride on 'Big Yellow Taxi.'" *The Morning Call*, April 26, 2003.

[220] Ibid.

[221] Kirk Baird. "Crows Still Counting on Duritz as Chief Visionary." *Las Vegas Sun*, June 28, 2002.

[222] Anna Roberts. "Guitarist Opens Up His Wings to Speak." *The Badger Herald*, October 17, 2002.

[223] Davide Poliani. "Interviews - Counting Crows." *Rockol*, July 29, 2002.

[224] Kirk Baird. "Crows Still Counting on Duritz as Chief Visionary." *Las Vegas Sun*, June 28, 2002.

[225] "Rock News: Music's High and Low Notes." *United Press International*, June 7, 2002.

[226] Kirk Baird. "Crows Still Counting on Duritz as Chief Visionary." *Las Vegas Sun*, June 28, 2002.

[227] Davide Poliani. "Interviews - Counting Crows." *Rockol*, July 29, 2002.

[228] Graham Reid. "Reading Their Riot Act." *Elsewhere*, June 20, 2008.

[229] Mike Seely. "Sensitive Swordsman." *Riverfront Times*, November 27, 2002.

[230] "Rock News: Music's High and Low Notes." *United Press International*, June 7, 2002.

[231] Evan Schlansky. "Hangin' Around with Adam Duritz." *Rolling Stone*, July 12, 2002.

[232] Kelefa Sanneh. "A Mainstream Cult Band." *The New York Times*, October 12, 2002.

[233] Patrick Schabe. "Counting Crows: Hard Candy." *PopMatters*, September 5, 2002.

[234] Geoff Harkness. "Counting Crows." *The Pitch*, July 25, 2002.

[235] Dale Price. "Counting Crows - Hard Candy." *Drowned in Sound*, July 9, 2002.

[236] Scott Silverstein. "Now Hear This." *The Washington Times*, July 6, 2002.

[237] Jim DeRogatis. "Listen Hear." *Salon.com*, July 30, 2002.

[238] Chris Willman. "Hard Candy." *Entertainment Weekly*, July 12, 2002.

[239] Barry Walters. "Hard Candy." *Rolling Stone*, July 2, 2002.

[240] Billboard staff. "Hard Candy." *Billboard*, July 13, 2002.

[241] James Sullian. "Crows Can't Raise a Flap." *SF Gate*, July 7, 2002.

[242] Kelefa Sanneh. "A Mainstream Cult Band." *The New York Times*, October 12, 2002.

[243] Matthew Despres. "Hangin' Around with Adam Duritz." *Massachusetts Daily Collegian*, October 4, 2002.

[244] Kirk Baird. "Crows Still Counting on Duritz as Chief Visionary." *Las Vegas Sun*, June 28, 2002.

[245] Evan Schlansky. "Hangin' Around with Adam Duritz." *Rolling Stone*, July 12, 2002.

[246] Mike Seely. "Sensitive Swordsman." *Riverfront Times*, November 27, 2002.

[247] Evan Schlansky. "Hangin' Around with Adam Duritz." *Rolling Stone*, July 12, 2002.

[248] Kelefa Sanneh. "A Mainstream Cult Band." *The New York Times*, October 12, 2002.

[249] Billboard Staff. "Duritz Headed to NYC as Crows Hit the Road." *Billboard*, October 15, 2002.

[250] Ibid.

[251] Michelle Edgar. "Counting Collector." *Women's Wear Daily*, March 25, 2008.

[252] Ibid.

[253] Evan Schlansky. "Hangin' Around With Adam Duritz." *Rolling Stone*, July 12, 2002.

[254] Ibid.

[255] Steve Hochman. "Crows Make the Best of Adversity." *Los Angeles Times*, December 13, 2002.

[256] PopMatters Staff. "Counting Crows." *PopMatters*, January 8, 2003.

[257] Neva Chonin. "Duritz Perfects an Imperfect Image." *SF Gate*, December 18, 2002.

[258] Mike Seely. "Sensitive Swordsman." *Riverfront Times*, November 27, 2002.

[259] Alan Tular. "Counting Crows Getting a High Profile Ride on 'Big Yellow Taxi.'" *The Morning Call*, April 26, 2003.

[260] Kirk Heynen. "Counting Crows & John Mayer." *Paste*, August 11, 2003.

[261] Steven Mirkin. "John Mayer/Counting Crows." *Variety*, July 20, 2003.

[262] Carla Hay. "Film Music Challenges Counting Crows' Duritz." *Billboard*, May 8, 2004.

[263] Sandi Davis. "Adam Duritz Finds Cure in Writing Shrek 2 Song." *The Oklahoman*, May 21, 2004.

[264] Carla Hay. "Film Music Challenges Counting Crows' Duritz." *Billboard*, May 8, 2004.

[265] Ibid.

[266] Sandi Davis. "Adam Duritz Finds Cure in Writing Shrek 2 Song." *The Oklahoman*, May 21, 2004.

[267] Ibid.

[268] Ibid.

[269] Adam Duritz and Corbis Images. "The Lonely Disease." *Men's Health*, April 16, 2008.

[270] Susan Ault. "Essential Reviews." *Billboard*, May 22, 2004

[271] Carla Hay. "Film Music Challenges Counting Crows' Duritz." *Billboard*, May 8, 2004.

[272] "Longevity is True Prize for Counting Crows." United Press International, February 25, 2005.

[273] Imaeyen Ibanga. "Counting Crows Take Flight." *ABC News*, March 19, 2008.

[274] "Correspondence: Love Letters & Advice." *Rolling Stone*, November 11, 2004.

[275] "How Sahaja Yoga Meditation Helped Matt Malley Maintain a Moral Compass in a Multi-Platinum Rock Band." *YouTube*, March 22, 2021.

[276] "The Matt Malley Story." *YouTube*, April 25, 2007.

[277] "How Sahaja Yoga Meditation Helped Matt Malley Maintain a Moral Compass in a Multi-Platinum Rock Band." *YouTube*, March 22, 2021.

[278] "Matt Malley: Life as a Counting Crow." *DIY Musician Podcast*, #57, April 27, 2009.

[279] Ibid.

[280] "Ampeg SVT Time Live with Matt Malley." YouTube, July 12, 2022.

[281] "CC & the Hollywood Bowl Orchestra." *Countingcrows.com*, August 31, 2005.

[282] Jesse Truesdale. "Concert, Other Festivities Mark KCK Center's Opening." *Shawnee Dispatch*, April 26, 2006.

[283] Adam Duritz and Corbis Images. "The Lonely Disease." *Men's Health*, April 16, 2008.

[284] Pete Crooks. "Long Play Version: An Interview with Adam Duritz of Counting Crows." *Diablo Magazine*, March 9, 2008.

[285] Brain Hiatt. "Why Can't Adam Duritz Get Any Respect?" *Rolling Stone*, April 3, 2008.

[286] Jon Bream. "Crowing Pains." *Star Tribune*, August 30, 2007.

[287] Liz Lawson. "Everything After August." *Paste*, March 24, 2008.

[288] Pete Crooks. "Long Play Version: An Interview with Adam Duritz of Counting Crows." *Diablo Magazine*, March 9, 2008.

[289] Billboard Staff. "Goo Goo Dolls, Counting Crows Team for Tour." *Billboard*, April 3, 2006.

[290] Liz Lawson. "Everything After August." *Paste*, March 24, 2008

[291] Pete Crooks. "Long Play Version: An Interview with Adam Duritz of Counting Crows." *Diablo Magazine*, March 9, 2008.

[292] Adam Duritz and Corbis Images. "The Lonely Disease." *Men's Health*, April 16, 2008.

[293] Liz Lawson. "Everything After August." *Paste*, March 24, 2008.

[294] Alan Sculley. "Counting Crows Back on Stage." *The Herald*, June 15, 2006.

[295] Michael Metivier. "Counting Crows: New Amsterdam." *PopMatters*, August 8, 2006.

[296] Adam Duritz and Corbis Images. "The Lonely Disease." *Men's Health*, April 16, 2008.

[297] Ben Wener. "For Adam Duritz, Creative Daylight Fading." *The Orange County Register*, June 23, 2006.

[298] Ben Wener. "Counting Crows: Rearranged, Revealing, Riveting." *The Orange County Register*, June 23, 2006.

[299] Linda Laban, "Bands Share a Bill But Not a Philosophy." *The Globe*, July 31, 2006.

[300] Michael Korb. "Goo Goo Dolls Review." *The Saratogian*, August 9, 2006.

[301] Adam Duritz and Corbis Images. "The Lonely Disease." *Men's Health*, April 16, 2008.

Notes

[302] Pete Crooks. "Long Play Version: An Interview with Adam Duritz of Counting Crows." *Diablo Magazine*, March 9, 2008.

[303] Ibid.

[304] Adam Duritz and Corbis Images. "The Lonely Disease." *Men's Health*, April 16, 2008.

[305] Ibid.

[306] Pete Crooks. "Long Play Version: An Interview with Adam Duritz of Counting Crows." *Diablo Magazine*, March 9, 2008.

[307] John Benson. "Counting Crows Blend Loud with Soft on New CD." *Billboard*, August 15, 2007.

[308] Imaeyen Ibanga. "Counting Crows Take Flight." *ABC News*, March 19, 2008.

[309] Jon Bream. "Crowing Pains." *Star Tribune*, August 30, 2007.

[310] Pete Crooks. "Long Play Version: An Interview with Adam Duritz of Counting Crows." *Diablo Magazine*, March 9, 2008.

[311] Ibid.

[312] Jonathan Widran. "The Counting Crows Singer Adam Duritz Discusses Their Album, *Saturday Nights & Sunday Mornings*." *Songwriter Universe*, April 28, 2008.

[313] John Benson. "Counting Crows Blend Loud with Soft on New CD." *Billboard*, August 15, 2007.

[314] Source Liz Lawson. "Everything After August." *Paste*, March 24, 2008.

[315] Jonathan Widran. "The Counting Crows Singer Adam Duritz Discusses Their Album, Saturday Nights & Sunday Mornings." *Songwriter Universe*, April 28, 2008.

[316] Jon Bream. "Crowing Pains." *Star Tribune*, August 30, 2007.

[317] Ibid.

[318] Kate Kiefer. "Counting Crows: Saturday Nights & Sunday Mornings." *Paste*, April 15, 2008.

[319] John Benson. "Counting Crows Blend Loud with Soft on New CD." *Billboard*, August 15, 2007.

[320] KC Baker. "Adam Duritz Talks About His 'Downward Spiral.'" *People*, March 27, 2008.

[321] Adam Duritz and Corbis Images. "The Lonely Disease." *Men's Health*, April 16, 2008.

[322] John Benson. "Ready For Takeoff." *Billboard*, March 15, 2008.

[323] Courtney Harding. "Counting Crows Bowery Ballroom." *Billboard*, February 6, 2008.

[324] John Benson. "Ready For Takeoff." *Billboard*, March 15, 2008.

[325] Jonathan Widran. "The Counting Crows Singer Adam Duritz Discusses Their Album, Saturday Nights & Sunday Mornings." *Songwriter Universe*, April 28, 2008.

[326] Adam Duritz and Corbis Images. "The Lonely Disease." *Men's Health*, April 16, 2008.

[327] KC Baker. "Adam Duritz Talks About His 'Downward Spiral.' *People*, March 27, 2008.

[328] Liz Lawson. "Everything After August." Paste, March 24, 2008.

[329] Brain Hiatt. "Why Can't Adam Duritz Get Any Respect?" *Rolling Stone*, April 3, 2008.

[330] Adam Duritz and Corbis Images. "The Lonely Disease." *Men's Health*, April 16, 2008.

[331] Jonathan Widran. "The Counting Crows Singer Adam Duritz Discusses Their Album, Saturday Nights & Sunday Mornings." *Songwriter Universe*, April 28, 2008.

[332] Adam Duritz and Corbis Images. "The Lonely Disease." *Men's Health*, April 16, 2008.

[333] "Counting Crows Release First Album in Five Years." *The Buchtelite*, March 25, 2008.

[334] Claire J. Saffitz, "Counting Crows: Saturday Nights & Sunday Mornings." *The Harvard Crimson*, April 11, 2008.

[335] "Counting Crows: Saturday Nights & Sunday Mornings." *Absolute Punk*, March 28, 2008.

[336] Kate Kiefer. "Counting Crows: Saturday Nights & Sunday Mornings." *Paste*, April 15, 2008.

[337] Andrew Reilly. "Album Review: Counting Crows, Saturday Nights & Sunday Mornings." *Room Thirteen*, January 30, 2008.

[338] Chris Willman. "Saturday Nights & Sunday Mornings." *Entertainment Weekly*, March 21, 2008.

[339] Andrew Gilstrap. "Counting Crows: Saturday Nights & Sunday Mornings." *PopMatters*, March 27, 2008.

[340] Paul Schrodt. "Review: Counting Crows: Saturday Nights & Sunday Mornings." *Slant*, March 25, 2008.

[341] Chris Saunders. "Counting Crows - Saturday Nights and Sunday Mornings." *Music OMH*, March 24, 2008.

[342] Caroline Sullivan. "Counting Crows: Saturday Nights & Sunday Mornings." *The Guardian*, March 20, 2008.

[343] Brain Hiatt. "Why Can't Adam Duritz Get Any Respect?" *Rolling Stone*, April 3, 2008.

[344] Imaeyen Ibanga. "Counting Crows Take Flight." *ABC News*, March 19, 2008.

[345] Brain Hiatt. "Why Can't Adam Duritz Get Any Respect?" *Rolling Stone*, April 3, 2008.

[346] Ibid.

[347] Ibid.

[348] Jon Bream. "Crowing Pains." *Star Tribune*, August 30, 2007.

[349] Michelle Edgar. "Counting Collector." *Women's Wear Daily*, March 25, 2008.

[350] Imaeyen Ibanga. "Counting Crows Take Flight." *ABC News*, March 19, 2008.

[351] Adam Duritz and Corbis Images. "The Lonely Disease." *Men's Health*, April 16, 2008.

[352] Imaeyen Ibanga. "Counting Crows Take Flight." *ABC News*, March 19, 2008.

[353] "Counting Crows." *A&E Private Sessions*, March 30, 2008.

[354] George A. Paul. "Contrasting Moods from Maroon 5, Counting Crows." *The Orange County Register*, September 13, 2008.

[355] Imaeyen Ibanga. "Counting Crows Take Flight." *ABC News*, March 19, 2008.

[356] Jon Bream. "Adam's Riff." *Minneapolis Star Tribune*, August 22, 2008.

[357] Clark Collis. "Adam Duritz Exclusive: Why Counting Crows Left Geffen." *Entertainment Weekly*, March 18, 2009.

[358] Ibid.

[359] Pete Crooks. "Long Play Version: An Interview with Adam Duritz of Counting Crows." *Diablo Magazine*, March 9, 2008.

[360] Clark Collis. "Adam Duritz Exclusive: Why Counting Crows Left Geffen." *Entertainment Weekly*, March 18, 2009.

[361] Sam Sessa. "Concert Review: Counting Crows, Michael Franti and Augustana at Merriweather Post Pavilion." *Baltimore Sun*, September 6, 2009.

[362] Eunice Oh. "What's the Secret of Adam Duritz's Sex Appeal?" *People*, October 1, 2009.

[363] "Counting Crows + Augustana: 18 August 2010 - The Wellmont." *PopMatters*, August 25, 2010.

[364] Sean Spillane. "Counting Crows Doing it Again." *Entertainment Weekly*, August 10, 2010.

[365] "For Now, Counting Crows' Future is Live Music." *The Morning Call*, August 5, 2010.

[366] Sam Sessa. "Counting Crows Singer Shares Memories of Baltimore." *Baltimore Sun*, July 8, 2010.

[367] Steven Kurutz. "Adam Duritz Asks Fans to Design Album Cover." *The Wall Street Journal*, March 15, 2011.

[368] Caryn Robbins. "Counting Crows Adam Duritz on His New Musical Black Sun." *Broadway World*, June 1, 2012.

[369] Jonathan Bautts. "Interview: Adam Duritz of Counting Crows." *Chorus.fm*, August 22, 2014.

[370] Gary Graff. "Counting Crows' Adam Duritz Mourns Lost Album Tapes: 'It's Disgusting.'" *The Hollywood Reporter*, October 23, 2012.

[371] Joanie Cox. "Adam Duritz of Counting Crows Strikes up a Conversation." *Sun Sentinel*, October 29, 2012.

[372] Alan Sculley. "Counting Crows Counting on a Few New Tricks." *Aspen Times*, February 28, 2014.

[373] Joanie Cox. "Adam Duritz of Counting Crows Strikes up a Conversation." *Sun Sentinel*, October 29, 2012.

[374] Keith Spera. "Counting Crows Embark on Busman's Holiday on 'Underwater Sunshine' Covers Album." *NOLA.com*, November 5, 2012.

[375] Patrick Flanary. "Counting Crows Want You to Hear New Album for Free." *Billboard*, February 6, 2012.

[376] "Counting Crows Back with Quirky Covers." *San Francisco Examiner*, March 6, 2012.

[377] Patrick Flanary. "Counting Crows Want You to Hear New Album for Free." *Billboard*, February 6, 2012.

[378] Brad Wete. "Counting Crows Frontman Adam Duritz Struggling with 'Severe Mental Illness' and Weaning Himself off Medication." *Entertainment Weekly*, June 28, 2011.

[379] Joanie Cox. "Adam Duritz of Counting Crows Strikes up a Conversation." *Sun Sentinel,* October 29, 2012.

[380] "Counting Crows Back with Quirky Covers." *SF Examiner,* March 6, 2012.

[381] Caryn Robbins. "Counting Crows Adam Duritz on His New Musical Black Sun." *Broadway World,* June 1, 2012.

[382] Ibid.

[383] Gary Graff. "Counting Crows' Adam Duritz Mourns Lost Album Tapes: 'It's Disgusting.'" *The Hollywood Reporter,* October 23, 2012.

[384] Adam Finley. "Live at Town Hall." *PopMatters,* October 25, 2011.

[385] Keith Spera. "Counting Crows Embark on Busman's Holiday on 'Underwater Sunshine' Covers Album." *NOLA.com,* November 5, 2012.

[386] Gary Graff. "Counting Crows' Adam Duritz Mourns Lost Album Tapes: 'It's Disgusting.' *The Hollywood Reporter,* October 23, 2012.

[387] Ibid.

[388] Ibid.

[389] Josh Langhoff. "Counting Crows: Underwater Sunshine." *PopMatters,* May 6, 2012.

[390] Caroline Sullivan. "Counting Crows: Underwater Sunshine - Review." *The Guardian,* April 5, 2012.

[391] Joanie Cox. "Adam Duritz of Counting Crows Strikes up a Conversation." *Sun Sentinel,* October 29, 2012.

[392] Sandra Barrera, "Counting Crows Gets Under the Covers for Songs That Shaped Its World." *Los Angeles Daily News,* November 23, 2012.

[393] Keith Spera. "Counting Crows Embark on Busman's Holiday on 'Underwater Sunshine' Covers Album." *NOLA.com,* November 5, 2012.

[394] Jon Bream. "Counting Crows Were More Indulgent Than Exciting at State Theatre." *Star Tribune,* April 23, 2012.

[395] Gary Graff. "Counting Crows' Adam Duritz Mourns Lost Album Tapes: 'It's Disgusting.'" *The Hollywood Reporter*, October 23, 2012.

[396] Joanie Cox. "Adam Duritz of Counting Crows Strikes up a Conversation." *Sun Sentinel*, October 29, 2012.

[397] Ibid.

[398] Matthew Hogan. "Crows Singer Spreads Wings." *The West Australian*, March 28, 2013.

[399] Brian Orndorf. "Freeloaders Review." *Blu-Ray.com*, December 13, 2012.

[400] Joanie Cox. "Adam Duritz of Counting Crows Strikes up a Conversation." *Sun Sentinel*, October 29, 2012.

[401] Matthew Hogan. "Crows Singer Spreads Wings." *The West Australian*, March 28, 2013.

[402] Gary Graff. "Counting Crows on Tour with Wallflowers." *Daily Tribune*, June 28, 2013.

[403] Jeff Giles and Matt Wardlaw. "Adam Duritz Talks About His 'Alien" Experiences with Counting Crows, Summer Touring & Plans for New Music." *Popdose*, June 3, 2013.

[404] Nick Hasted. "Counting Crows: Alive in Wonderland." *Louder*, December 17, 2014.

[405] Jeff Giles and Matt Wardlaw. "Adam Duritz Talks About His 'Alien" Experiences with Counting Crows, Summer Touring & Plans for New Music." *Popdose*, June 3, 2013.

[406] Erin Hill. "Counting Crows' Adam Duritz: 'Rock 'n' Roll is not a Popularity Contest." *Parade*, June 12, 2013.

[407] Jeff Giles and Matt Wardlaw. "Adam Duritz Talks About His 'Alien" Experiences with Counting Crows, Summer Touring & Plans for New Music." *Popdose*, June 3, 2013.

[408] Colin McGuire. "Start Again: An Interview with Counting Crows' Adam Duritz." *PopMatters*, November 13, 2013.

[409] Jeff Giles and Matt Wardlaw. "Adam Duritz Talks About His 'Alien" Experiences with Counting Crows, Summer Touring & Plans for New Music." *Popdose*, June 3, 2013.

[410] Adam Duritz. "Ask Me Anything." *Reddit*, July 30, 2013.

[411] Ibid.

[412] Jeff Giles and Matt Wardlaw. "Adam Duritz Talks About His 'Alien" Experiences with Counting Crows, Summer Touring and Plans for New Music." *Popdose*, June 3, 2013.

[413] Kelly Parker. "You Can Always Count on These Crows." *Los Angeles Times*, July 23, 2013.

[414] Gary Graff. "Counting Crows Working on First Album of New Material Since 2008." *Billboard*, June 12, 2013.

[415] Jeff Giles and Matt Wardlaw. "Adam Duritz Talks About His 'Alien" Experiences with Counting Crows, Summer Touring & Plans for New Music." *Popdose*, June 3, 2013.

[416] Gary Graff. "Counting Crows Working on First Album of New Material Since 2008." *Billboard*, June 12, 2013.

[417] Jeff Giles and Matt Wardlaw. "Adam Duritz Talks About His 'Alien" Experiences with Counting Crows, Summer Touring & Plans for New Music." *Popdose*, June 3, 2013.

[418] Michael Hardy. "No, Adam Duritz Will Not Play 'Mr. Jones.'" *Houstonia*, July 29, 2014.

[419] Jeff Giles and Matt Wardlaw. "Adam Duritz Talks About His 'Alien" Experiences with Counting Crows, Summer Touring & Plans for New Music." *Popdose*, June 3, 2013.

[420] Jeff Ignatius. "Unchained from the Plot of His Own Life." *River Cities' Reader*, December 9, 2014.

[421] Ibid.

[422] "Counting Crows Adam Duritz Finds New Songwriting Perspective." *San Francisco Examiner*, August 14, 2014.

[423] Adam Duritz. "Ask Me Anything." *Reddit*, July 30, 2013.

[424] "Counting Crows Adam Duritz Finds New Songwriting Perspective." *San Francisco Examiner*, August 14, 2014.

[425] Michael Hardy. "No, Adam Duritz Will Not Play 'Mr. Jones.'" *Houstonia*, July 29, 2014.

[426] Jeff Ignatius. "Unchained from the Plot of His Own Life." *River Cities' Reader*, December 9, 2014.

[427] Jonathan Bautts. "Interview: Adam Duritz of Counting Crows." *Chorus.fm*, August 22, 2014.

[428] Michael Hardy. "No, Adam Duritz Will Not Play 'Mr. Jones.'" *Houstonia*, July 29, 2014.

[429] Colin McGuire. "Start Again: An Interview with Counting Crows' Adam Duritz." *PopMatters*, November 13, 2013.

[430] Nick Hasted. "Counting Crows: Alive in Wonderland." *Louder*, December 17, 2014.

[431] Leslie Michele Derrough. "Adam Duritz of Counting Crows." *Glide Magazine*, June 12, 2014.

[432] Jonathan Bautts. "Interview: Adam Duritz of Counting Crows." *Chorus.fm*, August 22, 2014.

[433] Megan Waldrep. "Five Minutes with Adam Duritz of Counting Crows." *Santa Barbara Sentinel*, 2014.

[434] Leslie Michele Derrough. "Adam Duritz of Counting Crows." *Glide Magazine*, June 12, 2014.

[435] Jeff Ignatius. "Unchained from the Plot of His Own Life." *River Cities' Reader*, December 9, 2014.

[436] Grayson Haver Currin. "Live: In Raleigh, the Counting Crows Get Listless." *Indy Week*, June 26, 2014.

[437] Alison Jones, "Counting Crows singer Adam Duritz Battles Back Through Illness and Reveals the Cost of Fame." *Birmingham Mail*, October 9, 2014.

[438] Gary Graff. "Sound Check: Counting Crows' Duritz Happy to Get Outside Himself." *The Morning Sun*, September 9, 2015.

[439] Jeffrey Lee Puckett. "Counting Crows are 'Somewhere Under Wonderland.'" *Courier Journal*, December 3, 2014.

[440] James Rettig. "Will Somone Please Right Swipe Adam Duritz on Tinder?" *Stereogum*, August 27, 2014; Brennan Carley. "Adam Duritz Joins Tinder, Tells Fans He Joined Tinder." *Spin*, August 8, 2014.

[441] Emily Tess Katz. "Counting Crows Frontman Adam Duritz Explains Why No One Can Find Him On Tinder." *Huff Post*, August 27, 20143

[442] Erin Hill. "Counting Crows' Adam Duritz: 'Rock 'n' Roll is not a Popularity Contest." *Parade*, June 12, 2013.

[443] Helen Brown. "Counting Crows: Somewhere Under Wonderland Review." *The Telegraph*, September 14, 2014.

[444] Colin McGuire. "Counting Crows: Somewhere Under Wonderland." *PopMatters*, October 2, 2014.

[445] Matt Melis. "Counting Crows: Somewhere Under Wonderland." *Consequence*, September 5, 2014.

[446] Jon Dolan. "Somewhere Under Wonderland." *Rolling Stone*, September 2, 2014.

[447] Jon Carimanica. "Maroon 5 and Counting Crows." *The New York Times*, September 3, 2014.

[448] Jess Mayhugh. "Adam Duritz Talks Counting Crows, Black-Eyed Susan Concert." *Baltimore*, May 15, 2014.

[449] Leslie Michele Derrough. "Adam Duritz of Counting Crows." *Glide Magazine*, June 12, 2014.

[450] Jonathan Bautts. "Interview: Adam Duritz of Counting Crows." *Chorus.fm*, August 22, 2014.

[451] Michael Hardy. "No, Adam Duritz Will Not Play 'Mr. Jones.'" *Houstonia*, July 29, 2014.

[452] Jonathan Bautts. "Interview: Adam Duritz of Counting Crows." *Chorus.fm*, August 22, 2014.

[453] Alison Jones, "Counting Crows singer Adam Duritz Battles Back Through Illness and Reveals the Cost of Fame." *Birmingham Mail*, October 9, 2014.

[454] Kate Nalepinski. "11 Questions with Adam Duritz of Counting Crows." *Long Island Press*, July 8, 2016.

[455] Leslie Michele Derrough. "Adam Duritz of Counting Crows." *Glide Magazine*, June 12, 2014.

[456] Jess Mayhugh. "Adam Duritz Talks Counting Crows, Black-Eyed Susan Concert." *Baltimore*, May 15, 2014.

[457] Jeff Ignatius. "Unchained from the Plot of His Own Life." *River Cities' Reader*, December 9, 2014.

[458] Alison Jones, "Counting Crows singer Adam Duritz Battles Back Through Illness and Reveals the Cost of Fame." *Birmingham Mail*, October 9, 2014.

[459] Colin McGuire. "Start Again: An Interview with Counting Crows' Adam Duritz." *PopMatters*, November 13, 2013.

[460] Jonathan Bautts. "Interview: Adam Duritz of Counting Crows." *Chorus.fm*, August 22, 2014.

[461] Nick Hasted. "Counting Crows: Alive in Wonderland." *Louder*, December 17, 2014.

[462] Lauren Moraski. "Counting Crows' Adam Duritz Reveals the Real Story Behind 'Maria.'" *HuffPost*, April 12, 2018.

[463] Jeff Wilkin. "Counting Crows' Frontman Branching Out." *Daily Gazette*, August 27, 2015.

[464] James Rettig. "Counting Crows' Adam Duritz Explains Why He Cut Off His Signature Dreads, Which Are in A Bag Now." *Stereogum*, November 18, 2019.

[465] Jon Bream, "Counting Crows and the Wallflowers Deliver '90s Favorites and Then Some at the State Fair." *Star Tribune*, August 26, 2022.

Printed in Great Britain
by Amazon